KILL OR BE KILLED . . .

Kordt raised his trembling arm slowly, gripping the weapon and pointing it at Muller. In the little man's eyes he saw it all: forty-five years of life, a wife and two kids who were still waiting for him, despite everything. But he had to do it . . .

'I'll count to three,' the sergeant said. 'One . . . Two . . .'

'No!' Muller screamed, his voice cracked with fear. He began to howl like an animal. 'No! You can't . . .'

'Three . . .'

Also by Will Berthold in Sphere Books:

LEBENSBORN

DEATH'S HEAD BRIGADE!

WILL BERTHOLD

Translated by C. Magnus

SPHERE BOOKS LIMITED
30-32 Gray's Inn Road, London WC1X 8JL

First published in Great Britain by Sphere Books Ltd 1980

Reprinted 1980, 1982

Printed and bound in Great Britain by
©ollins, Glasgow

Chapter One

The barracks lay still and grave-quiet in the freezing air, their roofs smothered under a metre of snow. The whole area around them seemed deserted and desolate, for this was a place where there was no hope, no humanity, no life as normal men would understand it. The time: February 1943. The place: the headquarters of Dirlewanger's 'Special Commando' at Lahuisk, near Minsk, in the coldest, deadliest sector of occupied Russia. Here lived the punishment troops, the so-called B-soldiers, who had already carved themselves a bloody reputation with friend and foe alike. They were the infamous 'Dirlewanger Brigade'.

The buildings were cheerless, though they were heated after a fashion. And the men who existed in them? Take one room in that place at random . . .

The longest-serving man had been reprieved from the executioner's knife. His name was Petrat, an East Prussian and a killer of prostitutes. As the hardest case in the barracks, he was also the most popular – with his superiors. Petrat was as cunning as a fox and as dangerous as a viper. Now he stared at Kordt, the youngest there, with evil in his eyes. The failed student just pushed his ration of schnapps over to him – there was no need for the man to ask.

Petrat nodded and grunted.

'And when do I get my turn with the bottle?' asked Kortetzky, the one they called the 'gorilla'.

'The next time,' answered Kordt, trying to hide his fear.

'I'll remember this, Professor,' the gorilla roared angrily. 'You can depend on it.' Kortetzky really did look like his nickname, with his receding forehead, protruding lips, grotesquely out-of-proportion chin and tiny eyes. But compared with some he counted as harmless, almost good-natured. He had only eight years in jail behind him, which in the Dirlewanger gang made him very junior indeed.

The men in the room wore SS uniforms without tabs, shoulder flashes, rank markings, or even the 'death's-head' insignia. Their provisions were pitiful and their clothes little better than rags. These three had twenty years' jail behind them – and like their comrades they often wished they were back there. Here, in 'freedom', each mission meant murder, and any refusal to participate meant suicide . . .

'Find some for yourself,' said Kirchwein, the epileptic, to Kortetzky. Kirchwein was pale and sickly, and everyone knew he had been on the condemned list for a long time. He broke down before almost every action, foaming at the mouth, his limbs jerking and thrashing. His superiors dismissed his fits as 'cowardice in the face of the enemy'.

'Don't know what you're all complaining about,' Petrat laughed. 'This kind of action's ideal . . . there's booze and good food.'

'If the partisans catch us, they'll kill us like dogs,' Kordt replied.

'More'll be the pity for you, Professor!' The gorilla clapped him roughly on the shoulder.

To their left sat Fleischmann. A few short weeks before, Fleischmann had been an SS Hauptsturmführer, the equivalent of an army captain; now he was degraded to mere private. Rumour said it had something to do with women, gypsies or Jewesses. Aumeier, a beefy Bavarian, was already sprawled out on his straw palliasse. He slept easy: he was a convicted black-market butcher, and his profession guaranteed him a protected existence here, because Dirlewanger liked good meat. Aumeier was one of the Sturmbannführer's favourites, which meant that he at least knew that he would still be alive at the end of each day – for the present . . .

'A Siberian sniper on every tree,' Kordt was saying. 'And as we go past . . .'

'Half of us will get it,' the gorilla agreed.

Kirchwein looked at him, but did not move. His face was turning green. For a moment the others feared that his next epileptic fit was on the way.

'And for what?' the small, plump Muller shouted suddenly. 'Why the hell do we have to die like cattle?' He jerked his thumb over his shoulder to the castle where Dirlewanger lived. 'So that the . . . can booze and whore and . . .'

'Quiet,' said Petrat.

By rights he ought to report the man. Squealing was against the criminal's code. But if he didn't do so, then someone else would – not so much out of maliciousness as out of self-preservation. Dirlewanger's spies – his 'listening machines' – never missed a thing.

'We can be slaughtered and he sits there with his harem,' Muller continued, ignoring Petrat's warning.

The little fat man had been a book-keeper in a metal factory and was the father of a family. He had gambled on the horses, had helped himself to 100,000 marks from the till, and had received a four-year prison sentence. And now he still hadn't finished with his outburst. 'But this war is coming to an end,' he was saying, 'I tell you . . . and then they'll hang these Dirlewangers – as high as they can.'

No one said a word; they just looked at each other. But each knew what the other was thinking. Who would denounce Muller? Who would turn him in? If no one did, they would all catch it in the neck if it ever came out that he had said those things.

'Don't you believe me?' Muller roared, trembling with fury, to his horrified audience.

'I do,' said young Kordt.

'Keep your mouths shut,' said the wiry Paul Vonwegh from the background.

The others' gazes all went to the medium-sized man with the taut, manly face, who wore his rags like a gentleman. They hated him because he wasn't one of them, because he was an arrogant bastard who thought he was something better. He kept silent most of the time and never said an unnecessary word, showed no hunger, even when the rest of them were crazy with hunger cramps. He never seemed dirty, even when there was no soap. He was never tired out by the grind, and he had no fear of action. This Paul Vonwegh would never find favour with the high-ups, but the thought didn't keep him awake at nights. Yes, although he had only been there a few weeks they couldn't stand him – maybe because they knew, deep down, that this was a man who could be a real leader to them.

'One day I'll kill you, you swine,' snarled Petrat at Vonwegh.

At his side the gorilla nodded thoughtfully. His pinpoint eyes were already glassy.

Then a whistle was heard – lights out. They crammed themselves together on their straw mattresses, listening to the weird howl of the wind outside, and they weighed up their chances: would they survive or die tomorrow? And, hell, what was the point of worrying anyway? If they survived the action, then one sign from Dirlewanger would be enough to snuff them out. If they hadn't shaved properly; if their helmet wasn't straight; because the captured Russian machine-gun with the ancient water-cooled action had a spot of rust; because one of their tormenters had had too much schnapps or too few women. Because one of them farted out of turn or was unable to kill an old Russian grandmother. No reason was too trivial, no coincidence too coincidental.

Paul Vonwegh lay awake on his mattress and made an effort to penetrate the darkness. Who had betrayed little Weber, the man who had been hanged yesterday? Who would leave the barracks now and sneak over to Dirlewanger's henchmen? Who was the swine who put all their lives at risk because of a few drunken words? They had cut wood all day. Then there had been barley soup. Then schnapps on an empty stomach that couldn't cope with it. He didn't drink it, and the others shouldn't drink it, but then the Dirlewanger soldiers took no oath of allegiance, received no pay – only schnapps, to keep them going. He struggled against tiredness, ordering himself to stay awake. The thought kept punching its way through his weary brain: *I must find out who the informer is, before he sends all of us to the gallows, one by one . . .*

As the lights were going out in the other ranks' barracks,

candles were lit in Dirlewanger's headquarters in the 'castle'. They stood in massive candlesticks of pure silver, looted from a Polish church. Fifteen guests sat round the oval table: favourites from his own unit, or cronies from headquarters at Kiev.

Dirlewanger's bodyguard stood in front of the castle, day and night, an NCO and six men. These sentries, known as castle-gendarmes, were there as protection, not so much against the Russian partisans as against his own men. Dirlewanger had enough imagination to know how much he was hated.

Sturmbannführer Dirlewanger sat at the head of the table, half slumped in his seat and, as always, very drunk. Many of his own people hadn't seen him sober for months. Sergeant Weise, his right-hand man, watched him appraisingly. The chief was in a bad mood, he thought, and it was high time to do something about it. Weise stood up, went to the gramophone and put on Dirlewanger's favourite record, signalling to the guests as he did so. The conversation stopped, allowing the song to be heard loud and clear all over the room: 'Every Day Is Not a Sunday'. Sergeant Weise had done the right thing. Dirlewanger listened, fascinated. Somehow the emotion which took hold of his hawk-like face made it all the more terrifying and sinister. Then the mood was gone, and he tapped on his glass.

'Gentlemen,' Dirlewanger announced, 'I have a special treat to announce for dessert.' He winked, and those who knew him realised what he meant.

Even within the S S leadership it was considered bad form to have anything to do with Dirlewanger. Gauleiter Kube of the Ukraine in Kiev, himself not exactly squeamish in his treatment of his Russian subjects, continued to mobilise all his connections to try and drive Dirlewanger out of his area. Alfred Rosenberg, chief of the administration in the Eastern Territories, complained almost every month to Obergruppenführer Gottlob Berger at the S S security headquarters, the Reichssicherheitshauptamt. But Berger had 'discovered' Dirlewanger, and he stood by him. 'The man just has an ethical defect,' Berger would argue, 'he is the last of the free-booters, the robber barons who made this country great . . .'

And so whenever someone wanted to bring Dirlewanger to account for his atrocities, S S security headquarters in the Prinz Albrechtstrasse were presented with a success report – 1,000 persons liquidated, three villages burnt down, 2,000 Russian workers transported to Germany for forced labour, partisans ruthlessly eliminated from area X Y Z . . . And then Oskar Dirlewanger obtained a stay of execution, even decorations. No one could argue with success.

Who was this man, whose crimes place those of the extermination camp commanders and killer-squad leaders in the shade? Who was the man who embarrassed the party, the Wehrmacht, and even the S S, and yet was looked on as a necessary evil to keep Russia down by terror?

He had returned from the First World War as a first lieutenant of the Reserve, had joined a volunteer corps and fought with a self-styled armoured unit against the Reds during the chaos that followed the war. His friendship with Gottlob Berger stemmed from that time. Then Dirlewanger had studied political economy and took a doctor's degree, after which he was unable to find a job and became one of the many 'professional war veterans' who were the scourge of Germany in those days. In 1933, as a reward for his 'patriotism', he was made director of the Employment Exchange in the town of Heilbronn. He soon fell out with the local Nazi leader, accusing him of embezzling money belonging to the Winter Aid Fund.

In the meantime Dirlewanger was also in the dock for indecent assault on a fifteen-year-old girl. The president of the court, a fellow-National Socialist, sentenced him to two and a half years in prison for the crime. Dirlewanger's Nazi career seemed in ruins.

But Gottlob Berger, now a powerful figure in the S S, had kept a protective eye on the man with the 'ethical defect'. He sent Dirlewanger to the notorious Condor Legion in war-torn Spain, after having first arranged a shabby retrial for him where, under pressure from the S S, the court acquitted him owing to 'lack of evidence'. It was sufficient for Dirlewanger to be able to creep back into the ranks of the S S, even if in a more modest position.

Berger brought his old crony back into business full time during the partisan war that began to rage almost immediately after Hitler's invasion of Russia. As an experiment, a commando group of 180 poachers was put together in Oranienburg concentration camp – the S S security bosses, in typical cowboy style, thought that they would be effective in the forests. Dirlewanger was placed in command, and passed his test with flying colours. He wiped out his first villages and sent his poachers to the slaughter, almost to the last man. Then his proposal to recruit B-soldiers from among professional criminals was accepted. Thus, for the first time in history, a bunch of criminals was turned into a regular army unit under the command of a crook. A licensed murderer was created out of a born criminal, who 'for disciplinary reasons' was given total power of life or death. No red tape for Dirlewanger – he got results . . .

'Where are the girls?' Dirlewanger asked.

'They're coming now,' Weise replied, then added, as if in afterthought: 'There has been an . . . unfortunate event, Sturmbannführer.'

'Well?'

'Aumeier, the staff butcher, assaulted a Red Cross nurse in Kiev, where he was supposed to be organising . . .'

'Him again,' Dirlewanger snarled. 'I'll make him regret it . . .'

'The Reichsführer S S has ordered him to be shot.'

'Rubbish,' Dirlewanger replied. His hand began to tremble slightly as he reached for another glass of schnapps.

But Weise persisted.

'Report of the execution is to be made within forty-eight hours . . . tomorrow is the deadline. We shall have to kill him.'

'And then we'll starve, eh?' roared Dirlewanger. 'That man stays alive until you find a replacement for him, understand?'

'Yes, Sturmbannführer.'

'Then look sharp about it tomorrow. Find me a new butcher – and fast.'

Then he smiled, signalling that the subject was closed and that there were better things to do. Weise looked at him slyly. Three young Russian girls, kidnapped from a suspected partisan hideout that morning, were serving cream-cakes and liqueurs with hunted, terrified looks on their faces. Dirlewanger looked at them. Then he stood up and said to his guests with an extravagant gesture:

'Please, gentlemen, help yourselves.'

Minutes later the castle-gendarmes outside in the front heard the piercing screams of the Russian girls. They exchanged wolfish grins: another of the Sturmbannführer's 'parties' was under way.

Paul Vonwegh woke up with a start in the middle of the night. Despite his efforts, he had fallen asleep. He knew that the shadowy figure scurrying silently back into the barracks was the traitor and Weber's murderer, the Sturmbannführer's 'listening machine'.

But who was it? Vonwegh asked himself again and again, tense with frustration. There were thirty men in the room, and it could be any of them. Under the circumstances, any of them would do it – which was exectly the way things were planned. What a life, he thought: behind us lies prison, before us the partisans; above us are Dirlewanger's bully-boys, and beneath us are bedbugs, rats and killers.

He himself was trapped by love and kept alive by hate. He didn't know where she was, but he kept seeing the woman in his thoughts. He had no picture of her, but he could have painted her portrait. Paul Vonwegh had risked everything for her, and had gone to hell for it.

But he would risk everything a second time, at this moment, if he could see Karen again. How long was it since he had felt that way: a month? A year? An eternity? The feeling did not change, only the circumstances.

At this moment, Paul Vonwegh went back to the beginning, when he had crossed the border into Germany, fully aware of the consequences of what he was doing. Only a fool would behave like that, a suicide . . . or a lover.

He remembered how he had leapt from the boat into the waters of Lake Constance, seeing the border-patrol's searchlight sweeping the lake. Ten or fifteen times it had flashed across the water, until the tension had waned and the adventure became a child's game – for the moment. Then he had reached the bank and was back in his home country. In the realm of the perfectly–honed police machine that would now be hunting him. In a country where he was a wanted man.

His first stop had been Hanover, where she used to live. All the time he felt her attracting him, like a magnet. He hadn't seen her for years, but she would not have changed. Karen would never change. Vonwegh's angular face softened whenever he dared think of her. In his mind's eye she smiled at him with those bright eyes and tossed her shining hair, standing before him, tall and tender. Her skin, which she had inherited from her Swedish mother, was almost transparent, and then there was her assurance, her honesty, and her stubbornness – the inheritance of a German father.

Vonwegh had met Karen in the South and had been captivated by her from the first. They had looked at each other and it had felt right. With no time to lose, they had wasted none. Then Karen had asked Vonwegh to come with her, and he had had to refuse. It had meant separation.

Since then, the passage of time had trampled on his feelings, but it had failed to destroy them, which was why, that crazy day, he left Hanover station, heading for the Residents Registration Office.

'Karen Bäumler?' said a sullen clerk, shaking her head. Then she examined the man who stood before her more closely and disappeared to search. It took her ten minutes – ten minutes in which Vonwegh had to have his escape route planned and ready . . .

'She's moved to Berlin,' the clerk said when she returned. 'Her name's changed to Maybach.'

'How come?' he asked, stunned.

'She's married,' the woman replied.

Next stop, Berlin, and a building where the name Maybach stood on a metal plate outside. It seemed cold, alien, unreal. But the entrance to the apartment block was open, and so slowly Vonwegh climbed the stairs.

He rang the bell and heard steps. The hinges need oiling, he thought absently.

Then she stood before him.

'You,' said Karen simply.

'Yes,' he replied.

Amazement had struck the young woman dumb.

'Surprised?' he asked. God, he sounded stupid, he thought.

'I have been waiting for you, Paul,' she replied. Only then did she ask him to come in.

All Vonwegh could say was a mumbled 'oh'. He cursed himself twice over for his awkwardness.

'I knew you would come, you see,' she said.

'It was my fault, Karen,' he said at last.

She smiled, and then he got a proper look at her. Her eyes were still bright, her hair shining-blonde, her face still youthful, her mouth still tender.

'Can I offer you anything, Paul?' she asked.

It was a foolish question, a woman's question, and it made Vonwegh feel better.

'Yes, cognac,' he answered. 'Do you remember . . . the first time . . . ?'

'I could never forget it, Paul,' she said.

'Me neither,' he said, staring at the ground. Now he had to ask. 'You got married?' he enquired.

Karen nodded.

'Do you love him?' Vonwegh asked, staring at the cosy decor of the apartment with hatred.

'Not in the same way as . . .'

'As?'

'As you,' she finished, and looked up at him.

'I don't understand,' Vonwegh said.

'He's dead,' said Karen harshly. 'He fell in Poland.'

He went up to her. They looked at each other. He reached for her . . .

The whistle forced Paul Vonwegh back to reality in the bitter present. His waking dream was over. Roll-call was beginning. Outside the instructors were cursing, and he knew that those who didn't move at the double would get a kick in the backside. Somewhere, yet another shot was heard. A whisper went round that the sergeant had had a hard night and was still full of alcohol. They heard his animal roar: 'Roll-call!'

Then he came nearer: Weise, the chief's right-hand man, the slave-driver who had done his apprenticeship at the 'school' of Oskar Dirlewanger. He was the favourite, the 'spymaster', and the number one swine.

'Gather round . . . !' he was shouting. 'Muller!' he bawled.

'Here,' the fat man answered.

'Kordt!'

'Here,' said the student.

The informer had done his job, Vonwegh thought.

'Listen, for once in your miserable lives,' Weise roared. 'You pigs are here because our Führer in his infinite goodness has given you a chance you don't deserve. But instead of going down on your knees to the Sturmbannführer for tempering his justice with mercy, you incite the others against him . . . Lie down!' he bellowed at the pair of them. 'If I had my way, you'd be cut up into little pieces, hung up, have the skin torn off your backsides.'

The two men fell face down into the snow like spent cartridges.

'And no one reported it,' Weise went on. 'Just see, I'm going to have all your arses.'

They leapt to their feet again at his command. It was obvious that Dirlewanger had ordered an example to be made of them, but for the moment the sergeant wasn't letting on what was in store. He was looking at the chalk-white Kirchwein.

'Don't fall over, boy,' he bawled at him. 'If you do, maybe you won't get up again.' Weise guffawed harshly.

The others stared at Kirchwein. If he had a fit now, he was finished. Irrationally, they all found themselves fighting against an attack, though none of them had ever had one.

Meanwhile the sergeant had walked up to Kordt and pressed a pistol into the man's hand. Weise pointed to Muller.

'You agreed with him,' he said. 'Next time, you're for it.'

Kordt stood there like a ghost.

'Get on with it,' the sergeant commanded. 'Kill him.'

The boy didn't seem to understand what he was being ordered to do.

'Yes, you've understood all right,' Weise sneered. 'Are you going to do it soon?'

Kordt held the weapon irresolutely in his hand and shook his head.

'Ah,' said the sergeant gloatingly, 'so you can't do it . . . bleeding-heart humanitarian, eh? Fine. Then give the thing to Muller, maybe he'll succeed with you . . .'

'No!' the boy's voice became a howl of despair.

'All right then, son,' Weise said patronisingly, 'then get on with it.'

Kordt raised his trembling arm slowly, gripping the weapon and pointing it at Muller. In the little man's eyes he saw it all: forty-five years of life, a wife and two kids who were still waiting for him, despite everything. But he had to do it . . .

'I'll count to three,' the sergeant said. 'One . . .'

Kortetzky stared ahead in dull rage. Kirchwein's teeth chattered. His eyes were popping out of their sockets with the effort, but he held on this time. Petrat ground his teeth, his face twisted in an idiot grin. Fleischmann looked as though he was about to throw up. Only Vonwegh stood there calmly, composed and cold. He was supported by that hatred, the hatred that no other man could touch or see.

The gorilla gave him a poke in the ribs.

'You squealed on Muller, you bastard,' he hissed between his teeth.

'Two . . .'

'No!' Muller screamed, his voice cracked with fear. He began to howl like an animal. 'No! You can't . . .'

'Three . . .' Sergeant Weise called.

Chapter Two

There was no sun on this day, no light in the sky, no mercy in the scene. Muller knelt in the snow with his arms spread out before him, saw his death, and prayed for a life in which he was forced to act and die like an animal. His face was distorted, a shattered mirror of the terror that Dirlewanger created. They would all end like this, today or tomorrow.

'No,' Muller moaned feverishly, 'please, no. You can't do it.' His voice rose to a high-pitched wail. 'Kordt, listen, I'm your mate,' he gasped. 'Listen to me . . .'

'Get on with it. Hurry up.' Weise spoke mechanically, with complete disinterest.

And so Kordt, who had to murder if he was not to be killed himself, finally staggered towards his victim. The weapon in his hand trembled like grass in the wind. His finger on the trigger ached with cramp.

'Please Kordt . . . please . . . please don't . . .' Muller turned towards the sergeant and his pathetic words came tumbling out. 'I'll never say anything again . . .' he whined 'I'll never drink again . . . The Sturmbannführer is a . . . great man. I'll carry out every order, every one. I'll – '

Weise nodded to the hesitating Kordt and, prolonging the horror, slowly took a cigarette out of his pocket, lit it and smiled luridly.

'Well, is it going to be soon?' he asked, almost affably.

'Yes, sergeant, yes . . .' muttered the tormented boy.

Kordt's voice cracked with loathing and fear. He stretched out his arm to take aim but was unable to look at the whimpering man, his mate, who had given him a cigarette just the day before and was now his victim. But Muller's goggling eyes were fixed on him, beseeching, searching frantically, almost popping out of their sockets. It was the wild, lost look of a man damned.

'I . . . I . . .' said Kordt bleakly.

'Are you going to carry out the order?' Weise asked languidly, savouring every moment. 'Yes or no.'

'Yes, sergeant.'

'Then I would advise you to get a move on with it.' He came a step nearer the boy and gave him a kick on the backside with one highly-polished boot. Now, they all thought: it must be now. They stood and they listened, as if glued to the spot, their spines tingling with a shared terror that went right into the pores of their skin. It was nothing new. This was life with the Dirlewanger Brigade.

Some of the men there watched, unable to help themselves, as Kordt came to within three yards of his victim and stretched out his arm again. They saw madness flicker over Muller's face. The sergeant had half-smoked his cigarette, and the boy was not going to be able to gain any more stay of execution. For all the men who watched, there was only one question: whether they hated or feared Weise more.

Other eyes stared straight at the ground or stared up at the dull, weary sky. Even Kortetzky hung his head, and Petrat had stopped his grinning. Fleischmann crashed forward headlong on to the ground and lay there like a block of wood. No one took any notice of him: they were all too intent on Muller's whimpering and Kordt's gasping breath. Kirchwein was leaning against Vonwegh, the man from whom everything seemed to slide off, like water running down a stone wall.

And the shot finally rang out.

It sounded thin and paltry. The report echoed off the barrack walls, making it sound as if Kordt had emptied the whole magazine at once. Muller, the victim, slumped on to his back with his arms outstretched in front of him. Thank God, thought a few, who had long since given up praying, and in that first moment they felt relieved, almost released. All except Kordt, who looked like a child with an old man's head – so aged, so sad, so numb. He just stared uncomprehendingly at the pistol, fumbling with it feebly in his frozen hand.

Sergeant Weise went up to Muller, who lay there, the whites of his eyes showing, like a slaughtered animal. But he wasn't dead.

'You lousy shot!' roared the sergeant, swivelling on his heel to face Kordt. 'You idiot . . . you miserable coward!' Weise tossed his cigarette away and stared at Kordt with hatred and contempt. He saw fear of death in the boy's eyes and nodded, satisfied. He could enjoy that here, every day, every hour. The power to reduce a man's life to the fate of a fly. Weise had never achieved anything in his thirty years of life, but now he was a god: men went down on their knees in front of him, trembling, hoping, praying.

'So you want to finish the thing in instalments,' Weise said, and smiled crookedly. 'You've wasted ammunition!' he shouted suddenly. 'Sabotage! Draining the war effort!' His voice became dangerously soft. 'Now, be so good as to take that weapon and . . .'

Muller had only gradually realised that Kordt's shot had simply grazed his forehead. A thin, bright red trickle of blood ran from his left temple down his face, over his mouth and chin. But the little fat man with the nickel glasses wasn't going to let himself be hanged a second time. Suddenly he found a strength he never knew he had, the desperate will to live gave him energy. And Muller acted.

Suddenly the fat man was on his feet, passing the cursing Weise, running from the horrified Kordt, gasping for his life, sprinting as fast as he could. He felt the pain in his temples, saw red in front of his eyes, and stumbled on. His lungs prickled like knives, his knees wobbled and shook, his heart beat wildly. But fear was stronger than all that, and it drove him onward, though he knew he hardly had a chance. Muller, in that moment, was like an animal in a slaughterhouse, granted a last-minute chance to break free from the butcher's axe. He ran, and made it over thirty, forty yards of the treacherous, snow-covered terrain.

Behind him was Kordt.

The men from the first platoon stood there, stared at the

life-and-death chase with narrowed eyes. Some looked away to avoid showing emotion. They had long since learned to hide their feelings as carefully as their bread ration.

Kortetzky shot Weise a craven look from his button-like eyes. Petrat was secure in the knowledge that his stock was high with the sergeant. Fleischmann still lay motionless on the ground. Kirchwein shook with fear.

Only Paul Vonwegh remained aloof. He looked detached, almost arrogant, as if he was trying to say: what's this to me? What have I got to do with it? A man who lives, as I do, from hate to hate knows no pity. Why should I feel pity? Anyone who makes mistakes has only himself to blame . . .

Meanwhile, Sergeant Weise had found a new victim.

'Oh, look at this one,' he said, and his attention turned to Fleischmann, who was still lying on the ground.

'Haven't you slept enough today, Herr Hauptsturmführer?'

Fleischmann heaved himself up and stood to attention.

'A very good morning to you,' Weise continued in a dangerous soft tone. 'Step forward!' he bawled.

The man obeyed like an automaton.

'You're a shit, eh?' Weise said.

'Yes, sergeant,' Fleischmann answered dutifully.

'Well, tell the others what mischief you got up to that brought you here.'

The degraded officer didn't hesitate for a second.

'I attacked a female air force assistant with a gun . . . I wanted her to . . .'

The new game was, however, becoming boring for Weise. He remembered Kordt and Muller, but they were nowhere to be seen. He'd hear the shot soon, he thought. No one escapes from me . . . He turned to the gang again.

'Kirchwein!' he yelled to the epileptic. 'What is an officer who attacks a German air force assistant with a pistol?'

'A pig.'

'Come on, why are you being so modest?'

'A stinking pig!' Kirchwein shouted as loudly as he could.

'Did you hear what you are?' Weise turned back to Fleischmann.

'A stinking pig,' Fleischmann replied resignedly. A proud member of the master race had been turned into a shit-scared punishment soldier.

'A knowledge of your limitations is the first step towards self-improvement,' the sergeant continued. He looked again in the direction that Muller had fled, spat, and shrugged his shoulders. 'Pity . . .' He faced Fleischmann once more. 'I was going to make you platoon commander for the next engagement, but you're too soft for me.'

'Yes, sergeant.'

Weise pondered. There were no set groups or platoons among the Dirlewangers. Even company commanders were only appointed for one engagement. They remained ordinary B-soldiers, and were recognisable only by a single white stripe on their sleeves, which remained there only for the duration of that mission.

The sergeant went up close to the men of the first platoon, wandered along the ranks, peering at them, and then came to a halt in front of Paul Vonwegh.

'Hm,' he said, and stared the medium-sized, wiry man in the face. He saw no fear, and for a fleeting moment he considered.

'I'll try you,' said Weise. 'You'll take charge of the platoon.'

Vonwegh nodded.

'Get on with it,' Weise ordered. 'Move off with your gang and get busy on the wood pile. Right now, I have to see about the two birds who have flown.'

Vonwegh came to the front of the ranks to face the men. His voice was quiet but firm, as if he were used to command. The gorilla watched him defiantly, with treachery in his eyes, but Vonwegh just looked straight at him and Kortetzky followed the others, subdued. A minute later, they had reached their work place.

The new platoon leader kept a sharp eye on them, conceding them nothing. The quota would be met, Vonwegh left no room for doubt about that. He was neither a careerist nor a slave driver. But unlike the others he had an aim which went beyond filling his stomach, boozing, finding a cushy job, or staying alive. Hate held him up, drove him on and gave him strength.

Paul Vonwegh had lost the last of his illusions in Spain. He knew his enemies as well as he knew their victims, and he did not waste his energy on Muller or Kordt. They were beyond help now: it was much more important to know who had informed on them, who was the traitor. That was the life-or-death question, Vonwegh thought, as he urged his platoon on. Mechanically he looked back to try and see some evidence of Muller's fate, but he saw only the barracks, and the dark smoke rising from the chimney, falling grey, grimy and heavy to the ground, like the ash from Cain's sacrifice.

Then he winkled out Petrat, who had slunk off for a rest, and gave him a kick. He read the gorilla's opposition in his face, and hit him in the teeth. He noticed Kirchwein straining under his load. But he didn't move to help him: here, help was at best a weakness or cowardice; at worst it was suspect, subversive.

Vonwegh compared their progress so far with the total target. It was O K. At that point the first platoon had more than met their quota, and with ease. He walked past his men and studied them all, seeing, as he did so, how they were already swallowing their hatred and vying for his favour. It all left him cold. Nothing touched him. He was the best commander that the first platoon had ever had, but he did not encourage, or bellow, or promise, or threaten. The important thing was that in these first few minutes he had already got a grip on these men. He would get rid of the unfit ones and use the others. He would wait, watch, and select . . .

Vonwegh heard steps and stiffened. A Russian girl was being led past, and as he looked at her his face underwent a swift, fleeting change. The prisoner was still young. She seemed younger than Karen, her face was broader and her hair darker. But there was something about her that made her seem very like Karen. Perhaps every woman snatched away and dragged off like that was a Karen, Vonwegh mused. Every face was Karen's face when it was moulded by grief.

Karen . . . he thought longingly, and his glance followed the

Russian girl until she was out of sight.

That time in Berlin, he had held her in his arms at last. It had been like the first time, and yet quite different. They belonged together, even though the times had torn them apart. In Berlin, his hand, which for years had held only rifle butts, caressed Karen gently, as if she were made of expensive and delicate porcelain.

'I dreamt . . .' she said softly.

'I have been dreaming for years . . .' he replied.

Paul let her go but kept his eyes firmly fixed on her, as if trying to hold the image of her in his mind. They looked at each other and suddenly they felt afraid – not of the world outside; not of the neighbours; not of the police machine which was ruthlessly hunting Vonwegh, to find and destroy him. No, they were frightened, at that moment, for themselves, frightened that something might have changed, that one of them would say the wrong thing, that their tenderness might disappear as quickly as it had come.

'And now?' Karen began.

'You live here alone?' he asked.

She nodded.

Paul Vonwegh looked past her at the furniture, which had appeared so alien and unfriendly at first. But this was Karen, her taste, her essence, her lifestyle. Nothing was overdone, and nothing was left out. It was beautiful, practical, simple, and even a little bit playful. Yes, this room was Karen.

'Are they still looking for you?' she said abruptly.

'Yes.' His reply sounded hard and final. She looked up at him and there was both love and reproach in her eyes. There was one way in which she would never understand him: Karen wanted no part in politics; she defended herself instinctively against fluttering banners and noisy loudspeakers. To her it all seemed so crude, so inhuman, and so she rejected it.

Karen wanted to love and to be loved. There was nothing more important to her, and that was why she could never grasp what it was that Paul Vonwegh had gone to Spain for. No war was 'just' to Karen, all seemed equally hideous and pointless, and so even the side that he took in the Spanish struggle seemed cruel and hostile to her. Because she loved him so much, she had come to believe that she could hate him for his Spanish adventure. But with time her anger cooled and she had come to understand, gradually, that a man of his calibre could never give up risk and danger. For him there had to be something greater behind things, something great, strong and good . . . sometimes she would become jealous of it, this thing that kept him from her.

'I just wanted to see you,' Paul said softly, 'just once more, for a moment, to ask you a question.'

'You have . . . risked too much,' she whispered.

'Not too much,' he said, 'when it's about us . . . are dreams not beautiful?'

'Shouldn't we be getting used to reality?' Karen asked gently.

He nodded.

Stepping away from her, Vonwegh looked out of the window at the city. It had been so beautiful, and so stupid, to come to Berlin. It was stupid because of the police, and it was stupid, too, because of Karen. How could he achieve anything except another separation? But Karen had already come over to him and was standing by his side. She pulled him gently to her. Her hair was as shining as her eyes, her skin so finely textured.

'Would you . . . would you go to Spain again?' she asked.

'I . . . I don't know,' he answered haltingly.

He can't lie, she thought, *he still can't lie.*

They sat down together, feeling the shyness between them.

'No,' said Vonwegh suddenly. 'God, I would stay with you and never leave again. If –' his face was drawn and resigned '– if only I could . . .'

'And you can't?'

'No.'

'Why not?'

'Because you know I would only endanger you.'

'Do you still love me?' she said after a short silence.

'How can you ask that?' Vonwegh said.

'Because you must know that I don't care about all that.'

He took her hand.

'No,' he murmured, moved, 'I know that.'

'Then you will stay,' said Karen, almost harshly.

And then evening came. It came slowly, and they made no move to put on the lights. They let the dusk fall and the moon rise, bright and shining. Karen lit a candle, and they began to talk, to plan, to build castles in the air, test them, tear them down and then build them up again on more solid foundations. At first they would wait, they agreed, and then they would go to ground in a farmhouse in Mecklenburg. Finally they would get false papers and try to flee north to Sweden, where Karen's mother's relations would be waiting for them.

'But that's not today,' she said finally. The candle flickered, distorting the shadows on the wall. Smiling, they saw what it would be like in the shadows, fragmented and distorted, but a future.

There was a loud, piercing ring at the doorbell. They backed away from each other. It was probably only a casual visitor, but it showed Paul Vonwegh and Karen with a cruel and brutal clarity what a future on the run was going to mean . . .

Vonwegh looked round numbly, torn back to the present. He hadn't moved for several minutes, but he was suddenly alerted by the sound of voices, voices that he recognised straight away as belonging to Petrat and Kortetzky.

'I saw it with my own eyes,' Kortetzky lied. 'Vonwegh sneaked off to the castle . . . to squeal on Muller.'

'He'll get his, then,' hissed Petrat. 'Tomorrow . . . in action.'

'I'll divert his attention . . . and you kill him,' the gorilla muttered.

'You can rely on me.'

Vonwegh moved away, making sure he wasn't noticed. He had learned a lesson. There was no point in losing yourself in thoughts of the past when the present was a death sentence – from your own comrades.

*

Kordt felt a creeping sensation of panic in the back of his neck. He was still pursuing his friend Muller like a man possessed. It was no longer a hunt: it had turned into a crazy running-amuck.

He was running, stumbling, straight through Dirlewanger's headquarters, past the sweating B-soldiers creeping through the snow in their gas masks, past the staff butchery, where Aumeier, who had been personally condemned to death by the Reichsführer SS and was due to be executed today, lorded it over his private empire. He passed two Russian women, spreadeagled naked in the snow, having water poured over their shivering bodies to make them betray the hiding-places of partisans. He passed the block on which human beings' flesh was torn to shreds, and the bunkers which the Sturmbannführer had personally invented, where a man could be made to stand upright for days until the joints swelled and the body became obscenely bloated, even though the victim was starving.

Muller had disappeared from Kordt's view. Then suddenly he saw him and started after him. He was gaining. He was the younger of the two, and his former qualms had long been destroyed by his overwhelming fear of Sergeant Weise's brutal wrath. There were still thirty yards between them. He stood still and aimed with the .08, but whenever he tried to pull the trigger his aim seemed to become blurred and Muller leapt out of his line of fire. Then Kordt watched his quarry stumble and fall on a piece of ice. Now, he thought, and pulled the trigger once, twice, three times.

The shots rebounded crazily off the castle. The next moment Sturmbannführer Dirlewanger tore open the window and yelled to his castle-gendarmes:

'Who the hell's that shooting around the place like a lunatic? Go out and get those fellows – both of them!'

Minutes later, the Sturmbannführer had them delivered to his presence. He stood there, his tunic still unbuttoned, staring at them through those tiny, bloodshot eyes of his, but his mind was on the papers that were lying on the table in front of him. One of them was a complaint from Reichsleiter Rosenberg about Dirlewanger's methods of waging war; but another was a retrospective promotion to Obersturmbannführer and a simultaneous appointment to S S Standartenführer. He had been handed them ten minutes earlier, and the pleasure that they had given him – in their different ways – had driven the early-morning hangover from his head. The two men who stood before him would not have believed it, but Oskar Dirlewanger was in a good mood.

The boy Kordt stood swaying in front of his newly-appointed Standartenführer, trembling like a scarecrow in a storm. Muller's face was grotesque and smeared with blood. But he was quiet now. Unlike Kordt, he had no more need to fight for his life. It would soon be over for him, and already the energy was waning from him as quickly as the air from a decompressor . . .

'Where did you get that weapon?' Dirlewanger snapped at the boy.

'From . . . from the sergeant.'

'From which sergeant?' the chief interrputed him.

'Sergeant Weise.'

'And why?

'I . . . I was ordered . . . to kill him.' He indicated Muller.

'I see,' Dirlewanger said irritably. 'Then why is he still alive?'

'I . . . I missed,' Kordt answered, wishing the ground would open up under his feet.

'Fetch me Sergeant Weise,' Dirlewanger directed one of his men.

The Standartenführer was pale. His face was unhealthy and the skin stretched tautly over it like a thin film. His cheeks were hollow, despite the fact that he led a life of gluttony; he was forty-seven years old, but looked ten years older. And above those small, restless eyes one eyelid twitched gently.

Nothing – and no one – else in the room moved.

Then a few of yesterday's guests, attracted by the noise

from Dirlewanger's quarters, stuck their heads into the room.

'Come in, gentlemen,' the Standartenführer said affably. He was going to take this opportunity to show them a thing or two.

At that moment, Sergeant Weise entered the room. He knew he would survive this business if Dirlewanger's goodwill held out. And he didn't doubt that he would be finished if it did not.

'Weise,' snapped Dirlewanger. 'What's going on? You gave this fellow a weapon and he goes firing it outside my front door . . .'

'He missed at a distance of two yards,' the sergeant said when Dirlewanger had finished his complaint. Weise stood to attention. 'On purpose,' he continued. 'It was a deliberate refusal to carry out an order.'

Dirlewanger grunted and took his favourite to one side.

'That's the man who was slandering you, Standartenführer,' the sergeant explained quickly.

'Yes, I know,' Dirlewanger said impatiently, with a wave of the hand.

'There are, however, only two things that matter here,' Dirlewanger continued, 'either the fellows should be got rid of in private . . . or publicly, as a deterrent . . . in front of the whole gang.' His hawklike face distorted in a grin.

'Yes, Standartenführer,' Weise answered obediently.

'That's settled, then,' the commander said. 'But unfortunately at the moment we need every man we have . . We can't expend lives if we're not getting any replacements.'

'Yes, Standartenführer.'

'Get back to your gang,' Dirlewanger said with a satisfied smile. Then he turned back to his guests.

'Excuse me, gentlemen . . . I must sort this out.'

The officers made to leave, but Dirlewanger said:

'Please, by all means, stay . . . Perhaps it would be interesting for you to learn something of our methods.'

Then he poured himself a tumbler full of vodka. He ran his eyes over Kordt and Muller, luxuriating in their fear.

'You miserable coward,' he said to Kordt. Next he turned to Muller, 'And what have you got against me?' he asked, with something close to amusement.

'N-Nothing . . . Sturmbannführer,' Muller muttered quickly.

'Didn't you say that I ought to be hanged after the war?'

'I . . . I was d-d-drunk, Sturmbannführer.'

'Standartenführer from now on. How much did you drink!'

'Half a litre of schnapps, Standartenführer.'

'And you can't hold it . . .'

Muller nodded.

'I don't blame you for having something against me,' Dirlewanger said finally. 'But that you doubt our final victory is treason and desertion. And what is the penalty for that . . .?' He turned to Kordt enquiringly.

'Death,' the boy said, without hesitation.

'The right answer,' Dirlewanger said, pacing backwards and forwards, grinning at his guests. 'And you agreed with this fellow . . . you are also in favour of stringing me up?'

'No, Sturmbann – . . . Standartenführer,' the young man hastily corrected himself, stupefied with terror.

'I pardon you for wanting to put a rope round my neck,' Dirlewanger replied moodily. 'But there can be no pardon for missing your target four times. Come, gentlemen,' he waved to his guests and minions, 'let us take a walk over to the parade ground.'

He took a Wehrmacht colonel aside and commented:

'An old interest of mine . . . applied psychology as a means of maintaining morale and discipline. Watch carefully how we deal with things here – you might find this instructive.'

Muller followed the castle-gendarme without protest. Kordt on the other hand, had to be made to see reason with a hefty kick, and by the time they reached the 'standing bunker' he looked like one of the living dead.

'Well,' Dirlewanger said, 'we shall now undertake a morale-raising exercise.' He laughed humourlessly and pointed to Kordt. 'Get undressed!' he bellowed.

At least I'm not going to be shot, the boy thought, and tore the tattered rags off his body with a pathetic eagerness. Anything is better than that, he thought as they strapped him to the block . . .

'I hereby sentence you to twenty-five lashes,' said Dirlewanger casually. 'Thank my promotion . . .'

The newly-promoted Standartenführer took the whip and handed it to Muller.

'Let's see what you're made of,' he said. 'Spare him nothing, man.' He guffawed suddenly, revealing yellowed teeth. 'Imagine it's me there,' he said, pointing to the strapped-down figure of Kordt. 'If you do your bit properly,' he added, making a play of his tolerance, 'I might temper justice with mercy again . . . and you'll get away with just the bunker.'

Muller understood Dirlewanger's style of 'mercy'. He swung the leather thong back as far as he could.

Kordt had to count out loud at each stroke. He only got as far as the seventh, but everyone in the camp could hear his choking screams, and they counted for him. At the eighth, Kordt's howl became a whimper, and at the fourteenth he was unconscious and barely breathing, what breath he had coming in painful gasps.

'Just keep at it,' said Dirlewanger to Muller. 'I'm satisfied with you so far.' He turned to the castle-gendarme. 'Throw him in the bunker when he's finished . . . until further notice.'

Kordt, who had become conscious again during the brief respite, began to moan, but Muller swung the whip back as far as he could. The fat man was no sadist, and he felt nothing against his companion, but when his life was at stake . . .

Each man against his comrade. That was the system here. It broke their spirits, made animals of them all.

At the time, though, everyone in the camp judged it as an astonishing stroke of luck that Dirlewanger had not had the two shot or hanged on the spot. The promotion, they thought. The Standartenführer was not promoted every day, but the beatings, hangings and shootings took place here seven times a week.

In the middle of the night the whistle startled them from their straw mattresses. Turn out. Rumours buzzed backwards and forwards as they learned the news: they were *all* to report.

Paul Vonwegh led the first platoon. They left the barracks and marched for hours through the forest, over snow-covered fields. The new day dawned pale and distant, while somewhere on the horizon they saw a cloud of smoke rising. The sun broke through feebly and the first platoon tramped on . . .

A mother lay next to a house, holding her dead child tenderly in her arms. Both mother and child were dead, shot through the neck. The second platoon had been through here before them.

They headed off to the left, over frozen, marshy terrain, walking in single file. It was then came the first salvo of rifle-fire.

'Take cover!' Paul Vonwegh ordered.

They had run into the enemy's first line of resistance – snipers. If they didn't get past them, they had had it . . .

And so Paul Vonwegh was stuck in a swamp, with a bitter dilemma racing through his mind. If he led them forward, he would almost certainly be killed from behind; if he kept at the rear of his unit, no one would be prepared to advance.

Meanwhile, the firing went on. Two men were already dead, one was badly wounded. Vonwegh began to manoeuvre the machine-gun into position.

The gorilla, who had come up beside him, hissed: 'They're over there . . .' He pointed to where Petrat had sloped off.

And a short distance away the East Prussian sat, his weapon fire-ready, his eye on the notch on the bead sight. Aiming at Paul Vonwegh . . .

Chapter Three

The wind moaned across the boundless frozen wastes, whipping the icy marsh, rustling ominously among the treetops, as if it were the patient, tormented soul of Russia, crying softly to the heavens. Crystals of snow flickered blue, green, yellow and orange; if a man looked at them for long enough, they went through the whole spectrum of colours by which poisons are known. It was seven minutes before nine in the morning, and at this hour the light still came from the east.

And death came from the east, too. It perched in trees. It bided its time. And any man who wanted to cross the swamp had to pass it.

Paul Vonwegh scrambled up and instantly fell, half-smothered by a snow drift. A bullet hissed over his head, just missing him. He stood up and realised that the give in the ground had saved his life. What was more, the shot had come from the right, where Petrat was. The platoon leader crawled on quickly, glimpsing bullets burrowing into the snow to his right and his left – all coming from straight ahead. Vonwegh reached a tree stump which gave him cover, turned round and ordered Kortetzky to join him. It was better to have the gorilla by his side than behind him.

Kortetzky hesitated. Paul Vonwegh reached for his pistol and levelled it at the gorilla, in the easy way of a man who had a job to do, who would pull the trigger without pleasure but who would have no trouble in doing it if he had to. Kortetzky looked, he understood, and so, panting hard, he jumped through the sights of the Siberian snipers.

He crouched, more dangerously apelike than ever, in the snow beside his platoon leader. But Vonwegh crushed him with a contemptuous look. 'Fleischmann!' he called, without taking his eyes off the treetops. Fleischmann took longer than the gorilla, but he made it.

Vonwegh looked to his right, where the shots had come from: no sign of Petrat. Must be waiting until I show myself, he thought – he may not be a partisan sharpshooter, but he's only fifty yards away. 'Move to the right!' he called to the men with the machine-gun.

There couldn't be many partisans, Vonwegh judged, and their tactics were simple: to delay them for a while, pick off a few, and then withdraw before the Germans could get their range. Protected by white snow-camouflage suits, the Russians could only be spotted if they moved. In the meantime, they had other advantages: precise telescopic sights, sharp eyes, and trigger fingers that rarely missed.

Feeling the strain on his eyes, Vonwegh put down his field glasses.

'Target designation,' he said calmly, without turning to his machine-gunners. 'Distance four hundred metres . . . the second tree on the left . . . Hold the fire high.' Mechanically he added: 'Fire when you are ordered, understand?'

His men obeyed. An expert? they asked themselves. It was a novel experience for them, who had received their formal education in the underworld. They could steal, they could cheat and they could rob, but when it came to fighting a war they were innocents.

'Left wing!' Vonwegh ordered. 'Limited bound!'

He raised his hand slightly and brought it down in perfect time. Out of the corner of his eye he watched them jump from their cover. All wrong.

They jumped one after the other, instead of together. The first of them somersaulted twice, his arms and legs splayed wildly, like a man being tossed out of the door of a bar after closing time. And by the time he reached the ground he was dead.

'Target sighted?' Paul Vonwegh asked, throwing his field glasses to the machine-gun crew. Christ, in this bunch of clowns only every second man had a weapon, every fifth man a piece of bread, every tenth a cigarette, every fiftieth a machine-gun – and every hundredth a conscience . . .

'Target sighted,' came the report from the machine-gun emplacement.

Vonwegh nodded, noticing that the other men had joined up with him – all, that was, except Petrat, who was still lying in wait for him in some cosy corner on his right. 'Kortetzky,' he said harshly, 'go ahead with Fleischmann, carefully, first to the right, then to the left.'

The gorilla looked at him stupidly, but Fleischmann got the message, and his head sank between his shoulders. Vonwegh was intending to drive him and Kortetzky into the firing-line as decoys, to attract the snipers' fire.

'The machine-gun will take over fire support,' the platoon commander continued, turning to the two gunners, 'but only after the partisans have fired on Kortetzky and Fleischmann, clear?'

The men manning the machine-gun confirmed his order.

'Rest of the platoon spread out to the left,' Vonwegh called to those on the other flank. 'Keep twenty metres' distance, all right?'

Fleischmann was still staring at the snow, terrified to go forward and equally terrified to go back – one way or the other, he was going to get his. And the gorilla had understood things at last.

'That's lunatic!' he shouted. 'I'm not crazy!'

'Kirchwein!' Vonwegh called to the epileptic, 'you will be responsible for seeing everything goes to plan on the left flank.'

'Yes, sir,' said Kirchwein in amazement.

'You slimy bastard,' Kortetzky swore.

Ignoring him, Vonwegh unshouldered his machine-pistol and handed it to Fleischmann.

'Fleischmann,' he said coldly. 'I'll give you a chance. Drive Kortetzky in front of you, and if he doesn't go, kill him. That's an order.'

'Yes, sir.'

'Go in front yourself, you cowardly swine!' the gorilla screamed, in rising panic.

'Go! Now!' Vonwegh ordered.

Kortetzky hesitated, knowing that the man behind him had a machine-pistol pointed at his spine. Vonwegh nodded to him and the gorilla raised himself slowly out of cover – slowly, until a kick from Vonwegh sent him on his way.

The two men moved forward quickly, and the others followed them at a distance. The breakthrough seemed to be working as planned: either the partisans had withdrawn or they were waiting until the B-soldiers were nicely in range. Kortetzky managed fifty, sixty yards, with Fleischmann driving him forward like an animal.

'Move!' Vonwegh roared to Kirchwein on the left.

While the left wing swarmed out, swearing, creeping, squirming and jumping. Vonwegh left his cover, levered himself backwards as fast as he could, straightened again and went off to look for Petrat, making a wide curve to his right.

The first shots fell in front of him, and the machine-gun returned the fire. Vonwegh didn't waste his time glancing at the battle. His bunch would make it – the only question was who would die on the way. His estimate varied between four and nine dead, but the exact number was unimportant, he thought wryly: a Dirlewanger cost no more than a shot of powder, a length of rope, or a crushed-in skull . . .

Here, Vonwegh decided. He saw the trough in the ground from a way off. Petrat had to be waiting for him there, if he had an ounce of common sense. Ahead, in the direction of the enemy, he was shielded by a snow-covered bush, to his right the land sloped away slightly. Petrat would assume that he was bringing up the rear of his men, urging them on.

He went on a few paces, noting automatically that the machine-gun had opened up again and that his men were moving forward. The shouts and the curses seemed further away.

A few steps more and Vonwegh stumbled across Petrat. The East Prussian was staring hard to the left, in the direction he had last seen his platoon leader.

'Are you waiting for me?' Vonwegh asked.

Petrat started, turned, leapt to his feet, gun at the ready as he pointed towards Paul Vonwegh.

The camp looked like a winter paradise today. The chimneys were bizarre caps of snow. Under a thick layer of fresh snow the barracks looked pretty, almost pastoral. The alleys were empty.

To the left of the castle stood the 'standing bunker', to the right the smoking-chamber. Both were inventions of the Standartenführer: punishments to the left, delicacies to the right. Each came into force according to his mood and requirement. The sun might play with the light; Oskar Dirlewanger played with power.

Coming out of the dacha, he strolled, bolt upright and hands in pockets, leaving no doubt as to who was the master in his private hell. Dirlewanger walked for a while, heard voices behind the woodpile, smiled and nodded. He approached the men slowly, quietly, from behind, so that they didn't get a chance to see him. An emaciated B-soldier was chewing raw potato peelings. He raised his head as the Standartenführer stood there, unseen, and sniffed at the appetising roasting smell coming from the dacha's kitchen.

'Christ, there's something better cooking in the castle,' he said morosely. 'All stolen . . .'

'I couldn't care where it came from,' the second man replied, sampling the smell. 'Roast duck . . .' he said wistfully.

Then he saw the Standartenführer, sprang to his feet, stood to attention, and reported:

'B-soldier Haubach and a man from the . . .'

'Idle swine,' Dirlewanger interrupted him brutally.

They both stood there, pale, lost, and empty. Both knew that this conversation could cost them their lives.

'You have a complaint to make?' said Dirlewanger to the miserable Haubach, staring at a body swollen by malnutrition. 'You seem to have stuffed yourself already . . .' He summoned a castle-gendarme. 'Take their names.'

Then he went on his way, turned briefly to savour their fear, nodded and drawled: 'Carry on.'

Dirlewanger reached the smoking-chamber, dismissing the sentry who stood at its entrance, and strode into the room without a sound. Aumeier, his favourite, was snoring on the wooden bench, fat, full, and satisfied. His commander prodded him with the toe of his boot to wake him.

Quickly gathering his wits, Aumeier leapt to his feet and saluted.

The Standartenführer went over to a wooden tub.

'What's this here?' he called over to Aumeier.

'A new idea,' said the black-market butcher. 'I wanted to try smoking with saltpetre.'

'Why?'

'It's milder than salted meat . . . an old recipe of my grandfather's . . .'

'My God . . .' said Dirlewanger, with mingled admiration and apprehension. 'What if anything goes wrong?'

'You can depend on it, Standartenführer – nothing goes wrong when old Aumeier's in charge.'

Dirlewanger smiled mysteriously.

'You don't think so?' he said. 'And what about that little event in Kiev?'

Aumeier shook his head, then he winked slyly. We two understand each other, he was saying: we take what we want and we do very well out of it, eh?

'Well, yes,' he began cautiously. 'She was really something, Standartenführer, red-haired . . . I'm only human, after all . . .'

The Standartenführer nodded in agreement.

'The trouble is,' he said then, with an edge to his voice, 'that you attracted attention. The incident was reported to the Reichsführer S S. Bad luck.'

Aumeier hung his head. Six weeks ago when he had been in Kiev he had been caught by an MP patrol and taken in for attempted rape. The report had gone through official channels, but after three days he had been called back to his unit. With that, Aumeier had thought the whole thing was settled. But now . . . ?

'Get your gear together,' Dirlewanger said finally. He

offered the man a cigarette. 'I'm sorry, but I have to have you shot this evening.'

Aumeier laughed like a village idiot. It was a joke – a laugh.

Dirlewanger shrugged.

'All the better for you if you don't believe it,' he said.

Aumeier began to shake in a grotesque parody of hilarity. But now his laughter was leaden, and there was animal fear in his eyes as they met Dirlewanger's.

'Standartenführer,' he gasped. 'But that just isn't . . .'

Dirlewanger turned on his heel and strolled out of the smoking-chamber.

'But that can't . . .' Aumeier shouted after him. His voice rose to a soprano shriek, cracked and rose again until the sentries taught him some sense with a few swift, efficient blows from their rifle butts. The fall of the favourite was complete . . .

Now Dirlewanger had reached the 'standing bunker', where the Kapo in charge rushed out into the alleyway and spluttered out his report.

'What?' Dirlewanger asked in irritation. 'Twenty-seven prisoners? Deserters?'

'Eleven had been condemned to death,' the guard said.

'And the others? At any rate leave it until after the mission before locking them up.'

'They can't move,' the overseer answered with a grin. 'They've got legs like elephants.'

'I'll make them healthy,' the Standartenführer said. 'Instant healing . . .'

He had the first cell unlocked. Kordt keeled over flat on his face, powerless to break his fall.

'This one's had enough,' said Dirlewanger, satisfied.

'The other one's the same,' replied the Kapo, but he didn't have time to display the bespectacled Muller. Dirlewanger had already gone.

'Still no report from Sergeant Weise?' he asked a castle-gendarme when he got back to his headquarters.

'No, Standartenführer.'

'Damn it,' Dirlewanger cursed.

Then he went to eat. Today he had only five guests, since some of his favourites were in action. Despite the splendid meal, Aumeier preyed heavily on his mind. What should he do? He had to carry out his order. Dirlewanger drank without his usual enthusiasm, but slowly the alcohol began to take effect.

It was then that the chief castle-gendarme came and stood next to him, showed him a piece of paper with two names on it and asked:

'What is to be done with those two fellows from this morning, the ones from the wood detachment?'

'Ah, yes,' Dirlewanger smiled smugly. 'Bring them to me.'

Around the room, the conversation died down, and the Standartenführer's guests braced themselves for what was to come. Dirlewanger must have some 'special treatment' in mind for the pair who had displeased him.

Soon B-soldier Haubach and his companion stood before the master of their destinies, pathetic in their fear, men who had already given up hope.

'You have a good appetite?' Dirlewanger addressed the one with the body swollen by malnutrition.

'Yes, Standartenführer.'

'And you're famished, eh?'

'Yes, sir.'

'Please,' said the chief, pointing to the groaning platter of roast meats.

Terrified that this was some ruse that would lead to his being whipped, if not shot, the man dared not move.

'Get a move on,' said Dirlewanger, turning to the second man and giving him a push towards the table. 'Or do I have to shovel roast pigeon down your miserable throat?' He laughed at his own wit, and the men around him smiled.

'Stuff yourselves full, you idiots,' he said.

The two men stumbled to the table. For weeks now they had had nothing to eat but water, soup and raw potatoes. Now they saw the delicacies they had dreamt of all that time and they felt sick, horribly sick. It was more than their shredded nerves could take: a condemned man's meal without an execution – yet. With all eyes on them they quivered with terror and nausea as they stuffed the rich food into their mouths.

'God help you if you don't empty your plates!' Dirlewanger called to them. The Standartenführer beamed with brutal satisfaction. His entourage joined in. This was one of his better jokes.

The castle-gendarmes amused themselves by laying bets on which of the two men would vomit first, and Dirlewanger drank and followed the game until it began to bore him. His mood was just about to take a turn for the worse when he remembered something. Quietly he studied Haubach, who was seated to his left, still chewing dutifully.

'What's your profession?' he asked.

'Craftsman, Standartenführer,' the B-soldier said.

'And from where?'

'Lower Bavaria.'

A remarkable resemblance, Dirlewanger mused. The more he drank, the more striking it became, and gradually a way out of his predicament became clear.

A little while later, a castle-gendarme sidled up to him.

'What are we going to do with them, Standartenführer?' he whispered.

Dirlewanger smiled slyly and pointed to Haubach.

'We will swop that one with Aumeier,' he answered softly. The guard looked at him in puzzlement, and Dirlewanger grinned again.

'Brains,' he concluded, tapping his skull.

Paul Vonwegh reacted immediately and instinctively, hurling himself forward just as Petrat fired. He swiped at the gun barrel while still in the air and the bullet sped harmlessly to the left. Petrat was thrown to the ground by the force of the collision.

'You swine,' the East Prussian breathed, his lips dripping with saliva like a mad dog. He got to his feet again and prepared to jump, and as he launched himself Vonwegh caught him, spun him round, and then threw him over his shoulder on to his face into the snow. He waited until Petrat got up again, and then finished him off systematically, pounding the man with his fists with cool, unemotional precision – going for the carotid artery in the neck, the stomach, nose, and chin, always aiming to create maximum pain, the kind of pain that would break the man once and for all. The hair on Petrat's forehead was stuck to his blood-smeared face, and tears showed through the dirt and the bruises and the blood. His tongue lolled out of an opened, slack mouth. With a final uppercut, the platoon leader jammed that tongue back between his teeth.

Petrat collapsed, and the hatred suddenly turned to fear. The platoon's heavy now cried like a child, reaching a high-pitched crescendo as he saw Vonwegh unshoulder his weapon. Gasping for breath, he whined:

'You . . . It wasn't me . . . The gorilla's idea . . .' A look of pathetic cunning flitted over his ruined face. 'If you don't watch out . . .'

'What about Kortetzky?' Vonwegh cut in, waving the gun barrel between Petrat's eyes with a grim playfulness.

'The gorilla,' Petrat whispered, 'he wants to . . . kill you . . . but I don't . . .'

'Oh?' said Vonwegh sardonically.

'Not me . . . not at all . . .' Petrat whined on.

'On your feet,' Vonwegh commanded.

Still trembling, Petrat got up painfully.

'Here,' said Vonwegh contemptuously, and threw him the weapon.

Petrat stared at him in total incomprehension.

'Go on. Get up front and face the music,' Vonwegh said, pointing in the direction of the battle.

'You –' Petrat gasped, his face contorted with astonishment, ' – Are you going to report me?' Now the fear was creeping back again.

'Nonsense,' Vonwegh answered coldly. 'Just move. Join up with the others.'

Shaking his head, Petrat stumbled off, with Vonwegh behind him. The East Prussian's whole understanding of the world had collapsed. He could still feel those brutally efficient blows on his body, still know that his hatred had turned to craven fear, still smart with the awareness that he had whimpered for mercy like a dog. Why hadn't Vonwegh finished him off when he had the chance?

By now the pair of them had almost reached the main body. The ones in front were still being fired on, but the partisans' resistance was already beginning to crumble. Paul Vonwegh took in the battle-situation at a glance: the withering fire of the machine-gun; the death-leap of a Russian sniper from his tree top; Fleischmann's butt-strokes, driving Kortetzky on in his wild bursts of running – and the left wing moving inexorably up. Then he saw the gorilla fall, saw Fleischmann glance at him and then hurry on. A second later, the resistance had melted and they had reached the other side of the swamp. As for the six dead, that was average casualties . . .

Petrat was now going forward in the open, though still ducking for safety's sake, while the platoon commander ran beside him, as unconcerned as if he were going for a keep-fit run. Inside, however, Vonwegh knew that this was the crunch: the two men who had planned to kill him were the platoon's 'heavies', who had always had the others exactly where they wanted them. Whoever broke Petrat and the gorilla would have everyone else's respect and obedience. If he could do that, these men would follow him through hell and back.

Paul Vonwegh had worked and planned for this moment, though the way had been long and miserably hard. It had led through burning villages, past violated women and murdered children.

Anyone who could come through on top after that was a model member of the Dirlewanger Brigade.

Anyone who succumbed was destroyed.

Anyone who showed even pity was suspect.

Paul Vonwegh knew that he must not arouse suspicion.

Now, as they gathered on the other side of the swamp, they all knew that the breakthrough had succeeded and that the way ahead was clear. Vonwegh watched the one or two stragglers drifting in, then his thoughts were interrupted by

Petrat's harsh snarl as he leaned over the fallen body of Kortetzky:

'Well,' the East Prussian said through clenched teeth, 'he won't make it with women again . . .'

Vonwegh pushed him aside, crouched down beside the gorilla, felt his pulse and raised one of the man's eyelids.

'Move,' he ordered Petrat. 'Carry him over to the others.'

Petrat shook his head. 'He's already had it,' he grunted. Then he saw the look in Vonwegh's eyes and that was enough: in a moment he had heaved the unconscious Kortetzky on to his shoulders.

The platoon leader nodded to Kirchwein. He had taken the chance to display the new, tamed Petrat to the others, and now Vonwegh introduced another innovation unheard of in Dirlewanger's gang: he ordered Kortetzky to be bandaged. The men murmured in amazement. Up to now, only the less seriously wounded had been taken along – bad cases were left to the cold, the Russians, and the wolves.

And so they advanced, through country where nothing living moved, towards a goal that made even the most hardened criminals sick with foreboding.

Punctual to the minute, Vonwegh marched his men in to join the rest of the company and made his report to Sergeant Weise.

'Hm,' said the NCO, who was already drunk. 'Six dead.' He shot a gobbet of spit on to the ground. 'You've been a very efficient boy, Vonwegh.' Then he saw Kortetzky being carried on an improvised tarpaulin stretcher. 'What the hell is that?' Weise said.

'A serious casualty,' said Vonwegh expressionlessly.

'Oh yes?' the sergeant said sarcastically. 'Let's have a look at the bugger.' He recognised the gorilla and nodded.

More than a hundred men now advanced over a seemingly endless snowscape, their boots trampling terrain that was shroud-white, marching hour upon hour. Somewhere, far on the horizon, where the smooth sky arched over a predestined hell, rose the column of smoke that betrayed the village of

Smolwieski. It was 1 p.m. on 17 February 1943 . . .

Paul Vonwegh's body seemed to weigh more heavily on his legs with every step he took. Though he had imagined it a hundred times in his mind, this was his first direct experience of this kind of duty. Now that the reality was staring him in the face, he had to fight hard to remain the man who let things slide off him, who was never dirty, who felt no hunger and knew no tiredness.

The company approached to within three kilometres of the village and Sergeant Weise gave Vonwegh his orders:

'Your unit will be in charge of sealing off the village. If a single one of those Russian scum gets away, you're for it.'

Vonwegh nodded.

At least he wouldn't be directly involved in the massacre. But there would still be the screams, the frantic running, the gunfire . . .

Was there nothing against this bloody age, this brutal system? Were there no thoughts that could console a man, no hope at which he could clutch? Was there no God, to prevent such a thing? No men who would take arms against it? No future that would forgive . . . ?

Yes, there must be, said Paul Vonwegh to himself, and he drew himself up straight. They were at the village now, and he could see the peasants recognise the ragged gang, could see them rushing vainly, falling over each other in their panic. He saw women clutching children, heard their shrieks as commandos dragged them from them. He saw girls running towards the barricade on the other side, to be mown down by the men of his own platoon. His gaze took in the first houses as they began to burn, he heard the cattle bellowing as they searched desperately for a way out of their suffocating stalls.

He saw it, and he let it wash over him.

Paul Vonwegh held on to what he had lost. He focused his memory so hard that it hurt. He was not here, he was a long way away. At home. With Karen. Soon he saw and heard nothing more. It was their first evening after his return from Switzerland, and the doorbell had just rung . . .

Quickly, they moved apart from each other. It was something that they would do a hundred times more. This was to become their 'daily bread' – the price they had to pay for being together.

Paul Vonwegh went quietly into the next room while Karen answered the door. It turned out to be Frau Meier, her neighbour, returning a borrowed newspaper and angling for a chat.

When the woman had gone, the candle flickered again. This time, however, they saw only shadows – though they sat close, the mood was shattered.

For the next few days it went on: the milkman came, the man to read the gas meter, the air raid warden, the blackout inspectors. Even harmless tradesman became sinister, threatening figures. They told each other that it was all worth it if they could be together. They told each other that they were happy. The said it all too firmly, too often, too determinedly for it to be true.

They fled from Berlin, travelling separately to Mecklenburg, where Karen had a friend who lived in a small lakeside village. The man risked his life when he took in the stranger, Vonwegh, but in those times there were still people who were not informers.

In the village there was no telephone, no doorbell, and no air raid warden. At first their nerves were too strained for them to be able to enjoy it, but gradually they accustomed themselves to the peaceful life there. Time passed, nothing happened, and they became more confident; even though the war had reduced the village's tourist traffic to almost nil, they managed to have themselves accepted by the locals as summerlet holiday-makers.

They lived on the ground floor, in rooms that gave directly on to the lake, and they began to swim every day. Paul's face became tanned and healthy. As if there were nothing more important in the world, Karen kept telling him, over and over again, how young and handsome he looked.

'And you,' she would ask with a coquettish smile, 'do you still love me?'

He would smile back, and nod.

'I haven't grown old?' she would say.

'You will never grow old, Karen.'

'But you can see the years in me . . .'

'No,' he would answer. 'You're just as you were then . . . the first time . . .'

'Only because you are,' she would laugh, and lean her head on his shoulder.

Everything was so natural, as only complete happiness can be. They held hands as if they never wanted to let go of each other again. They swam in the lake from their own small boat, often staying out all day alone – the lake was their world, and the boat was their happiness. The summer was fine and warm, and they didn't bother to count the passing days. Had it been a day, a week, a month? The present had no form for them: it was simply a drop in the boundless sea of infinity, knowing no future and seemingly no past. There was only I and you, you and me, us, we, us . . .

But if they lived apart from the world, they could not ignore it. There were small things: a knock on the window because their blackout was not dark enough; the puzzled look of the postman because they received no mail; the ominous banner-headlines in the newspapers; a fatuous report on the radio; a bombastic military march – all the little pin-pricks that kept alive their awareness of the time they were living in.

On such occasions, Vonwegh would become disturbed and moody.

'What's the matter?' Karen would ask, and he would answer: 'Nothing'. But she knew that he was lying, because both of them were already beginning to think again about the same thing: the future. Soon it would be autumn, and then winter – and winter here would be no good for people without a warm, snug apartment.

Slowly, such thoughts began to take up most of Paul's waking time. As far as his own fate was concerned, he didn't care. But Karen was a different matter. True love must be unselfish, he told himself, and real, great feelings, such as they had, involve self-sacrifice. Karen must go back to Berlin. He had to disappear from her world. Karen would be sad, but she would weep and carry on living . . .

Vonwegh struggled with his emotions. For the first time in his life, his willpower, the thing that had always sustained Paul, failed him. He knew what he had to do, but instead all he did was to pull Karen to him, to caress her and hold her tight until she gasped for breath, to smooth the hair from her face and kiss that forehead and those lips until it chased the thoughts away from him.

And then, just when his feelings seemed to have won their final victory over reason, the blow came.

That day, he had gone for a walk in the forest, alone, leaving Karen to her domestic chores. He had soon become bored with his stroll and had come back earlier than expected. Hearing voices, he had gone into the next room.

'Yes,' the voice was saying – someone he didn't know – 'the whole family . . . to the camp . . . no one knows if they'll ever get out again.'

'Yes, but . . .' he heard Karen reply helplessly.

'It's a filthy business,' the man with her was saying, 'but what do you expect from these brownshirt bastards . . . just because they gave him some clothes for his escape . . . his own mother . . .'

'Please . . .' Karen said, and Vonwegh ached as he sensed the desperation in her voice.

Then the conversation became quieter, and Vonwegh could no longer hear what was being said. They must have noticed that he was back. Everything he had been suppressing these last weeks came rushing back to the surface of his mind: he was endangering Karen. He had to go, for her sake. Even if she didn't understand. Even if she broke down . . .

He, Paul Vonwegh, didn't break down so easily.

Vonwegh remembered how he had told himself that, ten times, a hundred times over. Now he told himself again as he stood there and ordered a line of guards to stop the human beings fleeing from the massacre. A few yards from him, a three-year-old child cried for its doll. Its mother made to fetch the toy, but she took too long for Weise; without even pausing, the sergeant pumped the whole magazine from his machine-pistol into the woman's body. She fell forward on her face, and still the child cried for the doll, not understanding what had happened to its mother.

'Russian scum!' Weise cursed, and swung his weapon back.

Paul Vonwegh turned to one side. At last, he had had enough. His hand clenched tightly on his own weapon, turning the knuckles white until the skin stretched so much that it looked ready to split. He levelled the gun at Weise, watching the killer through the sights. Petrat saw him. Kirchwein's eyes were fixed on him. Paul Vonwegh hesitated. He didn't break down . . .

Suddenly a woman and two young girls burst through the buildings and ran towards him, pursued by a bunch of whooping soldiers. Kirchwein looked at Vonwegh with an unspoken question in his eyes, but the platoon leader quickly shook his head. Then the girls were almost level with them, and he saw the leading one; she was about twenty years old, pretty, with long dark hair. All she desired in the world was written on her tormented face – she wanted to live, live, live . . . She threw up her arms in supplication and looked straight into the eyes of Paul Vonwegh.

Chapter Four

It all happened so quickly, yet seemed to last an eternity. In those few, paralysing seconds, Paul Vonwegh realised that he was in hell, and that the devil had found the first available opportunity to bring about his downfall.

He saw the Russian girls stumbling closer, straight to him, as if instinct told them that here was a human being among beasts, and he knew that there was no way out. Vonwegh could feel himself trembling, and his head was filled with a blinding pain.

Then, suddenly, he felt a dull anger dawning on him. From the faces of his men he could see that all eyes were on him, and in Dirlewanger's gang that could be, had to be, fatal. The first rule here was: merge with the crowd, stand in file as a total naught, a perfect nothing, a non-person. Vonwegh felt the bile rise in his throat.

He took the gun firmly in his hand again, feeling its sweat-sticky grip against his palm, and he came to a decision.

The foremost Russian girl had reached him now. Sergeant Weise, in full cry, paused briefly to ensure that the cordon was in operation and that no one would be able to slip through. Corporal Belle did the same on the other side.

Paul Vonwegh heard the first girl's gasping breath, saw her face, inhumanly pale and featureless in its fear of death. Behind her wide-open eyes, with their frightening, almost colourless pupils, lay the most total despair he had ever experienced in another. With horrified fascination he watched as she stretched out, reached for the toes of his boots, and tried to caress them.

The wind changed direction, driving the smoke into their eyes. The men of the first platoon quarrelled, cursed, laughed as they stood there – anything to make themselves impervious to what was happening. In the village ahead of them, a man tore himself free and ran headlong for thirty, forty yards, until a burst from a machine-gun caught him and flung him down, a bloody puppet, into the snow. The wretched Russian could not have known it, but in this lottery of death he had bought a winning ticket.

Meanwhile Belle reached the last Russian girl, pitched her on to her face with a kick from behind, aimed a few vicious kicks at the other, then called Vonwegh:

'Well, well, comrade!' he shouted, his voice slurred with looted drink, 'You're not exactly quick off the mark, are you, eh, friend?'

Paul Vonwegh stared for a moment at that plump, gloating face. He had his gun at his hip, he thought. At four paces' distance, he wouldn't need to aim, all he had to do was press the trigger . . . he could take a few of these butchers with him before it was all over – the hate, the revenge, the task he had set himself . . . Just one gentle squeeze with his index finger and that swine would cease to live, and afterwards he, Paul Vonwegh. At least he would die with decency, even though it would be futile. He would count to three, he thought: one . . . two . . .

'Man,' Corporal Belle guffawed, and then his booming laugh became a gurgling belch, as if someone's foot had trodden in the mire. 'You're lucky with the women, eh? Three at once, and well-stacked as well.' Belle stopped laughing for a moment and looked at Vonwegh enquiringly. 'Let's have a look at your harem,' he said, lurching up to him. He prised his schnapps-filled field canteen from his belt, handed it to the platoon leader, and said:

'Firewater. Go on, have a drop, mate.'

Paul Vonwegh shook his head.

'Band of Hope, eh?' Belle snarled. 'Or Salvation Army. Shit,' his patronising manner changed abruptly to menace, 'I've eaten bastards like you alive.'

Then, prising her head up with his heel, he forced the foremost of the Russian girls to look up at him. She was the youngest; the other two must have been a few years into their twenties. But they were all horribly alike in their suffering, in their pleading for a life, no matter what horrors it might bring. Were they still women? Had they ever laughed, hoped, dreamed? Were these still human beings cowering there in the snow, rigid with fear, begging like gods for an extension to their lives, if only for an hour or a day?

'Not bad at all,' Belle grunted. A shifty look came into his piggy eyes. We'll take these back for the Standartenführer, he thought to himself. Good party-fodder. Overcome with his own good fortune, Belle pressed his field canteen into Petrat's hand, and the East Prussian murderer drank greedily.

'Drink, children!' Belle shouted, his face distorted into a crazy grin. This was all grist to the mill, insurance that would mean Dirlewanger's goodwill, nights in the castle, invitations to the parties where there was music, vodka to drink, and living spoils of war to be enjoyed . . . And he too would become one of Dirlewanger's favourites, like Sergeant Weise over there, who a few months before had been busted down to nothing because of . . . well, what did it matter . . . and was now absolute master of Smolwieski, a man who had shown what he could do.

Belle turned to face Vonwegh again, watching him through tiny, vicious eyes, and said in a changed tone of voice that held a threat:

'What's your name?'

'B-soldier Vonwegh.'

'Well, Vonwegh, I've got a job for you . . .' Belle's grin broadened into an ugly leer '. . . of high importance to the war effort. I want you to make sure these women get back to headquarters . . . intact. If anyone tries to interfere with them, shoot them. Understood?' Then he was hurrying away, anxious to get back to the looting.

This was an ordinary mission for the killer-brigade. Death by the measure. Their daily blood. Every order was carried out, and there was no such thing as a crime while they were doing it. The way in which a village was exterminated was one of the Standartenführer's personal inventions, and there was even an official Dirlewanger guide to the method: surround the village; drive the people out of the houses; secure the livestock; sort out who was fit enough and the right age for forced labour; then drive the rest back, set fire to the village, and shoot down anyone who tried to escape from the flames. All very scientific, and calculated to take not more than two hours from start to finish, including personal looting – the troops' 'pocket money' for these special operations.

The sexes had been separated by now, with the men on the right and the women on the left. Women over forty went back into the houses, along with children under sixteen and men over sixty. In the meantime, the cattle were driven out of their stalls. Sergeant Weise had had a table brought out from one of the houses and was sitting there at it, acting like a presiding judge in a courtroom.

'What cretin lit the granary ahead of time?' he swore, and coughed.

Weise squinted at a broad-faced Russian peasant. 'How old are you, scum?' he bawled at him.

The man shook his head in bemusement. He was thirty-nine but looked older. He had lived his life in a remote village, a hard existence, and he hadn't the slightest idea what Weise was saying.

The sergeant shrugged and motioned to his underlings. They shoved the Russian to the rear to join the others – the ones who were destined to go back into the village before it was destroyed.

A section leader reported that the cattle had been safely rounded up.

'Get the chickens, too,' Weise said, taking a gulp from his bottle of vodka. 'And if anyone tries to sneak any into their knapsacks, they'll be for it – tell your men that.' The men had been dealt with now – all, that was, except for one boy. The boy had rapidly realised that the age limits meant life or death, and was now stretching himself up to appear older than he was, like an adolescent trying to see an 'adults only' film at the cinema. But this was no love story being shown here. This was a real-life drama: the massacre of a whole village, directed by Adolf Hitler, produced by Oskar Dirlewanger . . .

'I'm seventeen,' the boy was saying in broken German.

'Man, you're lying,' said Weise. He beckoned the young Russian over, ran his hand over the boy's chin and found only a light fuzz. Then he smiled almost kindly. 'I'll make an exception,' he said, and motioned the boy to go to the front.

Halfway there, the boy stopped in front of a woman. The likeness was unmistakeable. She had to be his mother, and there she was, standing with the condemned ones, clutching an ikon to herself as tightly as the others were clutching children. She understood that her son would live, and was happy; the boy, however, was in despair. Stretching the ikon out towards him, she said something, and the boy began to cry.

An S S guard stepped towards them.

'Get a move on!' he shouted.

As if in a dream, the boy walked on, then turned once more. As he did so, his mother reached out to hand him the ikon, but he dropped it. When he tried to bend down and pick it up, he was catapulted forward by a kick from one of the guards, and the picture continued to lie on the ground. The mother went slowly back towards the village, her face lit up by a smile because her son was going to survive. But the boy carried on staring at the ground.

'I'm only fifteen!' he yelled suddenly in Russian. 'I want to go back . . . to my mother . . .'

A few people heard him, but no one understood what he was saying. Perhaps Weise, in his present good humour, would let him die with her. Perhaps . . .

Meanwhile, the sergeant had moved over to the other side to deal with the women. He sorted them as if they were pieces of junk: here was the sale of a lifetime; first-class goods; every shelf stacked full, and dirt cheap . . . The price was a bullet or a jerry can of petrol.

Paul Vonwegh was breathing hard but he did not avert his eyes from the scene. He was forcing himself to memorise every detail. He would never forget anything. Don't weaken, he told himself, follow it all, note every face, down to the mugs of the three sub-humans raping a teenage girl in the corner, two holding her down while the other . . . Remember Belle's laugh, he thought; remember those eyes of his, day and night. Watch how the villagers are driven into the houses, count the number of beams used to ram the doors shut. Observe the machine-gunners getting into position for the final blood-letting . . .

The screams were the worst thing of all. They penetrated everywhere. There was no escape from that sound, mingled with the drumming on the walls of the houses, that was Smolwieski's death-agony. Everyone there had to hear, to see, and to suffer it. The flames, aided by petrol, shot higher and higher until the fire was a dazzling inferno. A few Russians, maddened by the heat, leapt out of windows to escape their torment, only to be mown down by a bark of fire from the machine-gun emplacement.

Then, suddenly, there was silence. Vonwegh's face relaxed for a moment. They are at rest, he thought.

As he surveyed the devastation, a man pushed his way up to him. It was Gruhnke, one of his own B-soldiers, an old criminal from Berlin.

'Those swine,' he was roaring, 'one day they'll pay for this . . . They'll go the same way when the war's over . . .'

Everyone nearby exchanged horrified glances. If anyone informed on Gruhnke now, he was for the high jump. And it was their 'duty' to denounce him . . .

'Not another word,' Vonwegh snapped at the distraut Gruhnke.

'You're as bad as they are,' Gruhnke shouted, beside himself with fury, 'and you even help them . . . instead of getting out your fucking gun and giving them a taste of their own medicine . . .'

Vonwegh took a deep breath. This man could ruin everything. 'Keep your mouth shut,' he said, for the second and last time.

At headquarters it was quiet. Outside it was clear and frosty, and the stars shone cold and distant. An east wind whistled through the camp's alleyways, sounding like a village cur wailing on the outskirts. All over the barracks there was a blanket of silence. Even the roofs of the buildings seemed to cringe, as if fearful of Dirlewanger's wrath.

A light was burning in Barrack VIII, the quarters of the first platoon, which was still away in action. There were five men in the room, and among those five were Kordt and Muller. To their surprise they had been released from the standing bunker – released to crawl back to their quarters like tortoises, urged on by the brutal laughter of the castle-gendarmes. They had dragged their swollen limbs on to their straw mattresses and now they lay side by side in total silence.

This was life . . .

In the Dirlewanger Brigade, there was no way of knowing what would happen next. Take one example: two of the three B-soldiers sitting in the room with Muller and Kordt playing skat with home-made cards had been summoned to Dirlewanger's castle that day, fearing the worst . . . and had been treated to roast duck until their starved stomachs could take no more, and the old man's favourites had laughed their fill.

'You never know your luck,' the third player was saying. 'When I'm picked on, you can bet your life it's a different kettle of fish.'

B-soldier Haubach, who had been one of the 'lucky ones', missed his turn at the pick-up.

'I don't know about that,' he said. 'The bastard kept looking at me . . . as if he was up to something.'

'Come on, he was just drunk,' his mate, Kleinschmidt, said. He and Haubach knew each other from a long way back – they had shared a prison cell in Straubing jail.

Haubach thought for a moment. 'No,' he said deliberately. 'It was as though . . . I got a funny shiver in my spine . . . He looked just like the old witch in "Hansel and Gretel".'

'Eighteen!' called the third man, in an effort to get them to concentrate on the game.

'That's mine,' Haubach said.

A hundred yards away, Dirlewanger received a radio report about the extermination of Smolwieski and the booty he could expect from the raid. It put him in such a good mood that even his staff-sergeant, Müller-Würzbach, managed to summon up the courage to get him to look through the 'for signature' file.

'You again,' the Standartenführer growled good-humouredly. 'How about a drink, you old sod?'

The staff-sergeant stood and waited, astonished by his chief's familiarity.

'Give me that rubbish,' said Dirlewanger, grabbing the papers. 'You've caught me in a good mood.' He signed document after document, taking no notice at all of the contents.

Müller-Würzbach, bureaucratic to the last, dried the ink carefully after each signature.

'Well then,' Dirlewanger grinned. 'Happy with me today?'

'Yes indeed, Standartenführer,' said the sergeant nervously, mindful of what he still had to bring up.

'Went splendidly, the mission,' Dirlewanger continued, beaming his pleasure at Müller-Würzbach, 'which gives us another good reason for a celebration.'

Exterminating villages was meat and drink to Dirlewanger – literally. He had established a regular shuttle to Germany, and he profited handsomely from the service he provided. He had even managed to send transportations of livestock to contacts in the butchery business in Württemberg.

Now, as he paced up and down the room, unable to contain his satisfaction, Müller-Würzbach stood there like a trained dog, eyes on his master. Dirlewanger's S S uniform, though made to measure by a tailor, flapped loosely around his body. It was strange how no uniform he had ever worn had ever fitted him properly – the field grey he had worn as a reserve officer, the mustard-coloured storm-trooper's uniform, or the black-and-white stripes of the convict.

In 1918 peace had brought unemployment for Dirlewanger. And he couldn't bear to take off his uniform. The Free Corps had offered him all a mercenary needed: the chance to give orders, to beat, to shoot, and to drink his fill. With a self-styled armoured unit, his gang had rolled into the small town of Sangershausen to fight Holz's Reds in the brutal civil war of 1919. After they had 'saved' the town, the terror had started: the victory orgy. The army took Dirlewanger to its bosom, and Sangershausen pronounced him an honorary citizen.

And he made a mess of things. Everything he did was pathological – from his obsessive hatred of the Left to his lust for women. Within a short time, the army would have nothing to do with him.

He slunk back home as an unemployed bully-boy, made a half-hearted attempt to live a normal civilian life, but found no real work and so became a 'professional veteran'. When the Nazi movement founded its so-called 'protection squads' – out of which the S S was later to grow – he was a perfect choice, and so he started his second career. The seizure of power by Hitler in 1933 found him in Heilbronn in southern Germany, but from there his next stop was a prison near Stuttgart. His head had been shaved, and he had been open to the abuse of the other jailbirds and the contempt of the warders. His sole income was fifteen pfennigs per day for stapling together exercise books. Dirlewanger ran the whole gamut of humiliation: he was in for rape, and rapists took the second-to-bottom place in the criminal hierarchy – they ranked only above pimps.

'Fall in . . . Stand to attention . . . Swab-buckets ready . . . Fight for your food . . . Grovel . . .' Dirlewanger went through it all, and he knuckled under just like the others. He sat in an ordinary cell with no name, just a number . . . as if he had never been an arrogant, privileged member of the Nazi elite, nor an honorary citizen of Sangershausen.

But he had not been forgotten by the Reichssicherheitshauptamt, his old S S security cronies, and that was why, nine short years later, Dirlewanger was at Lahuisk, near Minsk, completing his third and, for the present, final career. When he was in a good mood he made no secret of his criminal background. There were times when he smiled, as he did now, at the thought of how it shocked and intimidated his underlings.

Müller-Würzbach, the staff-sergeant, intercepted that smile now, and screwed up his courage to say what had to be said.

The Standartenführer saw the sergeant's unease.

'Come on then, tell me what's on your mind,' he urged him, continuing his pace up and down the roon.

'I just want to know what's going to happen about . . . Aumeier,' Müller-Würzbach muttered nervously.

Dirlewanger lit a cigarette, shrugged and shook his head.

'Aumeier,' he repeated. 'He doesn't exist any more . . . never did . . .'

The sergeant persisted.

'Yes, but . . .'

'Dead . . . shot . . . on the orders of the Reichsführer S S,' Dirlewanger said, a faint smile playing across his lips.

'But Standartenführer, he is still . . .'

'Good idea,' the Standartenführer said abruptly, and ordered one of the castle-gendarmes to fetch the staff butcher.

'And then,' the staff-sergeant continued hurriedly, 'there is another matter . . . Fleischmann, it seems, is to be transferred immediately to his old reserve unit . . . reinstated with the rank of Untersturmführer . . .'

'What the hell . . . ?' Dirlewanger bellowed.

'A pardon . . . he must have an influential friend in high places.'

Dirlewanger frowned and thought for a moment.

'Who the devil is this Fleischmann?'

'Only been here a few weeks,' the clerk-sergeant answered.

'Well, we'd better invite him here to celebrate with us,' Dirlewanger said with a sly smile, 'if he really does belong in better circles.'

'He is, of course, in action at the moment . . . with Sergeant Weise,' the clerk-sergeant said thoughtfully.

'Oh,' said Dirlewanger, catching the man's meaning. 'We can only hope that's gone well.' He grinned. 'At any rate, have Fleischmann report to me the moment they're back. I shall have to smarten him up before letting him loose among humans again.'

At that moment, the burly Aumeier careered into the room between two castle-gendarmes, quaking, half-mad with fear.

The Standartenführer looked at him with contempt, cutting in before the man could start the inevitable begging:

'Scared shitless, eh?' he said casually. 'Just try and keep on your feet, man.'

'But I'm not . . . I haven't . . .' Aumeier whined.

'Shut up and listen,' Dirlewanger said crisply. 'You died . . .' he checked his watch '. . . at 20.41.'

'No . . . No . . . .' Aumeier's voice rose to fever pitch.

'Don't mess up your chances, you cretin . . . Now, your name is Haubach, got that? . . . What is your name?'

'Haubach,' Aumeier answered uncomprehendingly.

'You'll be given the other details as soon as possible . . . For now, you're transferred to Block II, to the Russkies, understand? And if I ever catch sight of you again around here, then . . .'

Aumeier was not an intelligent man. He understood only that he wasn't going to be shot after all, and the sudden reprieve brought tears to his puffy eyes. What he didn't realise was that someone else had to die in his place – a man condemned by a chance likeness.

'You don't deserve it,' Dirlewanger said jovially to the cringing Bavarian butcher. 'Just be thankful you make such good sausages.'

While Aumeier was being led away by one castle-gendarme, a second was entering Barrack VIII. The trio playing skat played on at first, not realising his presence.

'Hearts flush,' said Haubach.

'Rubbish,' said the castle-gendarme behind him. 'An open grand of twos.'

The three men jumped to attention.

'OK,' said the gendarme to Haubach. 'Get your gear together. Everything – letters, pictures, clothes, personal papers . . .'

'Yes, but . . .'

'Shut up, you pansy . . . you're being transferred.'

No one said a thing as Haubach left three minutes later. He had no illusions, and neither had they as they watched him go. His hand lay on the table. He would win the hand if he didn't lose his life.

While Haubach was being taken to a remote spot in the camp, Müller-Würzbach was raising another delicate issue with the Standartenführer: Police Superintendant Prinz's inspection of the camp.

'Of us?' Dirlewanger asked, visibly taken aback.

The clerk-sergeant nodded.

'Special powers from the Reichsführer S S,' he said, cowering away from his chief.

'That's not good news, not good at all . . .' Dirlewanger murmured, with surprising coolness. 'Has he . . . got anything up his sleeve?'

'I gather he has,' Müller-Würzbach answered. 'His staff have been getting together material in Poland.'

'Material?' Dirlewanger was becoming agitated now. 'Against whom?'

'Against us,' the sergeant answered, and he seemed to shrink into himself.

Outside, a few hundred yards from the castle, a shot rang out.

Haubach had been transferred – into his grave.

The B-soldiers were on the march back, with the third platoon doing guard, the second driving the cattle, and Paul Vonwegh's unit responsible for keeping an eye on the Russian captives.

They marched for hour after hour. Though every man was ready to drop from exhaustion, the images of horror were as sharp as ever. Only Vonwegh experienced something else as well: an unconscious play of love and hate, a loose bond of fellowship, a first silent understanding, hidden but nevertheless there, of their common humanity. When they had stood there, forced to watch the barbarities at Smolwieksi, something had happened to those men, and it had shown in their faces. From now on, Paul Vonwegh would know whom he would be able to trust and whom he could not turn his back on. He had become aware of Fleischmann's brutal indifference and Gruhnke's rough decency. He translated his observations into practicality as he marched, and that meant: kick Petrat, keep an eye on Kirchwein, mould the gorilla, and take every chance to use and exploit that unconscious realisation of the others. The first step would be to goad them into rebellion – and then to strike, hard and decisively.

As they walked, the curious thing was that Petrat began to follow Vonwegh like a trained dog. And Vonwegh slackened the leash according to necessity.

'Fleischmann is always around the women,' Petrat reported during a rest period.

'Watch him,' the platoon leader said. As for Fleischmann, Vonwegh knew the type of old. He knew the arrogance behind the demoted Hauptsturmführer's servility. This man was a product of the system that he hated more than anything else in the world.

When they reached the edge of the forest, there was a cluster of broken-down huts. Vonwegh called a halt, posted a few men as sentries, and quartered the Russian women and girls in the largest hut. Then he and the others settled into a tiny shed to rest. But sleep did not come for him. Miserable, battered, exhausted as he was, his mind kept on working, conjuring up those sweet, dangerous thoughts, and it all came back.

The image of Karen.

That late-summer day in Mecklenburg, Paul Vonwegh made a decision. He only had to carry it out. 'Only' – he could have choked on that word. He tried to hide things from Karen, but he knew that she had sensed it in him. They would lie in bed at night next to each other, pretending to be asleep but wide awake. Sometimes they would talk; strange, elusive conversations that always skirted round the central problem of their lives.

'I know what the trouble is,' Karen said once. 'You feel caged in here . . . you ought to get out, among men. You need a change of company . . . I'm not enough for you.'

'Karen . . .' was all he said in answer. The way he spoke her name said everything, and she felt it. The shadows disappeared for that day – for the last day.

The next day, Paul Vonwegh went out and bought her some of her favourite flowers, marguerites.

'Oh, you . . .' she said.

'You know I would like to bring you flowers every day,' he whispered. 'Do you believe me when I tell you that?'

'You do anyway,' she said then.

He shook his head.

'Your words are like flowers,' Karen murmured. 'No,' she corrected herself, 'often they are even more beautiful . . . and . . .'

Paul looked straight into her eyes.

'You don't wither,' she continued softly. 'Or do you?'

'I'll never do that,' he said, and looked away, biting his lip against the pain inside.

Through the rest of breakfast, and through the day, everything seemed normal. Karen noticed nothing: over lunch she behaved normally, and in the afternoon they bathed in the lake as usual. Only Vonwegh knew that this would be the last time, and that there would be no good-byes.

The evening was magical, the night crept over them like a benevolent spell. They went to bed early, and Karen fell asleep while he lay beside her, feeling her warmth and her closeness, thinking of the happiness and the excitement they had given him. Suddenly, the church clock struck eleven and she awoke with a start.

'What time is it?' she asked sleepily.

'Not even midnight,' he said, pushing her gently back on to her pillow.

'Can't you sleep?' she said.

'It's all right, I'm just about to doze off . . .'

He had to be more careful . . . only two more hours to go. She had to be fast asleep. She mustn't suspect anything. Then, suddenly, the moonlight burst in through the window, bathing the room in its rays, picking out Karen's face like a beautiful, clear wax image. She looked so young, so fresh, so happy . . .

Paul stood up and looked at her. Karen was sleeping peacefully now, smiling as she dreamed of a joyful future at his side. He stared intently at her face. Wake up, he thought. Wake up, and this nightmare will end. He had heard that if you looked hard enough at someone when they were asleep they would wake up . . .but then maybe that only worked with strangers, people who meant nothing to you, whom you couldn't trust anyway.

For five full minutes he stood there, examining every detail of her as she slept, memorising her features as if they were some secret he would carry into an unknown future. Then, as he gazed, he began to see that face in other places – in a Gestapo interrogation chamber . . . in the dock in the 'Special Court' . . . in a prison cell . . . perhaps even on the scaffold . . .

It was time to leave.

Vonwegh crept carefully away from the bed, staring straight ahead, like a man in a trance. He had intended to leave without turning round, but as he reached the door the attraction was too strong. He looked, and saw the moonlight still highlighting every nuance of her face. She half turned over towards the place in the bed where he had been, smiling in her sleep, and she said something he couldn't quite catch – a whisper perhaps, or just a sigh.

Wake up, he begged. Say something. Look at me and I'll stay . . . Karen, wake up – wake up, or we shall lose each other again, this time for ever . . .

Paul Vonwegh stood there for a moment as if he had been carved of stone, listening to the gentle rise and fall of her breathing.

Then he opened the door, careful not to make a sound, looking straight ahead once more, and saw a night full of distant, glimmering stars, like this night in February 1943 on the endless, cruel steppes of Russia . . .

Vonwegh heard footsteps, a low moan of fear. He sat half up in his blanket, shaking off the numbness.

Within a few seconds the scream came. He recognised the

voice: it was Maria, the youngest and prettiest of the Russian girls. And she screamed in abject, helpless terror.

Before he knew it he was on his feet, gun in hand, covering the few yards over to the woodshed where the women were. Behind him stumbled the others, cursing and rubbing their eyes in the moonlight.

Petrat was already standing by the entrance.

'That swine has attacked her,' he said simply, and Vonwegh had no need to ask who he meant.

As he wrenched open the door he caught sight of those repulsive features, the caricature that was imprinted on his mind – the face of his enemy, who was the killer, the fanatic, the 'master race', the beast . . . Yes, Vonwegh knew that expression. He had left his country when men with those faces took over Germany and now, as then, he knew what to do when he saw one.

The Russian girl was putting up quite a fight against Fleischmann, but he was slowly forcing her to the floor. Calmly Vonwegh unshouldered his weapon and aimed carefully into Fleischmann's face. He used only one bullet as he shot the man clean between the eyes.

The former S S officer fell backward in a bizarre, twisted heap. What remained of his face was still contorted in an expression of gleeful lust.

The Russian girl looked at Vonwegh in amazement as he walked up to her. She met his glance and, in that moment, she actually smiled.

'What's going on here?' Corporal Belle bawled from the doorway.

'Just obeying orders,' Vonwegh said coolly, pointing at Fleischmann's corpse.

Belle looked at him in horror.

'Have you gone crazy?'

The platoon leader shrugged and said nothing.

'Did you know that Fleischmann was an S S officer?'

'A demoted one,' Vonwegh answered. 'And you ordered anyone who attacked the Russian girls . . .'

'You idiot!' Belle yelled. 'You'll be responsible to the

Standartenführer. I'll have nothing to do with it.' The corporal was still the bully, but there was fear in his voice too, fear of Dirlewanger's wrath.

Even Belle, though, hadn't quite realised just how far-reaching the consequences of the bloodbath in that little Russian hut would turn out to be.

Chapter Five

The raiders entered the camp again on the day following the destruction of Smolwieski. They were faint with hunger, exhausted, numb with cold – not a body of soldiers, but a rabble, wrecks in uniform dragging themselves along in a parody of marching. The sky was as grey as their faces. Then Sergeant Weise saw Dirlewanger waiting for them at the gate, ran to the head of the column and bawled out his order:

'Look smart there! Get in step!'

The men stopped and pulled themselves together for one final effort. Even then, it took them a few yards before they got into some kind of step with each other. Left, right, left, right, left, right . . . they dragged their worn-down boots over the parade ground, and any man who fell out of step got a hard kick from his neighbour. Those who still had the energy to look saw how Dirlewanger's eyes were focused on the booty as they made their pathetic march past. Did we rob enough? they asked themselves. Did we plunder, and kill, and burn enough to satisfy his appetites?

As a final insult, Weise ordered them to strike up a marching-song as they filed past the chief. Christ, when they heard the sound of their strangled, feeble voices, it broke their hearts . . .

The captured Russians hung their heads as they followed their captors, humiliated and dazed. Some must have been thinking of the deaths, the destruction. Others, the lucky ones, were incapable of thought, incapable of realising that they were now firmly in the grip of the most ruthless machine for human degradation ever devised by man.

In his position by the Russians' side, Paul Vonwegh sang the idiot marching-song. That part was easy – it was necessary, to survive. What was coming next would cause more problems. He had killed Fleischmann, the ex-S S officer, and Belle had served advance notice that he was having nothing to do with it.

But Vonwegh faced the decision coolly, almost indifferently. He was a professional gambler, he always had been. The only difference with this gamble was that the stakes were the highest any man could conceive of – his own life. Inwardly he shrugged as he marched and sang. One day it had to happen. One day he had had to come out into the open.

'Company, halt!' Weise bawled. 'Right turn!'

They obeyed him like string-puppets. And the strings that held them were bloody ones, nooses that hung round their necks, ready to be tightened according to the whim of Standartenführer Oskar Dirlewanger.

The sergeant strode forward and made a brief report.

'Good, Weise,' the chief said. Then he told him to stand easy and walked over to the ranks. It was an extraordinary, almost uncanny process, because as he approached the men in front they seemed to shrink, while Dirlewanger seemed to grow into a giant.

'Now, you band of villains,' he said as he went from one to the other, peering at them in the way they knew so well – the way that left no doubt who was master in this particular private hell. He paused, spat on the ground in front of them, then cleared this throat.

'You have fought like lions,' he rasped. 'Which is no more than I expect . . . and lucky for you.'

'Yes, Standartenführer!' they bayed in unison.

He started to walk the ranks again. 'You don't look so good,' he said, stopping to stare at Kirchwein, who was going green in the face, as if he was desperately fighting off another attack. But then Dirlewanger walked on to where Petrat was standing, with that stupid grin of his and his toady's eyes. A moment later he had turned back to nod to Corporal Belle and clapped his hand on Weise's shoulder.

'Big celebration tonight,' he said to his favourite. Belle, he said, was invited as well. Then suddenly Dirlewanger went over to B-soldier Gruhnke.

'Famished, eh?' he said to the Berliner.

'And how, Standartenführer,' the man said with feeling.

If anyone informs on him now, he's had it, Vonwegh thought. With any luck, though, Fleischmann had been the platoon spy until now. If he had, then Gruhnke might just get away with it – but then God knew how many spies Dirlewanger had in each unit.

'Ah, hunger . . .' Dirlewanger gave a cynical laugh. 'I can imagine. But the trouble is . . .' his face took on an expression of puzzled innocence: '. . . that if you eat too much, then you just get above yourselves – and I have to take responsibility for the things you bastards get up to. You have to be kept in order . . . and you all know why you're here,' his eyes narrowed, 'don't you? Robbery with violence, for instance . . . five years for a second conviction . . .'

Dirlewanger paused again and scowled.

'And now you're with us,' he said. 'Given the opportunity to serve your country . . . an opportunity you don't deserve, and all due to our Führer in his incomprehensible goodness.' Dirlewanger rolled the final words off his tongue menacingly and stared at Gruhnke expectantly.

'Yes, Standartenführer, sir!' the B-soldier shouted.

Now the Standartenführer had turned and was shouting, almost screaming, to the whole company.

'Yes . . . And he who has the good fortune to fight for Adolf Hitler,' he mouthed, 'is never hungry, never tired . . . the struggle is for the destiny of the whole race, and . . .'

Then Dirlewanger lost the thread of what he was saying, and with it his enthusiasm for speeches. He was silent for a moment, then grinned and said in a quite different tone of voice:

'If you're thirsty, then you're welcome to eat the snow!'

When he had finished guffawing at his own impish wit, the Standartenführer cast a brief glance at the loot. He smiled with satisfaction and said to Weise:

'Have a cow slaughtered for the lads . . . Aumeier will . . .'

For a moment he looked almost frightened. Weise looked at him questioningly, but Dirlewanger's recovery was swift.

'Of course,' he said quietly. 'Forgot. We haven't got a butcher any more . . . had to kill the fellow yesterday, on orders from the Reichsführer S S . . . some nasty business in Kiev . . .' He awarded the sergeant one of his best, yellow-teethed smiles. 'This rabble will have to fend for themselves . . . it's lucky I'm in a generous mood today. They can stand easy.'

With no further acknowledgement of the men's presence, the Standartenführer strode off to make an inventory of the booty. Sergeant Weise raised his hand, and the exhausted men fell – almost literally – out of line.

In the other corner of the parade-ground, Müller-Würzbach was already busy making a list of the livestock. Dirlewanger thumped a horse on its rump and pulled it towards him by its mane.

'Pity we can't make a riding mount of you any more,' he confided to the horse. 'Give this nag to the baggage train,' he said to the staff-sergeant.

'Yes, Standartenführer.'

'Notify the S S Administrative Bureau of the ten bullocks. The rest can stay here . . .' He watched Müller-Würzbach making notes briskly, then corrected himself: 'No, give them to section fifteen. They need something to keep them going on the canal project . . .'

Then Dirlewanger went on to the human booty.

'Send the men to Germany on the next transport,' he ordered.

The Russians looked at him dully.

'We've got enough Russkies in Camp II, and this bunch don't look as though they'll be much use to us . . .'

Now the Standartenführer had reached the women. He caught sight of Maria at their head and smiled.

'Where did you get hold of them?' he asked, the pleasure showing in his face.

'Reserved for you, of course, Standartenführer,' said the

eager Belle, who had been hovering at his side, waiting his chance.

'Good taste, man,' the Standartenführer nodded his approval.

'These three go to the castle,' he commanded. Then he cast a quick eye over the rest of the women, who were standing a little way off. 'The rest . . . all of them . . . can be sent to help out in the armaments factory.'

Sergeant Weise had been following his chief's every expression. Now he judged the time right to present him with another little treat.

'We have a report from an informant,' he said. 'B-soldier Gruhnke was heard making defamatory remarks during the raid . . . and slandering you personally, Standartenführer.'

'Right,' Dirlewanger said in cheerful anticipation. 'Stick the man in the detention block straight away . . . about time we settled all the pending cases. Fix a trial for tomorrow.'

'Yes, Standartenführer,' said Müller-Würzbach dutifully.

'Anything else?'

'Yes, Standartenführer,' the clerk-sergeant said, 'there's the matter of the man who was promoted to Untersturmführer . . .' he rummaged in his file and found the name '. . . Fleischmann – you said you wanted him pulled out of the gang.'

'Oh yes,' Dirlewanger said absently. 'Find him a respectable uniform and tell him he's invited to our celebration dinner at the castle.'

Belle winced, then stood as if nailed to the spot.

Noticing Belle's reaction, Dirlewanger turned to him shrewdly.

'Anything wrong, Corporal Belle?'

'I . . . I have to make a report, Standartenführer,' he muttered hoarsely.

'Well?'

'Fleischmann has been shot.'

'In action?'

'No, Standartenführer . . . he attacked one of the Russian

girls . . . and platoon leader Vonwegh immediately . . .'

'Shit, that's all we need!' Dirlewanger exploded. 'Do you know who Fleischmann was?'

Müller-Würzbach chimed in with the answer for Belle's benefit.

'He was restored to the rank of Untersturmführer and given full pardon . . . turns out that he's the nephew of a General.'

'You can get yourself out of this one,' Dirlewanger growled. 'I wash my hands of it. It's up to you and . . . that man . . .'

'Vonwegh,' the clerk-sergeant put in primly.

'You will present yourselves at the castle in half an hour to make a formal report. A formal report . . . understood?'

'Yes, Standartenführer,' the corporal said, and already he could feel the rope round his neck. The rope that Paul Vonwegh had put there . . .

The first platoon were back in barracks. Most had flung themselves on to their straw mattresses the moment they arrived. Other were too excited by the thought of a meat ration to rest. Everyone was amazed to see fat Muller and young Kordt back in circulation, but only a few dared welcome them – the others waited cautiously, just to make sure that being friendly wouldn't get them into trouble as well.

Paul Vonwegh, still platoon leader and unaware that he was at the top of Dirlewanger's blacklist, questioned Muller openly:

'Did you learn anything from all this?'

The fat man nodded wryly.

'Yes,' he said. 'To keep my mouth shut.'

'Good,' Vonwegh replied, making sure everyone in the room heard him. 'You do that.'

They realised only a few minutes later how right he had been to give them that public warning when a castle-gendarme turned up to take Gruhnke away.

The Berliner simply shrugged and followed the guard without a word. He was a tough customer. Then, at the door, he turned with hatred in his eyes.

'My compliments to the filthy swine who grassed on me,' he growled. Then he turned on his heel and was gone.

All eyes lingered on the door. Petrat cursed.

'He's right . . . that doesn't ever happen when you're inside.'

He met Vonwegh's ice-cold stare. 'Everyone knows . . .' he said lamely, then his voice trailed off into silence.

Everyone in the room knew that Gruhnke's life was less than worthless now. Despite their exhaustion, they mulled over the business, sounding each other out. Fleischmann hadn't been the informer, Vonwegh thought to himself – or at any rate, not the only one. Petrat wasn't the type: he was certainly capable of almost any kind of violent or anti-social behaviour, but betrayal of a comrade was strictly against the professional criminals' code. We can exclude Kortetzky, too, Vonwegh mused – in the first place, the gorilla had already been lying wounded when Gruhnke lost his temper at the village, and second he had been in a delirium since they got back to camp.

Thinking of Kortetzky, the platoon leader got up and wandered into the side room where the gorilla was lying. At first glance he could tell that the man was going to pull through: the worst of the fever seemed to be past. The gorilla had already had a few lucid moments and had discovered that he owed his life to Vonwegh, of all people. It was something unique for a badly-wounded Dirlewanger to be given a chance to recover – usually they were just left where they had fallen, or shot, while those that could walk or limp just tagged along with the rest of them as best they could. Kortetzky had been carried and cared for, if in the most primitive of fashions. Now it looked as if his brute strength would bring him through.

Vonwegh was turning to leave when the gorilla's eyes suddenly opened and focused on him, at first in fear but then, when he remembered, a thought seemed to strike him, and he smiled.

'You're the one who . . .' Kortetzky gasped '. . . we wanted to . . . to . . . kill you.'

'Don't speak,' the platoon leader said.

'But I just wanted to tell you . . .' the gorilla was struggling, but his face was determined '. . . I'm just a lousy, mean hoodlum, understand? . . . But you're . . . you're one of the good guys.'

Vonwegh grinned.

'Go to sleep,' he said quietly.

It's all working out, he thought; everything's going to be all right. Strange, but these hard-case crooks were turning out to be the most honourable of them all. They were going to be easy . . .

When he went back into the main barrack-room, there was a castle-gendarme there with the others.

'Are you Vonwegh?' the man asked.

He nodded.

'Present yourself in twenty minutes at the castle. Formal report!'

It had to be about Fleischmann. Now, one way or the other, the whole issue was going to be decided.

As the gendarme was leaving, Kleinschmidt, who had been sitting thoughtfully in the corner, suddenly came to a decision.

'You took my mate away yesterday . . .' he said, measuring his words. 'What happened to him? Name of Haubach.'

'Haubach . . . ?' The guard gave all the appearance of seraching his memory. 'Oh yes,' he said, 'he's in Camp II with the Russkies.' The man was obviously following instructions, Kleinschmidt thought. He'd heard that shot . . . The fact that Aumeier, Dirlewanger's private staff butcher, was no longer around either had not occurred to Kleinschmidt yet, but the man was no fool. He was going to follow this through.

The castle-gendarme seemed to guess the B-soldier's thoughts.

'Curiosity can be dangerous,' he said, and they all understood the threat in his voice. 'Take my advice, and stop asking dumb questions.'

Paul Vonwegh took the whole incident in, filing it away in his record of hate. Haubach – he memorised the name. And he wouldn't forget Kleinschmidt's reaction, either.

The others were silent as he prepared himself for his trip to the castle. But Kirchwein handed him his steel helmet, while Petrat gave his boots a polish – both of them unasked.

'Have you had dealings with the old man before?' Kordt asked, breaking the silence.

Paul Vonwegh shook his head.

'Just don't contradict him,' Muller put in. 'For Christ's sake, don't do that.'

'You've got nerves like steel-cables,' Petrat said, shaking his head in bemused admiration. 'No shitting your pants, eh?'

'No point in that,' Vonwegh said with a shrug.

Kirchwein walked with him to the door.

'Come back,' he said, very softly.

Vonwegh's first surprise when he arrived at the castle was the sight of Corporal Belle in the ante-room. The proud 'conqueror' of Smolwieski had turned into a nervous wreck in the face of the Standartenführer's wrath.

'I've got you to thank for this, you bastard . . .' he moaned, his voice heavy with self-pity, scuttling frantically round the room like a fly trapped in a glass of water.

Vonwegh gave him a crooked, contemptuous smile. When he got the chance, he knew he would finish Belle off without a second thought, with no trace of pity. He had lined up his gunsights on that sort of face before, in Spain. Every shot had hit home. But in those days there had always been more fascists than ammunition . . .

Sergeant Weise came out of Dirlewanger's office. He glared sourly at Vonwegh, pulled himself up to his full height in front of him and jerked a thumb in the direction of the door to the inner sanctum:

'OK, sharpshooter,' he sneered. 'Your turn. Have fun . . .'

A moment later, Vonwegh and the corporal were standing before the chief. Immediately Paul realised that he had a very important advantage – he cut by far the better, more soldierly figure. Dirlewanger might be a lecher, a drunk, and a mass-murderer, but he remained one thing above all: a militarist of the old school. From the Standartenführer's expression Vonwegh saw that he had a definite weakness for men of his type rather than the likes of Belle, who stood beside him now, like one of those squat target-figures in a shooting-gallery, and began to blurt out his side of the story before Dirlewanger had even spoken.

'Hold your tongue, corporal!' Dirlewanger snapped, and turned to Vonwegh. 'Now, man, what on earth possessed you to kill an S S Hauptsturmführer?'

Vonwegh spoke without hesitation.

'In the first place he was a B-soldier like the rest of us . . . secondly I was simply obeying an order . . . moreover . . .'

'Moreover?' Dirlewanger interrupted him with an expression of intense curiosity.

'I would shoot anyone who attacked a defenceless woman.'

'Myself included?' the Standartenführer asked, smiling broadly.

'You wouldn't do that,' Paul Vonwegh said, coolly but with just sufficient hint of contempt.

'I . . . I gave no such orders . . .' Belle cut in, but one look from Dirlewanger silenced him again.

'What were his orders?' the Standartenführer asked softly, with a wave of one clawlike hand in Belle's direction.

'That anyone interfering with the Russian girls was to be shot,' Vonwegh said crisply.

'But *not* Fleischmann!' Belle interrupted the questioning again.

The chief raised his eyebrows slowly, and his bird-face seemed more crane-like than ever. Strange, thought the platoon-leader, but birds of prey always seem to have that grin . . .

'Did you say,' Dirlewanger said, turning scornfully to the corporal, 'that he was to kill anyone . . . with the exception of Fleischmann?'

'No . . .' Belle stuttered '. . . I couldn't do that.'

The Standartenführer abruptly raised a hand for silence.

'For God's sake get some schnapps into you . . . you're a nervous wreck. Take yourself off and don't show your face again for a few days.'

Belle saluted smartly and hurried to the door.

'Be thankful for those Russian girls!' Dirlewanger called after him. 'And for your exceptional taste!'

Left alone with Vonwegh, Dirlewanger paced around the room for a few seconds, then turned and faced the platoon leader.

'Now, with regard to you,' he said, 'it seems your action was quite correct. God, I wish I had more like you . . .' He lit a cigarette and handed the packet to Vonwegh, lit the other's, drew on the smoke deeply, then continued: 'But you were unlucky. Not only did you choose a man who had been reinstated as an officer a week earlier, but you also shot an S S General's nephew . . .'

He came closer to Vonwegh, and noticed with surprise that the man's face was still showing no reaction.

'But I know you,' he said suddenly. 'Where have we met before?'

Here it comes, thought Vonwegh.

'Only here, in the camp. Standartenführer,' he lied.

'Nonsense . . . before that . . . somewhere . . . help me to remember.'

'I'm afraid I can't, Standartenführer,' Vonwegh answered. He knew that if Dirlewanger remembered that time in Spain he would end up in the deepest hot water there was.

'Why are you here?'

'I was transferred from Plötzensee prison,' said Vonwegh evasively.

'Come on, man, what were you inside for?' Dirlewanger barked.

'Forged documents and . . .'

'Oh, no!' the Standartenführer mouthed with a satirical smile. 'An intellectual!' Then he grinned and slapped his thigh. 'We've got all sorts in this camp, eh? . . . Well, look, if my superiors don't pursue the matter too hard, I'll let you off . . .' The grin widened. 'I'll fix Fleischmann's death up as a heroic sacrifice for Greater Germany.'

Then Dirlewanger summoned Müller-Würzbach.

'This man will go to the detention block until further notice,' he ordered.

'Standing bunker?' the staff-sergeant asked dutifully.

'No,' the Standartenführer continued. 'This is just a precaution . . . ordinary detention. With double rations – that's an order.'

Vonwegh clicked his heels.

'So,' Dirlewanger said, concluding the formal report. 'Get going . . .' Then he was already turning to Müller-Würzbach with an eager leer spreading over his face.

'Must have another look at that girl who's caused such a stir in the camp . . . she's reserved for me until futher notice.'

'Yes, Standartenführer,' the staff-sergeant replied, without moving a muscle.

Afterwards the victory celebrations took their usual course: dinner by candlelight, first-class cuisine, a procession of dishes. Tonight there were only the special favourites present. For dessert there was schnapps which, as usual, the girls had to serve. And for their special delectation they had the Standartenführer's favourite song, 'Every Day Is Not a Sunday', garnished with the girls' screams and their oppressors' curses. To the victors, the spoils . . .

In his cell in the detention block, Paul Vonwegh felt a growing certainty that he was going to survive. Dirlewanger had failed to recognise him, though there was always the possibility that he would ask for his file and find out about Spain from that. Vonwegh shrugged. There was no point in worrying. Here in the killer brigade's headquarters you counted your future in hours or, at best, in days.

'Special treatment' was a rest-cure. Double rations, a plank bed, and guards under orders to treat you well – what more could a man ask for in hell?

Four walls were his world: prison had him again. How long had he sat behind walls and barbed wire in the course of his life? He did some quick mental arithmetic: in the South of France, in Switzerland, in Germany, and now here in Russia – a total that could compete with any professional villain, he thought wryly.

If only there wasn't so much time to pass; too much time. Four paces forward: four paces back. Stop. Repeat from the beginning. To the side, two paces: two paces to the other. Three times two was six. It was six paces round the square, but you couldn't go right round because the bed and the bucket blocked the way. Forwards, backwards, left, right . . .

And all the time, over and over again, he told himself: once there was a time when I would have given anything for a secure cage like this one – for walls and locks that would have stopped me running away, that would have forced me to stay . . .

With Karen.

Paul Vonwegh would never know how much will power it took for him to shut that door. Five minutes later, he could still feel the imprint of the handle on his palm, as if it had branded itself into his flesh.

But finally he had gone, like an automaton, out into the night, swinging himself into a marching step as he set out to cover the thirteen kilometres to the railway station.

If he had gone during the day, he could have caught a bus, but buses were too dangerous. To tell the truth, risking the station itself was an idiocy – stations were places where 'they' checked, where 'they' kept their eyes and ears at their sharpest. But he had no choice. As he walked through the small hours and into the early day, he began to encounter people – too many people: early-rising workers, women on their way to market, men coming off the night shift, farmers' children walking to school .. .

None of it mattered to him. He didn't even have any idea where he was going. Maybe he would cross the border again and slip illegally into Switzerland. His choice was not very wide: there were no longer very many free countries left. No, the only important thing was to get away from her, from Karen, to protect her. He couldn't look back, and he dared not look ahead . . .

He went on, by fits and starts, until he reached the houses on the outskirts of the small town. Dawn was breaking in the East, the narrow silver strip of light that would nurture another glorious late-summer day – the kind of day that makes people love, and laugh, and thank God for life.

When he arrived at the station, he looked at his watch. He still had time, far too much time; there was still another hour and a half until the train left. Ninety minutes to think of Karen.

And so he sat on the hard wooden bench on the platform, until other passengers started to arrive and he could listen in to their conversations, involve himself, forget, Listen, he told himself, let these people's trivial lives wash over you: care about the fact that Frau Maier's baby is fifty-three grammes overweight; get interested in farmer Hinrich's cow; listen to how Frau Schmidt is against her daughter's going out with a corporal from the anti-aircraft unit; watch the signalman telling you all the marvellous things that Adolf Hitler is doing for Germany . . . Nod your head, or clap your hands in applause, or go to the lavatory, or be sick out of the window, or pull the emergency cord – do anything, but don't think about Karen.

In fact, the conversations were rather different from what he had expected. The local schoolmaster was the party stalwart, not the signalman. And Vonwegh heard a peasant woman, shielding her mouth with her hand, comment: 'He just wants to keep his soft job . . . so he doesn't have to go away and fight.' Her neighbour nodded bitterly and said that his sort should be the first to go. She talked of her husband, of her two children, and of the farm that she now had to run single-handed with the help of a French prisoner-of-war. The baby, it turned out, was underweight, and the anti-aircraft corporal was 'a nice young man'.

So this was the glorious Third Reich at war. Almost despite himself, Vonwegh shared these ordinary people's joys and sorrows as he sat there, staring at the platform. Most importantly, he managed not to think. That was the most important thing of all.

Then came the announcement. Train to Berlin . . . Like a man in a dream he watched the train pull into the station. Mechanically he stood, walked two, three paces . . . and then he saw her there, standing a few yards away, worn out, her face lined by worry. Karen. And suddenly her face was transformed by a smile . . . a smile he would see, in his mind's eye, over and over again . . .

He could still see it.

In his cell, Paul Vonwegh heard a commotion and looked at his watch. It was seven p.m. on the day after his interview with Dirlewanger. He went to the window and looked out, saw guards hurrying about, cursing. There seemed to be an atmosphere of excitement and tension in the camp.

What Vonwegh did not know was that Dirlewanger had a very important visitor. At 8.53 that morning the high-ranking S S and police officer Prinz had entered the camp, accompanied by a small staff and equipped with a special authority from Himmler, the Reichsführer S S. Prinz's task: to instigate an official enquiry into the doings of Dirlewanger and his henchmen.

Prinz was tall and lean, with a shorn skull, an intimidating figure. As many of his victims could tell the world, this was a stubborn investigator, a man who spared neither himself nor others, a fanatic about detail, a man who worshipped 'the book'.

The head of the sentry detail at the main gate had been the first to feel the lash of Prinz's tongue. The man had tried to delay the old police chief until a warning could be got to Dirlewanger.

'You are to refrain from informing the Standartenführer,' Prinz had snapped.

'Yes, but . . .'

'You will carry out orders and hold your tongue, understood?'

'Yes sir,' the castle-gendarme had answered with a nervous gulp. 'Heil Hitler!'

Prinz left one of his staff behind in the guardroom to ensure that the line to the special commando chief remained firmly cut.

From the first moment he entered the barracks at Lahuisk, Police Oberst Prinz acted like an avenging angel.

Chapter Six

Even while Police Oberst Prinz was taking the short route from the outer security perimeter to Dirlewanger's dacha, the camp began to seeth with rumours.

From the windows, the B-soldiers of the first platoon watched the investigator's progress. They found little for their comfort. This, they saw quickly, was not a man to be messed with, whether you were innocent or guilty. They looked at him, and they kept their thoughts to themselves.

Kirchwein, the epileptic, left the window, shaking his head. His skin was as sickly-pale as verdigris. Only the pupils of his eyes were alive – bright pinpoints of light, like those of a child afraid of the dark. Muller and his friend Kordt watched the Oberst as if mesmerised.

They all knew what was in store. An inspection, an assurance that there would be no victimisation. There would be requests to report any irregularities. This could – just could – be the chance they had been waiting for. The chance to topple Dirlewanger. But they needed someone to give them the courage, to enforce solidarity. Paul Vonwegh was such a man, but he was in the punishment block for shooting that bastard Fleischmann, and not a man in the first platoon would lay a cigarette butt on his survival.

'It won't make any bloody difference,' Petrat said. Then he caught the eyes of his room-mates and pulled himself up sharp, as if he had been caught in the act. He – and they – remembered Gruhnke, the old criminal from Berlin-Wedding who was facing death today because he didn't keep his mouth shut yesterday.

Police Oberst Prinz halted in front of the neighbouring barracks and motioned for an officer of his escort to stand guard. There was no need for a verbal order – everything had been prepared and practised. The young lieutenant, who had a wooden leg, was there to prevent any attempts to get to the B-soldiers before Prinz did.

Then Prinz strode on to the 'castle', where his arrival was more like an assumption of power than an inspection. He saw two guards dozing in front of the dacha, one smoking while the other leaned lazily against a wall, helmets askew, shouldered guns pointing at the ground. Then the guard on the left caught sight of the police chief and blinked sleepily, forgetting, in his surprise, to acknowledge the officer. The other managed to stand sloppily to attention, but his cigarette still hung from the corner of his mouth.

'Well, do you salute officers round here?' the Oberst said imperiously.

'S S Röttenführer . . .'

'You miserable apology for a soldier!' Prinz thundered. 'At least stand to attention!'

Ignoring the incredulous smiles on the castle-gendarmes' faces, Prinz turned to his adjutant.

'Take their names,' he growled. Then he turned back to the guards. 'Take me to someone who's awake,' he said contemptuously, 'and carry your guns properly, you shambling idiots . . .'

In the guardroom the same theatre was repeated, almost word for word. Before the sergeant had a chance to announce Prinz's arrival, he was ordered to report formally with the rest of the garrison and sent on his way.

It didn't take much imagination to reconstruct what had gone on during the 'victory celebrations'. The whole house reeked of stale alcohol. Pieces of broken glass and smashed furniture littered the rooms. The carpets were soaked through with schnapps. Discarded items of uniform lay around in the corridors. As a centre piece, an S S victory-rune nestled in the midst of a heap of half-eaten food.

The Oberst took in everything as he entered the house. Standing there, expressionless, he committed the whole scene to memory before bending over a body wearing a grey Wehrmacht sweater. The body began to snore loudly.

'Who is that?' Prinz asked.

'S S Sergeant Weise.'

'Hm,' the Oberst muttered. 'I can see we've stumbled into a real pigsty.'

Bergmeier, the castle-gendarme whom Prinz had appointed as his guide, took him on a roundabout route through the house. Prinz seemed not to notice. Despite himself, he was nauseated and shocked by what he found. He had known a lot about Dirlewanger, and it was all in the case file 'Poland/A. IX DORA' which he had presented to Himmler – the file that had finally persuaded the reluctant S S chief to give him this special authorisation. But as he wandered around the 'castle', even Prinz had to succumb to a grim sense of wonder . . .

The Oberst opened a door at random. On the carpet a naked, drunken man snored, his schnapps bottle still next to him. And a Russian girl was there too, awake and terrified, retreating as the Oberst gazed, trying desperately to cover herself, to hide in the farthest, darkest corner of the room. There, finally, in despair, she sat and wept.

'Make a note of every detail,' Prinz said to his assistant.

The Oberst was a military man, not a pussyfooting diplomat – he always had been and always would be. From the beginning he had been an outsider in the S S, who had in fact simply 'taken him over' when they absorbed the police.

To Prinz, the greatest virtue was obedience to orders. It was why he had been prepared to serve the Weimar Republic before Hitler's seizure of power – correctly, but without enthusiasm. He had inflicted the rubber cudgel of the riot police on many a demonstration and, while he preferred to hit the Left, he was also prepared to give the S A brownshirts a thrashing if need be.

After '33 he was left in his post, but there were no promotions, though when Himmler took over the State Police he was given an additional – and as far as he was concerned, unwanted – S S rank. Even under the Nazis, he carried out his duties by the book. Of course, he wasn't liked at S S headquarters, but they could find no excuse for getting rid of him – until war offered the perfect opportunity. Prinz was transferred out of the way to the East, where he was given the unenviable job of keeping order during the rape of Russia.

By now the Oberst had reached Dirlewanger's private bedroom. The two gendarmes in front of the door stood to attention in amazement and saluted.

Prinz nodded curtly to them and went straight to the door.

'No, Herr Oberst,' one of the guards said. 'No one is allowed in these quarters.'

'Have you gone mad?'

'Orders from the Standartenführer, Herr Oberst,' the man answered.

Prinz paused, then nodded. Orders were there to be obeyed; the man was right, he thought . . . and it was the first sign of military correctness that he had seen since he came into this crazy place.

'Very good,' he continued, 'then be so good as to report that Police Oberst Prinz is here to carry out an inspection . . . on special orders from the Reichsführer S S.'

The Standartenführer was sprawled diagonally across the bed, still hopelessly drunk, his mouth open to reveal incisors that looked like the fangs of a beast of prey. And Dirlewanger was not alone. Beside him cowered Maria, the 'reserved' Russian girl, and on her face was the same expression of fathomless suffering of every woman who ever entered Dirlewanger's private hell.

'Standartenführer!' said the castle-gendarme, ignoring the naked girl and shaking his commander energetically.

Dirlewanger grunted, gasped and let out a curse.

'Standartenführer!' the guard said a second time. 'Oberst Prinz . . . inspection . . . special authorisation.'

'Kill him,' Dirlewanger muttered, and sank back on his pillows again.

Then suddenly it penetrated his brain, and he sat bolt upright with a stream of oaths.

'Where is he?'

'Outside the door,' the bodyguard answered, lowering his voice.

'Here? . . . Outside my door? . . . How the hell . . . ?' Dirlewanger's face was twisted with fury and – yes – fear.

'He cut the telephone connection,' the guard explained shame-facedly, 'and occupied the guardroom . . .'

'And you let him?' the Standartenführer spat. 'You . . . you cowards . . . you useless arselickers . . .'

But furious as he was, Oskar Dirlewanger was already thinking his way out of yet another tight situation. The skin tightened in his crow-like face. His eyes seemed to sink deeper into their bony sockets.

'Shit!' he roared, and took a swig from his bottle. Then he became decisive.

'Release the men from the standing bunker,' he ordered, the words streaming from him in a feverish torrent, 'and everyone who has no proper judgement against them as yet.' He considered for a moment and continued in a low, dangerous drawl. 'Anyone squeals, I'll personally tear them apart . . . afterwards. Make sure they know that.'

Dirlewanger laughed nervously, went to the window and spat.

'And get those Russian bitches out of the house. Quietly . . .' he said. Then the guard was dismissed.

As the Standartenführer stood silently in his room, trying to think what other tracks needed to be covered, he heard the gendarme doing his duty outside with Prinz.

'The Standartenführer will expect you in his office in twenty minutes, Herr Oberst,' the man was saying.

Dirlewanger managed a crooked grin. He wasn't out of it yet, but at least he had made time . . .

Half an hour later, Dirlewanger entered the corridor that led to his office. He was greeted by Müller-Würzbach, suddenly sober and immaculately dressed. The staff-sergeant sprang to his feet.

'All in order,' he reported. 'He's already . . .' he jerked a thumb in the direction of Dirlewanger's office.

'Ridiculous,' the Standartenführer said quietly, 'for us to

be frightened by such a pompous cretin, of course.' Then he became thoughtful. 'Only the . . . er . . . women are worrying me.'

'Liquidation?' Müller-Würzbach said quickly.

'Careful,' the chief said with a shake of the head. 'Use your brains, man . . . see that they disappear, but be quick about it, and discreet . . . If they were to talk . . .'

The staff-sergeant nodded. They understood each other.

Then the Standartenführer flung open the door to his office. He gave the Oberst, who was standing coldly opposite him, a cursory glance, then said in a rasping voice:

'Dirlewanger . . . You wished to speak to me?'

Oberst Prinz made to present his credentials.

'I believe you,' Dirlewanger growled, handing back the document without even glancing at the contents. 'So . . .' he said briskly. 'What do you want?'

'To investigate certain complaints that . . .'

'Complaints against me?' the Standartenführer cut in.

'Yes,' Prinz answered simply.

'Have you witnesses?' Dirlewanger's face had taken on a sinister jocularity.

'I am here for that reason. It is my intention to find some . . . in your camp.'

'The best of luck!' the Standartenführer said. Then, without any more ado, he clapped his hands and called for Müller-Würzbach, who entered the room as if on a prepared signal.

'Sergeant,' Dirlewanger ordered, choosing his words carefully. 'You will ensure that all the Herr Oberst's questions are answered. He is to have unrestricted access to all parts of the camp. You will be responsible to me personally for seeing that not the least difficulty is placed in his way.' He turned to Prinz. 'Good day, Herr Oberst.'

Before the astonished officer could make any reply, Dirlewanger swept out of the room, leaving him standing there like a disgraced schoolboy.

The camp was restless. It was a tangible, eerie feeling. No B-soldier said a word, but they were all hoping, thinking, fearing. No one behaved abnormally, there was no excited chatter – just that expectancy, spreading through the rows of barracks like a psychic force.

Paul Vonwegh could feel the tension, even in the detention section. He stood at the tiny, barred window and placed private bets with himself on Dirlewanger's fall . . . Yes, he thought, there would be pleasure in that. But if this commander was removed, then another one would come . . . and even a humane version of Dirlewanger would still be a monster.

Vonwegh turned from the window and threw himself on to his plank bed. Aimless hope ate at a man's strength, he thought. And he switched off, in the way he had taught himself so long ago in his first hell, in Spain. He had worked on it, that 'switching off' – and had combined it with the iron self-discipline that was his gift, his trick, and his power.

Suddenly he heard steps outside, and subdued commands that sounded as if they were being filtered through cotton wool. Then they died away again and he slept.

He slept and the face came again. Her face . . .

They had stood opposite each other in that little crowd on the railway station in the depths of Mecklenburg. They had stood, and they had waited – until the train for Berlin left.

They went out of the station together. Karen asked no questions and he said nothing. The sun rose brightly, singing its song that gave the lie to war, to hunger, to bombs and destruction. It lit up the children in the playgrounds and shone on the recruits in the grey barracks courtyard. Its rays burst on to the sparkling fuselage of an allied bomber. It darted like a will-o'-the-wisp over the helmets of Stormtroopers. It bathed the swastika flags and the barracks of the concentration camps . . .

'What a beautiful day,' said Karen, as if to herself.

Paul Vonwegh nodded.

'Karen,' he began, forcing the words out of himself, 'you . . . you must . . . I mean . . I wanted to tell you . . .'

'It's all right,' she said simply. 'I understand everything.'

He saw how that strange, translucent skin on her face

seemed drawn, how her eyes gleamed with sadness.

'It's just the way that you went without saying goodbye . . .' she said, and for the first time there was a plaintive note in her voice. 'If I hadn't managed to get a lift to the station . . .' she smiled faintly. 'And our last cigarettes are gone, too.'

'It was the only way I could do it,' Vonwegh said thickly.

Karen just stopped, stood still, and pressed herself quickly, shyly against him.

On the other side of the road a peasant boy on an oxcart whistled, raised his whip in salute, and called out at them.

'Hey you two . . . and at this hour in the morning . . . !'

From there on, Vonwegh was lost. They walked quickly together now.

'Paul Vonwegh,' Karen said tenderly as they walked, 'you are a complete idiot. You simply run away from everything, without money, food, or identity papers . . . and I bet you didn't even know where you were going . . .' She read in his face that she was right.

When they reached a small wood she pulled him over to a tree stump.

'We have to have a serious talk,' she said. Vonwegh just looked at her sadly and fiddled in his pocket. Karen smiled and took out a cigarette, which she broke in two. While he lit the halves for them, she continued:

'No solo flights, understand?'

He stared straight ahead, expressionless.

'If there's going to be a getaway,' she persisted, 'then it's got to be in partnership . . . the two of us . . .'

Vonwegh nodded miserably.

'I know what you're thinking,' she said, cutting into his thoughts.

He shook his head dumbly.

'You're thinking that I won't make it,' she concluded.

'It's not easy,' Vonwegh burst out, 'in fact it's . . .'

Karen cut in again.

'I've got a proposal,' she said determinedly. 'I can see a possibility – one that might even mean we don't have to go anywhere but here.'

'How come?'

'I have a cousin,' she explained. 'His name is Wulf-Dieter Brillmann. At the moment he's a civil servant in the police department, about to be appointed to the public prosecutor's office. He's still young . . . a big noise in the Hitler Youth . . .'

'No,' Paul Vonwegh said, looking away in disgust.

'He's not a fanatic,' she explained quickly, 'he's got no time for those animals . . . it's just that he wants to get on, that's all . . .'

He bit his lip until the blood came.

'Darling, I know what you're thinking,' Karen said. 'I can't stand him either, but . . .'

'But?'

'Beggars can't be choosers . . .' she said. If it was meant to sound cheerful, then it failed badly.

He stood up without a word and she followed him, holding tightly on to him, leaning against his arm.

'Wulf-Dieter Brillmann isn't some monster,' she said, with a bright laugh, 'the most you can say against him is that he wants to get on. There are a hundred stupid fools like him, but they're not wicked . . .'

Paul Vonwegh remained obdurate. He had to refuse. The one group he hated more than the fanatics were the boys who just wanted to get on. They were the cornerstones of the whole system.

On the other hand, there was Karen – and she was a woman, not a matter of political principle . . .

In the end he gave his agreement, though only if she promised to flee along with him if Wulf-Dieter Brillmann refused to help.

On the day she went to see her oh-so-influential cousin he had waited at home, watching, guarding in every direction, so that he could react instantly if the doors swung open.

As they were opening now . . .

Paul Vonwegh jumped to his feet and recognised the face of the prison Kapo.

'Christ,' said the man admiringly, 'all this and he's taking a kip. The man's nerve . . .' Then he laughed, a low, throaty rasp. 'Well, you might as well know you're in luck. The Standartenführer's letting you all go.' The Kapo watched indifferently as two B-soldiers, their legs grotesquely swollen from a spell in the standing bunker, were carried past. 'But make yourself scarce and button your lips – because otherwise you can look forward to another stay here.'

Gruhnke had been released too, and he and Vonwegh walked back together to the barracks.

'Do you think they'll have us back in again?' the Berliner asked.

Vonwegh shrugged his shoulders.

'Could do,' he said briskly.

'Christ, you can be an irritating sort of bugger,' Gruhnke muttered. 'Doesn't anything matter to you at all? Don't you give a toss for anything?'

'What's the point?' the platoon leader said, as easily as before.

Gruhnke burst out laughing.

'What the hell,' he said. 'Guys like you are all right. They have a lot of trouble chopping you down to size, eh?'

The Berliner paused.

'Maybe nothing makes much difference to me now, either,' he said thoughtfully. 'Except that bastard who grassed on me . . . I'd still like to get my hands on him . . . I'll tear the sod apart . . .'

They were at their quarters.

Kirchwein stared at them as if they were ghosts. 'Good to have you back,' said Muller simply. Petrat grunted agreement. Kortetzky, the gorilla, was back in the main room now: he raised himself laboriously up from his mattress and gave Vonwegh a broad smile.

Almost straight away, they heard the whistles and bawled commands that meant a full parade. They fell in, cursing among themselves, but the edge had gone from things. Today there was no need to watch themselves. Today, mysteriously, no one was driving them.

It was the mysterious Police Oberst who was standing on the parade-ground and giving the orders: fall in, come into line, count off . . . He was doing it as though it were his only reason for being here, and as he watched the emaciated, ragged figures going through their paces he left no doubt that he wouldn't want to touch these B-soldiers with a barge-pole.

By the time Prinz had received the final reports, though, it was clear that he was surprised by the rabble's correct behaviour. Maybe they might be soldiers after all . . . He told them to stand at ease and form a square around him.

'Men,' he began, 'I am here on orders from the Reichsführer S S to undertake an investigation. You are to report any irregularities to me . . . any at all, do you understand?'

'Yes, sir!' they shouted back. Hope flitted between those ranks like an electric charge. There was only the sergeant with them, and he was powerless against a man like the Oberst. Christ, they all wanted something to happen. There wasn't a man among them who didn't want to dig his neighbour in the ribs and come out with their own particular choice item: how they'd seen once that Dirlewanger . . . how he'd had your mate killed . . . what had happened to those Russian girls they'd seen carried out of the 'castle' after a party . . .

'Anyone failing to present himself when ordered will be brought by me before a military court,' the old police chief shouted. 'In return, I guarantee every one of you immunity from prosecution. No one will be allowed to suffer for speaking up.'

The man's a fool, Paul Vonwegh thought as the Oberst roared on. For the first time he found himself seeing eye to eye with Dirlewanger and his cronies. As if everyone didn't know that the Oberst would be gone in a day or two . . . He could see it all: before Prinz had got as far as the exit gate, every witness he had found would be dead . . . and every poor bastard who so much as made the wrong face, nodded at the wrong moment, or batted an eyelid out of place would be in for it too . . .

'My officers will interrogate you individually,' Prinz continued. 'I must emphasise once more that no one needs to be afraid . . .'

Behind him, Sergeant Müller-Würzbach had to turn and

stifle a smile. At first the sergeant and the other bully-boys had been scared for their skins as this man with the lean body and the cropped hair had stomped around the place like a bull in a china shop. For a moment, they had really thought that he might put an end to their little empire. Then he had asked for lists of casualties, ration statistics, battle reports, and records of arrests, just as if he were dealing with any old Wehrmacht unit that had got a bit out of hand. As if Dirlewanger didn't have complete power of life and death . . .

'Official channels are suspended until further notice,' the Oberst concluded. 'They will be assumed completely and absolutely by myself and my officers.'

Prinz paused to let his words sink in, then said sharply:

'Anyone wishing to report now, raise your hand.'

No one moved. It was a miracle that the Oberst was not greeted by a massive wave of laughter . . . the scathing, bitter laughter of final despair.

Heads were bowed as the parade broke up. The electricity was gone, and with it the hope. This man was no match for Dirlewanger, whatever plans he might have.

Around mid-day, a rumour went round that Oberst Prinz was just a trap of Dirlewanger's to test people's reliability. And in the castle, around the Standartenführer's well-stocked table, the mood was hilarious. Only Müller-Würzbach still looked a little concerned.

'Come on, pessimist,' Dirlewanger said, and his manner was jolly. 'It's all going absolutely as planned . . .'

'So far,' the sergeant muttered.

'Everyone here will keep quiet,' the chief replied with perverse pride.

'Any one of them could be made to talk,' the clerk-sergeant rejoined cautiously.

'Yes,' Dirlewanger said, turning to the rest of them with a loud guffaw, 'if they were prepared to use *our* methods . . .'

The interrogations went on until late in the afternoon. The results everywhere were nil. But the B-soldiers consoled themselves with a day off, better food, and good treatment.

It was evening before Kleinschmidt found a chance to be alone with Paul Vonwegh.

'I have to talk to you,' the man said.

Vonwegh was non-committal.

'Well?'

'Haubach has disappeared,' Kleinschmidt said quickly, 'two days ago . . . I'm sure they've done him in.'

The platoon leader gave him no encouragement to say more.

'Proof?' he said simply.

Kleinschmidt shook his head.

'And why are you telling me this?' Vonwegh asked.

'Well . . .' Kleinschmidt said lamely '. . . this business . . . I mean someone should . . .'

'Planning to commit suicide, eh?' Vonwegh said sharply. looking closely at the other's eyes. 'How come you're telling *me* this?'

Kleinschmidt thought for a moment.

'Because I'm not frightened of you,' he said with a shrug and a smile. 'You wouldn't squeal on anyone. Pity you're not in charge of this investigation – we all know exactly where you stand . . .'

Vonwegh could have been flattered, but he was horrified. It had already got around this far, he thought. I must be more careful. At the same time, his brain was working feverishly. Haubach had been shot. So why all the secrecy? Why was he supposedly 'transferred'? They never usually used kid gloves like that – there was always a good reason for shooting someone. But this 'transferred to Camp II' . . .why?

Suddenly, in a flash of pure intuition, Paul Vonwegh grasped the connection – Aumeier was missing, Dirlewanger's butcher, his favourite. He had supposedly been shot on orders from the Reichsführer S S . . . Aumeier was the same height and build as Haubach, there was a facial resemblance – and they both even came from Bavaria . . .

Just as Paul Vonwegh realised that Kleinschmidt had placed a deadly weapon against Dirlewanger in his hand, the call came for him to see Oberst Prinz. Unhurriedly he went into the side room in which the policeman was personally conducting the interrogations of B-soldiers from the first platoon.

Paul Vonwegh saluted with his usual brisk precision. Good day, Herr Oberst, he was thinking. What a pity that men like you only go by the book . . .

Chapter Seven

The whole day had been a story of failure. As the old police Oberst reached to take a sip from his glass of water, his mouth was set in an even more disgruntled line. The veins on his face stood out with suppressed frustration and anger.

He stood up and watched as the next B-soldier saluted him. He walked round the man, could find nothing out of place, and was momentarily placated.

Finally he looked at Paul Vonwegh's face. Character there, he thought.

'Stand at ease,' the Oberst said. He went back to his desk, sat down with his boots stretched out casually, and lit himself a cigarette.

'I suppose you've got nothing to tell me, eh?' he muttered.

'No, Herr Oberst.'

'No irregularities?'

'None, Herr Oberst.'

'I can imagine,' Prinz snarled sardonically.

He knew their answers by heart. Vonwegh must have been the fiftieth man he had talked to today. Every one of them had stared at him with those big, dead calf's eyes, and had lied through his teeth. But sometimes he had seen their lips quiver; behind their servility was a germ of pride, behind the lies was hope. But he couldn't make the breakthrough, couldn't penetrate that wall of fear . . .

'What's your profession?' Prinz asked.

Paul Vonwegh hesitated. What indeed? Adventurer, professional soldier, criminal, refugee?

'Student,' he answered, just as the policeman was preparing to bawl him out.

'And what dirty business did you get up to?'

'Falsification of documents.'

Prinz raised an incredulous eyebrow.

'Hm . . .' he said reflectively, 'and for that you ended up with this lot?'

'Yes, sir.'

Outside, Sergeant Weise passed by, apparently by chance. He stopped for a moment and looked through the window. His eyes met Vonwegh's in that particular expressionless stare that he knew only too well. But Prinz had seen the sergeant too.

'Now listen carefully, Vonwegh,' the Oberst said. It was typical of him that he kept the platoon leader standing up – even though he knew that a more casual form of interrogation would bring better results, it went against his strict code as an officer to sit at a table opposite a convicted criminal. Prinz paused again and scratched his head. 'I'm assuming that you have a few more brains in your head than we usually find in this crowd. You're certainly above this . . . milieu . . . and I give you my word now that I shall protect you completely and absolutely, whatever you may have to bring against the leadership of the Special Commando . . . Do you follow me?'

'Yes, Herr Oberst.'

'I am even prepared to take your statement anonymously,' he continued. His distaste was showing, despite himself.

Paul Vonwegh did not avoid the Oberst's eyes. Here was a typical old warhorse, he thought – straight, correct, and stupid. What he had not yet noticed was that Prinz was deliberately going round the point, that this was all a prologue to the real interrogation, a piece of harmless bluff, cheap theatre. Vonwegh had not yet realised that this man, who looked like a caricature of an old-school officer, was as sharp as a razor – or that the Oberst was only going to use its cutting wedge when it would do his mission some good.

'Well?' his interrogator pressed.

Vonwegh kept his silence.

'Talk, man . . .' the policeman said, slowly and dangerously.

'Nothing, Herr Oberst,' the platoon leader answered, as if he were standing out on the parade ground.

'You pansy . . . you coward . . . you lily-livered swine!'

Oberst Prinz raged, and he roared so loudly that Sergeant Weise heard it. It was enough to send Dirlewanger's henchman away with a nod and a crooked, self-satisfied smile.

Officially, of course, the killer-brigade commander had given Prinz a completely free hand. Since that first meeting he had ignored him, as if he no longer existed. But in reality he was having his every step watched. Dirlewanger knew exactly how the investigation was going so far . . . and he and his cronies were already patting each other on the back.

Oberst Prinz stood up, walked right up to Paul Vonwegh, and looked him hard and long in the eyes. He read something there, a faint glint, a quiet deliberation, and he sensed: this man is no idiot, and no coward.

'Sit down,' Prinz said, breaking with his principles. He shoved a cigarette across the table and threw Vonwegh some matches, without taking his eyes off the man for a second. He saw how the B-soldier smoked the long-withheld cigarette without fuss, as if it were the most natural thing in the world, and he noted: this Vonwegh is in control of himself.

The Oberst's tone became almost conversational as he continued.

'You do realise,' he said, 'that if you do not talk, then I shall go away from here empty-handed.' He paused. 'Do you want that to happen?' he asked softly.

'No, Herr Oberst,' Paul Vonwegh answered.

'I see,' Oberst Prinz said. 'I think we are . . . beginning to understand each other . . .'

'Yes, Herr Oberst,' Vonwegh replied, just as expressionlessly as before.

'It may well be that you personally know nothing . . .' Prinz went on carefully '. . . but you know this man . . . or that man . . .' He stubbed out his cigarette in the ash tray, took another sip of water, and this time his face stayed calm. 'If . . . send him to me . . . he doesn't need to let on who told him . . .'

'Yes, Herr Oberst.'

'By the way, there's something else,' Prinz said as Vonwegh turned to leave. 'How long have you been with Dirlewanger?'

'A few weeks.'

'Do you know anyone who has been with him from the beginning?'

Paul Vonwegh considered.

'In Poland, I mean,' Prinz said coaxingly.

That's it, thought Vonwegh. I see what he's aiming at.

'Yes . . .' the platoon leader answered quietly. 'Petrat . . . killed his wife . . . pretty tight-lipped sort of character . . . might talk if you gave him a hard time . . .'

'Thank you,' the Oberst said, then continued in an undertone: 'Look out. Someone coming.' Then, without a pause, he bellowed: 'Stand to attention! . . . Don't just stand there like a stuffed dummy! . . . Get out of here before I have you locked up . . . I don't want to see you again, you numbskull, you cretin, you . . . !'

The platoon leader responded straight away by leaping to attention and delivering a Nazi salute.

Afterwards, as Paul Vonwegh made his way back to his quarters, he felt as stupid as any raw recruit. To think that he took the Oberst for a fool . . . and, God, it was going to make his whole charade even more difficult.

Suddenly someone clapped him on the shoulder from behind. Vonwegh turned round slowly to see Sergeant Weise standing there, that satisfied grin on his face again.

'Don't worry,' Weise said smugly, 'he'll soon be packing his bags . . .'

'Yes, sergeant.'

'And if there are no complaints about the business with Fleischmann, I'll propose you for promotion.'

'Yes, sergeant.'

'We can use tough nuts like you,' Weise said finally. Then he took up his observation post again.

A few of the others from Barrack VIII had seen the incident, and feelings were mixed. The platoon leader found himself caught up again in a welter of sentiments: envy, distrust, fear.

'Just be wary of Weise . . .' growled old, honest Gruhnke when they were alone. 'He's a real two-faced bastard . . .'

'And you watch they don't put the finger on you again,' Vonwegh said with a laugh.

'Let 'em . . . Before they do, I'll have some bugger of a grass's neck . . .' answered Gruhnke, spitting carefully on to the barrack-room floor.

Vonwegh knew that there would still be those secret watches at night for the unknown 'listening machine'. But at least from now on he wouldn't have to mount them alone . . .

Twenty-four hours had passed since Police Oberst Prinz's arrival in the camp before he and Standartenführer Dirlewanger had their first substantial discussion. Dirlewanger felt himself so safe, and so superior, that he was already beginning to feel pity for this wretched cop.

'Now . . .' Dirlewanger began patronisingly 'Have you discovered anything?' He gave a drunken laugh. 'After all, any irregularities would obviously be of burning interest to me . . . it's impossible to keep an eye on everything.'

Oberst Prinz nodded glumly.

'No,' he said. 'Absolutely nothing, Standartenführer . . . and that is really the only thing that makes me suspicious . . .'

'How come?'

'I have never yet come across a unit where everything is perfectly in order . . .'

'Well, yes, Oberst,' the Standartenführer cut in hastily, realising the irony of the man. 'But then we are a special kind of bunch . . . most of them are criminals . . . the sort that can only be controlled with the kind of powers that have been officially assigned to me by the Reichsführer S S . . . They are not pleasant, I know that.'

Prinz lit a cigarette. He knew all about Dirlewanger's absolute powers, and how real they were. The thought sent cold shivers down his spine. There were no historical precedents, even in the case of mercenary bands or freebooters. Here was a lunatic with more power even than a concentration camp commander. But nevertheless he would catch him – he, Prinz, would catch him . . .

'I don't know if you are aware that we operate on a loss

ratio of more than eighty per cent . . .' Dirlewanger was saying.

'I have seen the casualty lists.'

'It's unique,' Dirlewanger carried on, as if in triumph. 'You may think my lions a rough bunch . . . in prisons or in concentration camps, of course, they are just useless scroungers . . . but here they do something for us – for the Führer – for Greater Germany . . . do you understand that?' The Standartenführer laughed harshly. 'And if they get killed in the process, what does it matter? There are replacements enough in the prisons, aren't there?'

'I am not competent to judge the measures undertaken by the Reichssicherheitshauptamt,' Prinz replied stiffly.

Dirlewanger nodded and poured himself a schnapps. He offered the Oberst a drink but the man declined firmly, in a way that made it quite clear that he would never accept one from Dirlewanger, however much he might want one, or need one . . .

'I know,' the Standartenführer said comfortably, 'that you're one of the old school . . . and our times are not always easy to understand . . .' He toasted the Oberst, emptied the glass with one gulp, and continued:

'The main thing is that we fulfil our duty . . . each one in his place.'

Oberst Prinz nodded grimly.

'When do you leave?' Dirlewanger asked suddenly.

'Tomorrow, probably,' the policeman said. 'However, I would like to have one more try . . . I want to see the brigade once more, but privately . . . this afternoon . . .'

'Please. Go ahead,' the Standartenführer said with an airy wave of the hand. He called to his staff-sergeant. 'Müller-Würzbach,' Dirlewanger intoned gravely, 'you will be at the Herr Oberst's disposal once more, should he need you.'

'Yes, sir.'

'My thanks,' Prinz said curtly. 'And now if you will excuse me . . .'

Dirlewanger watched the Police Oberst leave.

'I'll do for him one of these days,' snarled Weise, who stood next to him.

'What for?' Dirlewanger asked cheerfully. 'I think we have more important things to do. He's just a blabberer . . . a do-gooder . . . he belongs in the Salvation Army.'

'Or in the heavenly host . . .' Weise said, with a feral smile that revealed shark-like teeth.

Prinz went straight to the office he had been allotted. He didn't need to refer to file P.A./IX DORA – he had it in his head. It was just one of Dirlewanger's atrocities, but it was the one, if he was lucky, that he might just be able to prove . . .

The case dated back to the year before.

At that time, the Special Brigade was looting its way through occupied Poland. Just behind what had once been the demarcation line, in a small village, Dirlewanger set up his headquarters. The Sturmbannführer, as he was then, gave his men some punishing drill-routines and went hunting. So it was that one of the B-soldiers got around to distilling some illicit schnapps in a cellar. The stuff tasted terrible, but they drank it until they fell about – under the influence, even regular soldiers forgot that they were supposed to be a cut above Dirlewanger's bandits.

It was the night in which a blind-drunk SS corporal set fire to the village church, while another wielded a whip to keep the fire brigade away from the blaze. It was the night in which dogs howled and children cried, shots rang out and women screamed. It was the night when Dirlewanger, three kilometres away and mad with alcohol, breathed fire.

The woman who reported to him in the morning was thirty-one years old, but looked forty. In that woman's face, the war years counted threefold . . .

'Seven soldiers . . .' she said. 'They dragged my Nadia out of her bed . . . she is nine . . . still a child . . .' The mother pummelled at her face with her own hands. 'And they . . .'

'All seven of them?' Dirlewanger asked.

The woman nodded. Her gaze was empty, her eyes could cry no more.

'Monstrous!' Dirlewanger bellowed. 'Would you recognise the men again?'

She said she would.

'Get them lined up!' Dirlewanger ordered Müller-Würzbach. 'All of them – right down to the domestics and the headquarters staff.'

Ten minutes later, the staff-sergeant reported that they were all waiting.

'Good,' said Dirlewanger to the woman. 'Now come and find the men.' He accompanied her along the ranks.

At first the woman couldn't concentrate. Then she thought of Nadia, her child, lying there half-dead and hideously mutilated at home, staring, wordless, perhaps for ever . . . Nadia, whose face would contort and who would suddenly, terrifyingly, scream out that single, same word: 'No . . . No . . . No . . . !'

'That one,' she said pointing to a red-haired B-soldier with freckles. 'Him,' she said, recognising his neighbour. 'And him,' she stopped in front of an S S lance-corporal, a favourite of Dirlewanger. She went on to the fourth . . . and the fifth . . . and the sixth . . .

Then the woman paused in front of a seventh man and looked at him closely. He had a receding forehead, strangely darting eyes, a thick lower lip and hair shorn down to the roots. The mother hung back – hadn't they all looked like that when they had flung themselves on her Nadia? She read the fear in the B-soldier's bulging eyes, the doglike pleading . . . she couldn't be certain, and so she moved on.

If the woman had looked at him even more closely, she would not have missed the nose with the wart on it – the ugly wart on the face of Petrat, the woman-killer.

Dirlewanger had the six delinquents arrested and put together a firing-squad from among their comrades.

'I shall take drastic measures,' he assured the mother. 'I won't tolerate such outrages . . . Have you any other witnesses?'

The woman nodded.

'Bring them here,' the Sturmbannführer ordered. He sent a few of his trusted henchmen with her.

An hour later the woman came back, accompanied by four men, three women, two boys, and a girl.

'Are they all here?' the brigade leader asked.

'My husband is still working in the fields . . .'

'Fetch him,' Dirlewanger demanded.

'All of you saw the incident?' he asked when the Polish peasant was brought to join the rest of them.

They confirmed that they had.

'Then let's see if you can identify the fellows again.'

Every single one of the witnesses picked out the same men – but they still didn't manage to find the seventh. As it turned out, Petrat was back distilling potato schnapps in the cellar . . . And in any case, Dirlewanger was getting bored with the whole business by now.

The firing-squad, put together by a reluctant Müller-Würzbach, stood ready now. A hole was dug. A large hole. The place of execution was set away from the buildings, to avoid eye-witnesses.

First the six men who had raped the nine-year-old girl were shot.

Then the child's mother.

Then the child herself.

Then the five men, three women, two boys – all the witnesses . . .

'That was a close shave,' Dirlewanger said afterwards. 'Someone might have sent a report to Himmler, and the Reichsführer can be a bit fussy about these things . . . Anyway, spread word round the village that the ones we shot have been deported to Germany.'

Oberst Prinz knew exactly what Dirlewanger had said. A B-soldier had written everything down conscientiously in a notebook. He had smuggled it out of the camp and given it to an old schoolfriend, who sent it to his local District Leader at home. But before the document reached the hands of Oberst Prinz, the witness B-soldier had died . . . or had been killed –

it amounted to more or less the same thing in the Dirlewanger Brigade, thought Prinz.

At mid-day there was meat for the men again. Dirlewanger's motives were rather more subtle than mere bribery. He was eager to pre-empt any charges under SS regulation IV (against profiteering) which he knew was one of Reichsführer Himmler's obsessions. Dirlewanger need not have worried, though. Oberst Prinz was far more concerned about making progress on the file P.A./IX DORA . . .

Kortetzky, the gorilla, was asleep at the time of the mid-day meal. Petrat had wanted to have his meat portion, but Vonwegh had stopped him. Now the criminal with the wart – the toughest, meanest B-soldier in the whole group – was watching Kordt with his spiteful eyes. He didn't need to speak, but as usual the boy understood the hidden threat and shoved him his plate furtively under the table. Paul Vonwegh noticed it.

'Eat your food yourself, Kordt,' he said quietly.

The boy hesitated for a moment, weighing up his trust in Vonwegh's authority against his fear of Petrat. Then he went on eating, gingerly at first, then wolfing the food down as if he would never eat again.

'If you don't leave him alone, Petrat . . .' the platoon leader said, and he didn't need to finish his sentence.

Vonwegh left the room, and Gruhnke watched him as he went.

'That man's learned how to behave,' he said meaningfully, with his eyes on the East Prussian. 'Being inside can improve people . . . sometimes . . .'

Petrat sat in a hunch, staring straight ahead. Everyone knew he didn't dare say anything against Vonwegh. Then he heard a voice behind him:

'He wanted to pinch your share . . . Vonwegh stopped him . . .'

Petrat didn't have to turn round. He recognised Kleinschmidt's voice, and he knew he was telling the gorilla about the meal.

'Well,' Kortetzky grunted savagely, 'I'll be fit again some time . . .'

There was silence in the room until Kirchwein spoke up: 'This inspection business is not so bad, eh?' he said with forced brightness.

Kleinschmidt looked at him contemptuously.

'The best is yet to come,' he muttered, getting to his feet and making for the door.

Outside he found Vonwegh. It was strange, he thought, but he was the only one whom the platoon leader used the familiar 'du' to. A weird fellow, Vonwegh, all round – always acted as if he was wearing gloves . . . some kind of invisible shield that protected him from the blood and the muck . . .

'Watch out for Petrat,' Kleinschmidt said to the platoon leader.

'A small fish,' Vonwegh retorted with a shrug, 'a very small . . .'

'A shark,' Kleinschmidt cut in, 'if he's given a chance.'

They walked a short distance from the hut, and Kleinschmidt looked cautiously around him – Vonwegh realised that he was about to raise the subject they had discussed earlier.

'Have you found out anything . . . about Haubach?' the man whispered.

'Yes,' said Vonwegh quietly. 'But I've no desire to stick my head in a noose.'

'Well, what?' Kleinschmidt said, with an edge of anger to his voice.

Vonwegh shrugged again.

'You could burn your fingers very badly . . .' he said, feeling his way with the man, cautiously sounding him out.

'Look,' Kleinschmidt muttered, 'I know you're a loner . . .' The platoon leader did not react. '. . . But Haubach was my mate, a good friend . . . he once did a three-year stretch on my account, and not a peep out of him . . . do you understand that?'

'Yes, I think I do,' Vonwegh said gravely.

'I mean, I'm not stupid,' Kleinschmidt continued, 'and I'm not about to do anything crazy – but I do owe Haubach something . . .'

'Come on, you won't change anything . . .' Vonwegh said, goading the man on now.

'Hell,' Kleinschmidt said, obviously riled. 'If you ask me, we're all for the high jump – that's what I bloody well think . . .'

'Me too,' said Vonwegh matter-of-factly.

'But beforehand, I'll even up the scores for Haubach,' the other fumed, raising his voice so that Vonwegh had to give him a sharp poke in the ribs to keep him quiet.

Kleinschmidt stood in silent frustration for a moment, then said again:

'Look, do you really know something?'

Vonwegh considered.

'OK,' he said. 'The fact is that your friend looked a lot like Aumeier . . . you remember – Dirlewanger's pal, the staff butcher . . .'

Kleinschmidt stared at Vonwegh, still uncomprehending.

'Well,' the platoon leader went on, 'Aumeier got into some trouble . . . attracted attention, right at the top . . . had to be shot . . .'

'And?'

'He's now called Haubach . . .' Vonwegh said simply. He had delivered his bombshell, now he had to wait for the explosion.

At last the B-soldier understood. Trembling with rage, he started to rave about taking his gun and going straight into Dirlewanger's dacha and . . . Vonwegh cut him short.

'If you do anything,' he said calmly, 'at least use your brains, you idiot.'

'What, then?' Kleinschmidt snapped impatiently.

'You'd better think it over,' Vonwegh said, putting a brake on the man again.

'That's up to me – and I've thought . . .'

Vonwegh nodded slowly, and then he proceeded to give 'advice' that sounded uncommonly like orders. Kleinschmidt lapped up his directions greedily, swallowing them whole. They were precise, as follows:

1. Only make contact with Oberst Prinz when there are no witnesses present.

2. Only make disclosures if the officer guarantees you protective custody under his personal direction and promises to take you to his headquarters on his departure.

3. Ensure that Oberst Prinz arrests the fake Haubach in Russian Camp II and then transfers him along with you.

'If you make one false move, you're dead,' Vonwegh said finally. 'For God's sake, be careful.'

'I will be,' Kleinschmidt answered, in a voice like iron.

The B-soldier began to walk away slowly, taking care that no one saw him.

'Kleinschmidt . . .' the platoon leader called after him.

The man came back again.

'You're a good man,' Vonwegh said softly.

Kleinschmidt flushed deep red, then went off again, cursing to cover his embarrassment.

I would have made a prison governor, or a criminal psychologist, thought Vonwegh sourly. His bomb was ticking now, and if there were any problems he was in a position where he could reset the mechanism. The sense of satisfaction that pulsed through him was intoxicating. He breathed deeply, feeling the frosty air in his lungs. But he felt no cold: he was warmed by the fire of the hate inside him. That fire had to be.

If only a woman had understood that fire . . . and if only he had trusted to it then . . .

From the way in which Karen had torn open the door, he had known that her meeting with Wulf-Dieter Brillmann had been a success. Even after they had kissed, while he was stroking her forehead the way she liked, she took a few seconds to recover her breath. And all the time he was looking out of the window, checking that she hadn't been followed. She looked up and saw him doing it, and she laughed:

'I saw a Western film once,' Karen said, 'and there was a man in it just like you . . . just as suspicious, always with his gun at the ready, always keeping a look out on all sides . . .'

'And?' Paul Vonwegh asked drily.

'He was right . . . and he got the baddies in the end.'

'Chance'd be a fine thing . . .' Vonwegh muttered sarcastically.

'But that was in a Wild West film, of course,' she said reproachfully.

'The Wild West is nothing to the country we live in,' he said softly, and his face darkened. The girl's innocence was so beautiful – and so dangerous . . .

'You might be right,' Karen said then, 'but there are still some decent people, aren't there?'

'Sure. Some!'

'Like my cousin Wulf-Dieter, for instance.'

Vonwegh unwrapped her arms from round his neck and pressed her gently into an armchair, then stood there expectantly.

'Well, I didn't say anything about you personally . . .' she began.

He smiled wryly.

'No,' she continued earnestly, 'I talked about a hypothetical case – the case of a girl-friend who . . .'

'Devious stuff,' Paul cut in, and couldn't help laughing.

'Otherwise I told him everything about you,' Karen said. 'Only I left out names . . . and I made you older . . .' she smiled roguishly. 'I gave you a pot belly and a big nose, all red with, you know, little blue veins.' She saw the incredulous grin on his face and knew it was time to get on to the serious part. 'Well, and, as I told you before, Wulf-Dieter has contacts . . . even with, and don't be too horrified, with the G-G-Ges . . .'

'Gestapo,' Vonwegh completed the word for her, and the way he said it was like a spit in the face of the system.

'Yes,' Karen said. 'And don't look at me like that. He's well-trusted, and contacts are very important in that business . . . he's got something with some old friend from univeristy that's worked wonders for him . . .'

Paul Vonwegh nodded. He understood sure enough.

'And what did he propose?'

'That you should give yourself up,' Karen replied.

'Brilliant!'

'But they would guarantee you immunity . . .'

Vonwegh stood up and went over to her. He stretched out one hand to stroke her hair and looked into her eyes.

'And if they don't choose to keep their promise, Karen?' he said, as if to a wilful child.

'There's still Wulf-Dieter,' she answered, almost angrily.

'Oh yes . . . the cousin with the hyphen in his name, the Hitler-youth hero with the bully-boy friends . . .'

'But you don't know him!' she protested.

'Not personally, no,' Vonwegh said, 'but from the company he keeps . . .' He realised that he was making her miserable and confused, and changed his tone. 'Don't take too much notice of me,' he said gently. 'I'm just an old cynic.'

'I suppose so,' she said, mollified. 'But then you have had experiences . . .'

He nodded.

'But he means it honestly, believe me . . . He wants to speak with you first . . . on neutral ground to start off with, and then with the Gesta – '

'Gestapo.'

'He'll bring up your problem as a theoretical one, you understand,' Karen continued, 'as a sort of textbook case . . . and if they agree . . . please, Paul, be reasonable.'

He nodded again, but said nothing.

'Wulf-Dieter has heard of a few cases . . . even people who have come back from Spain . . .'

Into a concentration camp Paul Vonwegh thought. Yes, he knew about all that. But still he said nothing.

'It's entirely your choice,' Karen said, reaching over to ruffle his hair. 'Will you go?'

'When would it be?'

'Tomorrow.'

He nodded and tried to look confident. He appraised his

chances of success – 10%, maybe 15% if the go-between turned out to be a decent sort. At that thought, he felt a pitch in his stomach. A decent sort! Yes, some bastard who, of course, was too fine to be a brownshirt – but who tripped over himself to be nice to them when it came to his career. A type . . .

Paul Vonwegh knew that he thought in black and white. It was inevitable after that time down in Spain; the white was the flag of surrender after the bitter struggle, and the black belonged to the violated sisters of the dead, the mourning mothers, the dark night of fascism . . .

Back in the present. The platoon leader heard whistles, and the next moment the barrack doors were flung open. 1500 hours: the time had come for Oberst Prinz's investigation to make its decision.

The men shuffled in dull anguish on the parade-ground. The time of reckoning for S S-Standartenführer Dirlewanger and his crew. Now or never.

Chapter Eight

By their sides, the men's hands were clammy in spite of the cold. Neatly lined up in three ranks at attention, they stared stubbornly straight ahead. There was fear, and hope, in those faces after two days of rumours, of wild expectation.

The military regulations were followed to the last detail. The men standing on the camp's parade ground would have shone in any military parade – except that they were convicted criminals.

'Form a square!' the police Oberst ordered.

The left and right flanks wheeled in at once, and lined up at the double. Behind them Sergeant Müller-Würzbach made notes; the scavenging hyena. Going up close to the men so that they would all be able to hear him, the Oberst studied the ranks with chilly detachment, his face stern and expressionless.

'Men . . .' he began carefully, 'as you know, I came here on the instructions of the Reichsführer S S to . . . make certain enquiries.' He broke off and gazed along the lines of men, as if he were consciously screwing up the tension. For a moment his eyes rested on Vonwegh's taut face, then they wandered on to Kirchwein next to him; his eyes flitted on, to Petrat, the sly one, then to Guhnke, who had come to see the policeman as a prophet, a miracle-worker, and from there on to the others.

Without turning his head, Vonwegh followed Prinz's gaze. One man was missing: B-soldier Kleinschmidt, his own remote-control bomb, the witness in the Aumeier–Haubach affair.

'My officers and myself . . .' the Oberst continued then, stiffly, 'have given every one of you the opportunity to talk to us . . . even outside the usual official channels. Anyone with a complaint to make was offered my personal protection . . . we selected over one hundred B-soldiers and interrogated them . . .' he paused once more '. . . it is now my duty to inform you of the results of my investigations.'

The first rank of men seemed to swell, and then to sink back together again, like some organic force. Now, they all thought: someone, somewhere, must have talked; someone with more guts, or better nerves than I . . .

'It is with pleasure that I can confirm that . . .' the Oberst's words rattled like hailstones on the ranks of the B-soldiers '. . . here everything is in extraordinarily good order.' His face was impassive.

The men's illusions and dreams collapsed like soap-bubbles. Their heads sank; their eyes became dead again; their backs hunched as if they were already feeling the strokes of the whip.

'I have inspected many units in my time,' the officer continued, with a snarl in his voice, 'but such . . . exemplary qualities as this one displays I have never seen before.' Oberst Prinz felt the disappointment in the hundreds of men and nodded grimly. Now his feelings came out into the open, and he became scathing in his scorn: 'Yes, you get the best provisions, you have the most superb non-commissioned officers, your treatment is excellent . . . I will report that to the Reichsführer S S without reservation . . .'

Again the policeman enjoyed the effect of his words. 'You all have something to make good, and according to your own statements you are on the best road to doing so. I can only congratulate you all: you have found a better unit than you deserve.'

Oberst Prinz watched as Müller-Würzbach and Sergeant Weise grinned at each other in satisfaction, then continued loudly:

'It only remains for me to state categorically that all the rumours which led to this investigation are completely unfounded. I believe that you are on the right path, and I wish you all well during your continued service.'

The officer broke off and nodded. A few faces had still not managed to regain their composure. He noted them. In the front rank a man keeled over, sprawled full length, gasped, twitching his arms violently in a St Vitus' dance: Kirchwein, the epileptic, had suffered the long-dreaded attack.

It was quiet, uncannily quiet. The only sound was the sick man's strangled gasps . . . It hadn't escaped Sergeant Weise's notice that the man had drawn attention to himself at the worst possible moment. This time he'll pay for it with his life, the NCO thought grimly.

Oberst Prinz moved closer.

'Why don't you help the man?' he called to Vonwegh.

'Only on orders, Herr Oberst,' the platoon leader answered.

'What are you waiting for then?' the Oberst shouted angrily.

Vonwegh bent over Kirchwein at once, wiped the foam from the man's mouth, whispering to him reassuringly, trying to hold his arms still.

The sergeant came up from the rear.

'An epileptic, Herr Oberst . . .' he explained to Prinz.

'I can see that for myself, man. Why hasn't he been taken to hospital?'

'We haven't got one, Herr Oberst,' Müller-Würzbach cut in, almost contemptuously.

'Then transfer him back to the parent unit until he's recovered.'

'We don't have one of those either, Herr Oberst,' the sergeant replied triumphantly. 'Move,' he said to Vonwegh and Gruhnke, 'take him to his room.'

While Kirchwein was being carried away, Prinz seemed to be making his mind up about something.

'Shall I dismiss the men?' Müller-Würzbach asked.

'Just a moment,' the Oberst said, like a man who had just remembered some trivial point.

'Who has been with this unit for more than a year?' he said suddenly.

No one moved; no one wanted to stand out from the crowd.

'Who was in Poland?' Prinz asked then, his voice edged with menace.

Again no one moved.

'Shall I refresh your memories?' The Oberst went over to Petrat and stood pointedly in front of him. 'Do you want to be put in the detention block?' he asked quietly.

'No, Herr Oberst,' Petrat said hastily.

'Am I going to have to look through all your service records?' Prinz said, turning to the others again.

A second B-soldier slowly raised his hand.

'Right. At last,' the officer said coolly. 'Any more?'

'Yes, Herr Oberst,' replied Müller-Würzbach, the staff-sergeant. 'I . . .'

'Another,' the visitor concluded with a satisfied nod. 'Now you can dismiss them. Then report to me, along with the two others.'

'Yes, Herr Oberst,' the sergeant answered miserably.

Paul Vonwegh bent over Kirchwein as the epileptic moaned in his delirium. Suddenly the cramps eased and the patient became quieter. The platoon leader got to his feet. As he did so, Gruhnke shrugged his shoulders as if to say: so what? Kirchwein was finished anyway, and it would be better for him to go this way.

Vonwegh nodded absent-mindedly and accepted a cigarette from Gruhnke.

'Black market,' he explained with a grin.

The platoon leader hesitated for a moment, and the good-natured crook misunderstood the gesture.

'I'll keep a lookout,' he said, and went to the door.

As they were carrying Kirchwein away they had just heard that the police Oberst was looking for B-soldiers who had been with the brigade in Poland. It didn't surprise Vonwegh.

He weighed the situation coolly: three men were involved, because Müller-Würzbach would certainly keep his mouth shut. Perhaps Petrat could be made to talk, with the right approach – and the right approach meant brutally, because violence was the only language the East-Prussian killer understood.

Kirchwein was speaking, more quietly and clearly. Syllables were becoming words, and the words were taking on meaning. The epileptic kept on repeating something – haltingly but insistently, as if his fear of death were spurring him on.

Suddenly Paul Vonwegh began to listen carefully. He concentrated on making sense of the garbled stammering of the sick man. For a moment he was thoughtful, then he understood. As he straightened up and turned to Gruhnke, his face wore a tight smile. Luckily the Berliner had not been paying attention.

'The others have got to make up a wood-gathering detail,' Gruhnke said with a grin, 'but we're still nursemaids.'

The platoon leader nodded. The fuse had been lit, the bomb was primed. It *had* to go off . . . For a moment, the man with the iron will felt a pitch of uncertainty. Maybe I've done it all wrong, he thought. Maybe I shouldn't have relied on Kleinschmidt . . . Maybe this is the kind of coup I should have carried through myself . . .

His thoughts went back to another time of torment, of indecision. That time, too, he had had to make a knife-edge decision. When normal, everyday things are involved, you can throw a coin and ask: heads or tails? But then it had concerned the two of them – him and Karen. And it had been life or death. You don't leave that sort of thing to the toss of a coin; you worry about it until your head feels like bursting, as he had done then. In the night before the decision.

They were lying next to each other, both pretending to be asleep. Karen was breathing firmly and evenly. He had his eyes clamped tight shut.

Paul Vonwegh felt Karen's gaze on him and forgot to keep breathing evenly. She noticed, and he started breathing deeply, too deeply. He abandoned the struggle and sat up.

He studied her lying there, so beautiful and young. It was a crime to involve her in all this, he thought. She was so brave, she had so much to live and hope for . . . Perhaps she was right about her cousin. She had to be right.

'You're nowhere near asleep,' she said, and her voice was like a little girl's.

He made no answer.

'Fake!' she reproached him, and dug him in the side playfully.

Paul Vonwegh smiled and drew her to him.

'You really ought to sleep,' Karen said, as if he had some control over whether he slept or not. 'You know,' she continued, 'my cousin . . . he was so nice as a child . . . we used to play together . . . he was a real little knight in shining armour when he was only five or six . . .'

And secretly Karen was thinking: Wulf-Dieter was already disgusting, selfish, a cry-baby. Once he threw a sand-shovel in my face and laughed at me. How can anyone be such a swine at seven years old? she thought despairingly. And he has always been one, right through school and university.

'I know all about your cousin,' Vonwegh said. 'And if you say another word . . .'

They didn't speak again. They were silent in the morning as well, over the flower-decked breakfast table. Karen handed him a roll spread with jam – he never managed to work out where she got such things in wartime – and he pretended to enjoy it, though every bite was torture. His attempt was as pointless as her pretence of boundless optimism.

Time to go. Vonwegh stood in front of her, hesitating for a moment.

'Don't say good-bye,' Karen said with a sad smile. 'I know you'll come back . . . and you have to believe that, too . . .'

'Yes,' he answered, and swallowed hard.

He left, aware that Karen hadn't turned round to watch him go. She must be crying, he thought, as he made his way down the stairs. He carried on, making a conscious effort to hold himself erect, though he knew that she wouldn't be watching him. When he was out of sight of the house he walked hunched, like a lame man. He travelled by bus into the town, then had to steel himself, twice, before he could make his final approach to the café where he was to meet the go-between.

In the end, he made it to the entrance of the place. Vonwegh had no photo of Karen's cousin, only her description of him, but he recognised the man at once, went up to him and inclined his head inquiringly.

'My name is Brillmann,' the man said shortly. 'And yours?'

Vonwegh shook his head.

'Names are not important,' the man said, and laughed.

The other's voice was not unpleasant. His face was soft, almost feminine. Vonwegh's first reaction was one of pleasant surprise, though he knew that something had to be wrong with this smiling perfection . . .

'So you are . . .' Brillmann began, 'not the first case . . . tricky, but not impossible . . .'

He offered Vonwegh a cigarette. 'But I'll be glad to help you.'

'Why?' Vonwegh interrupted him.

'Because of Karen,' he answered. The smile widened in his pretty face. 'Do you know, I was head over heels in love with her once . . . when she was a schoolgirl. Yes, I suppose cousins are always first loves . . .' he continued. 'But why am I telling you all this?'

Paul Vonwegh looked sharply at him, but saw that he was behaving in a quite relaxed and normal way. Vonwegh glanced furtively at the waitress a few times, twice he checked his watch. By now they would have made their move if this was a trap, he reflected.

'I like you,' Brillmann said suddenly. 'I don't usually have much time for . . . idealists.' He made a dismissive gesture. 'You obviously take me for a Nazi,' he continued, playing with his spoon in his empty coffee cup, 'but then these days that is quite a useful thing to be taken for. Yes,' he said, 'Karen . . . nice girl, good Nordic stock . . . I mean first-class character, you understand.'

Paul Vonwegh nodded. He was beginning to hate this man who was to be his 'benefactor', beginning to want to sink his fist into that soft, smiling face . . . *Pull yourself together* he told himself.

'What do we do now?' he asked matter-of-factly.

'You must, of course, reveal your identity,' Wulf-Dieter Brillmann replied. 'You know that I have nothing to do with the matter directly, but I do have a few contacts in the Gestapo . . . old student friends, and so on . . . you understand.' He dug into his pocket and pulled out a prepared statement. 'Here,' he said. 'If you will sign this, then the hunt for you will be called off . . . whoever you are.'

Vonwegh glanced quickly through the statement. It was propaganda of the worst kind, aimed at public opinion abroad. The black letters zoomed and flitted in front of his eyes like a swarm of flies, but he forced himself to stay calm.

'And if I don't sign it?' he asked.

Wulf-Dieter Brillmann stubbed his cigarette out slowly. He was still smiling.

'You don't have very much choice,' he said, and then he stood up. 'Send Karen my regards . . .' He gave Vonwegh his visiting card. 'The decision is yours,' he continued. 'I won't push you . . . I won't even advise you . . . ring this number when you have made your decision.'

Then he shook hands with Vonwegh; his palms were moist and flabby.

'All the best,' he said quietly, then, raising his voice: 'Heil Hitler!'

Vonwegh watched him leave. Then he just sat there and gave himself over to apathy. An old man came in, looked round and reached deliberately for a newspaper from the rack. Now, Vonwegh thought, and another one will be waiting outside. They must be hoping I'll lead them to Karen, so that they can get us both together. That must be it, after all . . .

Vonwegh saw an informer in every passer-by. But at least it helped him to shake off that terrible lethargy. He had a small purpose again, something to fight for. He had to protect Karen.

The man with the newspaper didn't follow him. Two soldiers who had seemed to be staring at him walked calmly on, and Paul Vonwegh walked and walked, from east to west, from west to east, straight through danger, past patrols, looking everywhere for pursuers. He did not understand that the trap had yet to be sprung.

By late afternoon he was famished, and there was still no

direct threat to be seen. He sat down at a table in a street café; it was only then that he felt someone looking at him and stood up, startled. It was a young girl of about eighteen, cheerful, unsuspicious, a brunette.

'You look troubled,' she said.

Vonwegh nodded distantly.

'Problems?' the girl asked.

'Yes,' he replied.

'Can I cheer you up?'

He shook his head and walked away.

'I didn't mean it like that . . .' the brunette sulkily called after him.

Paul Vonwegh spent three hours shaking off his imaginary pursuers. He ran the gauntlet through his fantasies. He fought pointless battles with shadows. He was exhausted by the time he crept back into the house like a thief.

His first feeling was one of surprise when he saw that Karen was still there. Then he saw her face, the marks of her crying, and realised just what he had been doing to this woman.

'My god,' said Karen. 'Where have you been all day?'

'I thought . . .' he began.

'You didn't trust him?' she asked abruptly.

He nodded.

'Idiot,' she said tenderly. 'Did you come to an arrangement?'

'I have to sign something,' he said, feeling the crack in his own voice.

'And then everything will be all right?'

He nodded stiffly.

'Well then,' she concluded with an air of triumph.

Did she really trust Brillmann? Vonwegh thought. Could he ever sign the statement? Of course, he told himself – Karen's safety must take precedence. But he could not trust this man, he . . .

'Look out!' Gruhnke hissed from the door.

Paul Vonwegh bent quickly over Kirchwein.

'So,' said Sergeant Weise as he appeared in the doorway. 'The gentlemen have already finished work for the day, eh?'

He went over to the epileptic and smiled as he pointed to him. 'I'll take care of him myself . . . I'm a miracle-worker, you know.'

Vonwegh and Gruhnke left the barracks, keeping at a run until they were out of sight.

'So long as the Oberst is here, he won't kill him . . .' panted the Berliner.

No one heard it; no one saw it; but they all felt it. Some time that afternoon, the bomb had exploded.

The explosion was silent, invisible; the timing was unpredictable. Yet, just as the most optimistic among them had given up hope, a subconscious flicker seemed to go from man to man. The old man had made his fatal mistake, and he was finished. The end of Dirlewanger.

The whole camp was filled with an atmosphere of intoxication, giddiness, rebellion – and all the signs were there. Dirlewanger's henchmen kept out of sight. Corporal Belle started offering people cigarettes. Castle-gendarmes hurried aimlessly backward and forward, like rats in a poisoned trap.

The upheaval grew like a river at storm time, rising into a torrent and sweeping everything with it. Crude laughter echoed in the barrack rooms. No one took any more notice of whistles. Orders were lost in a babble of voices. Someone was dishing out potato schnapps . . .

Hell was celebrating Satan's death.

Questions, everyone was full of questions, but Paul Vonwegh still wasn't opening up to anybody. In Barrack VIII things were quiet compared with the rest of the camp. But was Dirlewanger really going to be arrested? What should they do? What was really happening?'

A quarter of an hour before the upheaval, around 16.00 hours, the mood in the castle ranged from sleepy confusion to malevolent pleasure. Prinz, the police and S S bigshot, was making a fool of himself; his last shot at finding out the truth about Poland was rebounding on him. Müller-Würzbach, the first man he interrogated, knew nothing. Executions? Of course, they happened quite often; but it was either partisans or a matter of liquidations ordered on the highest authority.

The second B-soldier was able to prove that he had not been serving with the Dirlewanger Brigade at the time in question.

Petrat, the last one, knew nothing, he said. He hid behind a mask of puzzled stupidity. The police Oberst bawled his head off at him, but got nowhere. Prinz may not have been at the end of his investigation, but he was at the end of his tether – and everyone could hear it.

Meanwhile, Dirlewanger, his usual self-confidence unchanged, was kept informed on every step of the interrogations.

'Petrat? Who's he?' he asked Müller-Würzbach. 'Never heard of him . . .'

'He was there at the time.'

'And he's still alive?' said the killer-brigade leader with mingled disbelief and irritation.

'He won't tell. Totally reliable . . .' the sergeant soothed him.

'Be that as it may,' Dirlewanger cursed, 'I've had enough. Come with me.'

Taking a few men from his staff, he stormed into the other wing of the dacha, entering the interrogation room without knocking.

Prinz turned round angrily.

'If you think,' began Dirlewanger, without greetings or apologies, 'that you can carry on with this farce any longer, then you're . . .'

'What do you think you're doing?' Prinz said quietly.

'I will not be made to look a fool in front of my men,' the Standartenführer snarled. 'I don't know who's behind this business, but it can't have been the Reichsführer's intention for you to ruin the discipline of my unit . . .'

'I have my orders,' Prinz replied, with an edge of steel in his voice.

'Orders!' Dirlewanger barked. 'What do you know? You're just a visitor.' He laughed weirdly, a laugh full of hate. 'You think that everything that stinks is shit . . .'

As he raved, Oberst Prinz stared indifferently out of the

window. Then, suddenly, his face was creased in a satisfied smile. Officers of his staff were coming back from Russian Camp II, leading a stocky B-soldier who was having to be dragged struggling towards the dacha.

Dirlewanger followed the Oberst's gaze, and stared at the man as if he were a ghost. His eyes nearly popped out of their sockets; the veins stood out in his temples; for a moment he had to support himself on the table and take a deep breath, like a swimmer coming up for air.

Now everyone in that room realised what the visitor had uncovered: it was B-soldier Haubach, alias Aumeier. No one spoke. No one moved. They all understood what that meant.

Outside in the passage, steps were heard. Then the doors were thrown open.

'Orders carried out,' the young police lieutenant reported.

'Thank you.'

Prinz followed the exchange of looks between the newly-arrived B-soldier and Dirlewanger, glanced at the faces of the favourites and the castle-gendarmes, nodded and said:

'Would you leave me alone now, at last?'

Still no one moved.

'All right,' Prinz continued placidly, 'as you wish.' He went up to the man. 'What is your name?' he said, almost kindly.

'B-soldier Haubach, Herr Oberst.'

'Ah . . .' the policeman said. 'And have you been with this bunch long?'

'A year and a half, Herr Oberst.'

Prinz turned to the staff-sergeant.

'Bring me his personal records,' he said calmly.

Müller-Würzbach marched stiffly out of the room.

'Well,' the interrogator continued. 'One and a half years . . .' Then, quickly, he moved in: 'Have you been called Haubach for a long time?'

'Y-y-yes, Herr Oberst,' the man stuttered.

'Think carefully about it for a moment,' Prinz replied. He lit a cigarette and turned to one of the sergeants on his staff.

'You will make a verbatim note in shorthand,' he said. 'Tell me at once if you miss anything. I want every single word . . .'

'So far I have a complete record, Herr Oberst.'

Prinz nodded approvingly, then went right up to the B-soldier and looked at him with a cold stare; he saw how the man avoided his eyes, how he paled and wiped his forehead with the back of his hand.

'You're sweating, Haubach,' the Oberst murmured. 'At least stand to attention!' he bawled at him the next moment, his voice like thunder.

Meanwhile, Dirlewanger seemed to have pulled himself together after the first shock. But everyone there could read his face and what it said: Who told? And who has dared to confront me openly?

Just then Müller-Würzbach returned – empty-handed.

'Well?' the Oberst asked him.

'There are no papers on file,' the sergeant reported. 'They've probably been sent by mistake to some other unit . . .'

'Probably removed by you,' the policeman cut in. He turned to the Standartenführer. 'If you don't get out of here immediately, I shall have you placed under close arrest,' he said coldly.

'You'll regret this . . .' Dirlewanger hissed as he left the room, followed by his entourage.

Oberst Prinz turned again to the man who called himself Haubach.

'Well,' he said. 'Now, I think, we two can have an honest talk together . . .'

Chapter Nine

Straight away, a state of emergency came into being in Dirlewanger's camp. All contact with the outside world was broken off. The witnesses were taken into protective custody, and no outsiders were allowed into the interrogation sessions. Even the adjoining rooms were cleared; the corridors were sealed off; as a precautionary measure, a neighbouring police unit was alerted and put on standby, ready to intervene if there were any disturbances at Dirlewanger's headquarters.

Now the policeman could get down to his task. At last he was in his element. At last his investigation was beginning to come alive. The police machine hummed. Now this incorruptible, relentless prosecutor had something to go on. And with every minute of Prinz's enquiries, the noose tightened around the neck of Oskar Dirlewanger – the man who counted as a pariah even among the bloodthirsty hounds of the S S.

The B-soldier who had been arrested slumped wild-eyed in his chair, listening to Oberst Prinz's orders. He stared at the ground, paralysed with fear. Then he looked up. Everyone seemed to be ignoring him; he was dirt . . .

My name's Haubach, he kept telling himself; I've never been called Aumeier . . . I come from Lower Bavaria . . . my father is still alive . . . my mother died four years ago . . . I'm a car mechanic by trade . . . I was convicted of housebreaking and sentenced to six years' jail . . .

He repeated it all to himself a dozen times, clinging to the words, well aware that he would be finished if he remained silent, and that he would die if he ever talked . . . It didn't matter whether he was hanged by Prinz or by Dirlewanger. All he wanted to do was to live, live . . .

I'm called Haubach, he started again. And then his thoughts stopped – his consciousness choked, like a blocked hourglass.

'The police company is to wait at the perimeter of the camp,' Prinz ordered, 'and should only intervene on my express command . . . see that we remain in full contact.'

'Yes, Herr Oberst,' the young police lieutenant replied crisply.

'And now to you . . . Haubach . . .' Prinz began the interrogation proper. 'That is still your name, is it?'

'Yes . . . yes indeed, Herr Oberst.'

'Are you afraid of me?'

'N-no, Herr Oberst.'

'Then look at me.'

'Yes . . .' the man stuttered.

The policeman slowly took a packet of cigarettes out of his pocket, lit one unhurriedly, observed the prisoner for a few seconds, as if he were making his mind up about something, and then gave him a cigarette.

'You do smoke, don't you?'

'Yes, Herr Oberst,' the man answered eagerly.

Prinz threw a box of matches over to him.

'Why is your hand shaking like that?' he asked with a cold smile. 'I can assure you,' he went on, 'that I will get to the bottom of everything. If you want to make things difficult for me, feel free . . .' he dropped the ash from his cigarette into an empty tin that served as an ashtray '. . . but of course it will do you no good personally in the end . . .'

Then he handed the B-soldier over to the lieutenant for further interrogation.

The man who called himself Haubach came through the first round quite well. He had learned all the facts about his new personality by heart. But his answers came too quickly, too pat. He was like a model pupil who, by doing too well, betrayed the fact that he had been copying.

The police officers took turns; the interrogation became tougher. But it remained within regulations. Even when it came to nailing Dirlewanger, Prinz would tolerate no infringement of the rules – particularly in a case where there were bound to be accusations of intimidation of witnesses.

His lips were cracked. Spittle rimmed his mouth. His

throat was dry. He almost spat out his words. The man who called himself Haubach felt as if every joint in his body were swollen; but Dirlewanger's favourite and private butcher was not in the 'standing bunker' for which he now longed.

Yet another hour passed. The suspect was slurring his words.

'Give him a glass of water,' Prinz said contemptuously, 'and then continue . . .' He looked at his watch. 'Well, Haubach, or whatever your name is,' he said, returning to the fray again himself. 'How about a little confession?'

'I . . . but . . . I haven't anything to . . . confess,' the man whined.

'You haven't changed place with anyone, perhaps?' the Oberst asked.

'No . . . no,' Haubach muttered, choking on the word. 'No . . .' he moaned. 'No,' his voice cracked as it tried to shout; then he made an effort to rise from his chair, only to fall back helplessly. 'No . . .' it was a whisper, a compulsive twitch of the lips.

'It's not your fault,' the policeman continued conversationally. 'Or is something sticking in your gullet?'

The B-soldier shook his head grimly. His eyes darted to and fro in his hunted face. He was struggling against dizziness, short of breath; his fingers went to his collar, stroked his neck, as if to make sure that the noose wasn't already there . . .

'Well then,' the Oberst sighed, 'we shall have to see for ourselves what we can do . . .' He motioned to an orderly officer.

There was dead silence in the room. Even this pause was calculated to shred the nerves of the man who called himself Haubach. The B-soldier closed his eyes, trying to shut everything out. My name is Haubach, the voice in his head raced on. My mother is dead . . . my father is still alive . . .six years' jail . . .

Why is it so quiet? he thought. What can I do about it? I'm only a poor butcher, after all . . . yes, nothing more, just a . . . nobody . . . He had to stop the thoughts. Summoning his final reserves of strength, he leaned back in his chair. Pull yourself together, the voice in his head commanded; they can't do anything to you . . .

He felt quite calm now. He reached for a glass of water and drank slowly, savouring every gulp, and the lump in his throat seemed to dissolve. What an idiot I am, he mused. Everything's going to be all right; they can't pin anything on someone who has Dirlewanger's support. Even the pain in his joints was suddenly no longer there.

The man who called himself Haubach heard the sound of steps, but he took no notice of them. His face was set in a twisted smile. He noticed that everyone was looking at the doors as they were pushed open.

Then he saw who it was.

He collapsed into his chair, until he was half-hanging from it. It's not possible, his terrified face seemed to be saying; it can't be . . .

'Go right up to him, Kleinschmidt,' the Oberst ordered.

The B-soldier who had just come in stood just two metres from the prisoner. He was still wearing Dirlewanger-issue rags, but there was something about him that made him strong; he had a comrade to avenge – Haubach, who had once done three years inside without grassing on him, and who had been killed like a dog so that this bastard could live . . .

'Yes, Herr Oberst,' he stated firmly, his voice flat and toneless with hate. 'That is Aumeier. He was . . is the staff butcher.'

'What is your name – your real name?' asked Prinz. 'Is it Haubach . . . or Aumeier?'

The fat man was finished. A soft groan escaped his lips; his eyes were starting to plead . . .

'You are quite certain of what you said?' the Oberst asked, turning to Kleinschmidt again.

'Certain, Herr Oberst,' said the witness.

The whole thing was, of course, just a formality. Kleinschmidt's statement had long since been taken down in writing and locked away in a safe place. He had reported to the police Oberst during the afternoon, before their parade, and in giving his evidence he had followed to the letter the sequence which his platoon leader, Paul Vonwegh, had explained to him. First he had succeeded in getting into the building without being noticed. Then he had had himself taken into protective custody before making his statement. Finally, he had insisted that the man in Russian Camp II who called himself Haubach be arrested at once, before Dirlewanger got wind of things and had time to spirit him away.

Prinz had at once realised the monstrous implications of the Haubach/Aumeier affair. He knew that an incident like this would be much more deadly in Himmler's hands than the whole file P.A./IX D O R A. And the only thing that mattered to the Oberst was destroying Dirlewanger – as thoroughly as possible. So, that afternoon, he had staged the enquiry about the massacre in Poland only half in earnest; a strategic retreat, so to speak, something that would occupy the Standartenführer's attention for just as long as it took to get Aumeier into his custody.

'Are we going to get a confession from you at last?' the lieutenant with the wooden leg demanded.

'We're checking your fingerprints – that will be the final proof,' another of the policemen called over to him.

'And we'll bring you face to face with *all* the rest of them,' the Oberst joined in.

Aumeier could no longer think straight. There was a whirlwind in his head where his brain should have been. Question on question . . . he couldn't take any more. He wanted to block his ears, but somehow his arms were too weak, they wouldn't move . . .

'Stop,' he moaned. 'Just stop, for God's sake . . . I can't . . .'

'Admit that your name is Aumeier,' said the Oberst's voice, cold, inhuman.

'Yes,' the man who had called himself Haubach gasped. 'Yes . . .'

Prinz glanced at his stenographer to check that everything was being recorded.

'Interesting,' he concluded. 'Fetch me the sergeant.'

When Müller-Würzbach entered the room a few minutes

later, he saw at a glance what had happened. That's it, he thought; Dirlewanger for the high jump. From now on, his only concern was to save his own skin.

'Do you know this man?' Prinz asked, without even bothering with the preliminaries.

'Yes . . . that's B-soldier Aumeier, the staff . . .'

'And why does he call himself Haubach?' Prinz cut in.

'I . . . I don't know, Herr Oberst.'

'Then we shall have to ask Haubach, won't we?' the policeman said crisply. 'Call him in.'

'That's not possible . . .'

'I have given you an order. Carry it out . . .' Prinz roared at the sergeant.

'Haubach is . . . dead.'

'Of appendicitis?' the Oberst asked, with merciless sarcasm.

'No, Herr Oberst. He was . . . shot.'

'Shot? Why?'

'On the orders of Standartenführer Dirlewanger.'

'Instead of Aumeier, wasn't it? Surely you know that?'

'No, Herr Oberst,' Müller-Würzbach lied.

'I'll put an end to your games . . . !' For the first time, Prinz lost his objectivity and allowed the fury that was inside him to boil to the surface, 'All of them! As sure as I stand here, I swear it . . .'

The sergeant made to go, but one of the Oberst's men barred his way.

'First you will sign a statement,' Prinz said, calmer now.

I've done it, he was thinking at that moment. I have Dirlewanger. No one could get out of a situation like this one – no matter who might be protecting him . . .

After the shock appearance of Aumeier, Dirlewanger shut himself up in his bedroom, insane with fury. The most bitter realisation was that he had been duped by a fossilised bureaucrat like Oberst Prinz, a man he had taken for a fool. He didn't say a word to his castle-gendarmes as he entered his room.

The men of his entourage speculated that the chief would choose a pistol-shot as his only way out. Even his closest lackeys could see that his bloody career was finished. The gendarmes in the passage outside his room stood for hours, waiting for the shot that would mean the end. But there was no sound.

Then, finally, they heard soft, shuffling steps. The two guards cast each other meaningful looks. Now, they thought.

At that moment, the door opened.

The S S Standartenführer was grinning. Drunk. His yellow eyeballs were deepset in their sockets, and bloodshot. The two guards clicked their heels.

'Well,' said Dirlewanger, 'shall we eat? Or have you lost your appetites?'

'Yes, Standartenführer,' they rasped simultaneously.

Either he was drunker than he ever had been in his life before, or he had gone crazy.

It was arranged. The food was brought in, but there were gaps in the guest list. Sergeant Weise was missing. Belle, the corporal, was nowhere to be found. The clerk-sergeant had not yet returned from his interrogation.

'Music!' the Standartenführer roared.

They all sat down to eat. Dirlewanger seemed to have only one aim: to find out who showed less appetite than usual. Such a man would prove that he was an opportunist, a traitor. And so they ate, simulating heartiness, competing for his favour – just to be on the safe side . . .

During the meal, an ordinance officer explained to Dirlewanger about the police unit that had been moved into position near the camp, ready to intervene.

'Pity . . .' was Dirlewanger's only reply. 'Then we won't be able to kill those fellows straight away . . .'

A second later, Sergeant Weise burst into the room.

'Open revolt!' he yelled, panting. 'The men have got hold of some schnapps . . . they've even looted the bacon-smoking chamber . . .' He paused to gulp some air into his lungs, then went on: 'A bunch of them have attacked Corporal Belle and . . .'

'Don't waste your pity on him,' the Standartenführer said. 'Have you made a note of the mutineers?'

'Almost the whole camp is involved,' Weise answered, trembling with fury. 'Only the lads in Barrack VIII are keeping quiet.'

'The first platoon?' Dirlewanger asked drily.

'Yes . . . that Vonwegh has his lot firmly in hand . . . you remember, he's the fellow who killed Fleischmann.'

The Standartenführer nodded, then got on with his meal. The others ate, and drank, for tomorrow . . . Dirlewanger, however, seemed to have some sort of plan worked out. Otherwise, how could he seem so relaxed? On the other hand, it was always possible that the drink had robbed him of his last remaining senses . . .

'Women!' the chief yelled suddenly.

'But they've been got rid of,' the Hauptsturmführer sitting next to him replied, horrified.

'Bring them back here . . . We won't be cowed by these miserable idiots of policemen, will we?'

'No, Standartenführer,' they all chorused, but already they were wondering how all this would look when they were in the dock . . .

By the time Müller-Würzbach made his appearance, the whole lot of them were drunk.

The Standartenführer took the staff-sergeant to one side.

'Well?' he demanded.

'Aumeier confessed.'

'That's what happens when you give a man a chance,' Dirlewanger said wrily. 'That's what you get for humanitarianism . . . And you?' he asked sharply.

Müller-Würzbach shrugged.

'He has a B-soldier as a witness . . . Haubach's mate . . . you know, Standartenführer, the one with the roast duck that time.'

'You're all getting old and soft!' Dirlewanger screamed. 'Since when have we allowed witnesses?' He took a schnapps bottle from the table and hurled it at the wall. 'I'll smash you to pieces – like that! All of you – if you don't get the message!'

Suddenly his mood seemed to change, become calmer.

'Well, Weise,' he said, turning to the sergeant. 'How do we get ourselves out of this shit?'

'You should take some leave somewhere, Standartenführer,' his confidant advised carefully.

'Good idea,' Dirlewanger muttered. 'And what then?'

'Perhaps this stupid Oberst Prinz will get himself killed by the partisans . . .'

'Are there any of those left, then?' Dirlewanger asked sarcastically.

'They come by the yard . . .' Weise answered.

'You're drunk,' Dirlewanger said with a grin. He picked up a tumbler full of schnapps and drank it half-empty. 'Courage, children!' he roared, and turned to Weise again. 'Bad . . . if the Oberst gets the files to Berlin . . .'

'Berlin is a long way,' the sergeant answered mockingly.

The noise from Dirlewanger's table penetrated to Oberst Prinz's quarters, where interrogations were continuing through the night.

He heard the laughter, caught snatches of conversation, went to the window and heard them all yelling: 'I don't know anything about anything . . . !' they bawled in chorus.

He recognised Sergeant Weise's voice, which rose above all the others.

Prinz slammed the window shut.

Sing away, he thought. But I know a thing or two about you . . .

Today there was no reveille. The duty officer who wanted to sound it came close to getting himself lynched. Outside, in front of Barrack VIII, there was a cacophony of noise. The only commander in the camp at the moment was General Alcohol. The fear and the hate that had built up inside the B-soldiers was bursting free, sweeping out through the dams in a raging torrent of fury. It was open season on Dirlewanger's henchmen, and all the regular staff had made themselves scarce.

The third platoon got together to storm the castle, causing

panic among the gendarmes, who fired wildly into the B-soldiers. The schnapps-fuelled madness became a headlong lust for blood. The Dirlewangers swarmed off to storm the armoury.

In Barrack VIII the men looked at each other. No one said a word. Paul Vonwegh had a hard task in front of him today. He had bent these men to his will, by threats or by reason, ready to lead them to a goal of which only he was aware. He knew too that what was going on outside was the revolt's last, bloody gasp. Yes, he would have to take care that the first platoon came through this crazy day unscathed; and he himself was walking a tightrope – between being seen as one of Dirlewanger's lackeys and being seen as a coward who dared not confront him.

So for the first time the men in Barrack VIII began to kick against the unquestioned authority of Paul Vonwegh. Gruhnke made the first move.

'The others are settling with those bastards,' he said, 'and we're sitting here twiddling our thumbs – from nothing but sheer bloody cowardice.' He went to the door.

'Stop there,' the platoon leader said coldly.

'Don't you tell me what to do!' the Berliner yelled. He carried on his way.

Paul Vonwegh decided on a change of tactics.

'Look,' he said. 'Do you want to go home or not?'

'I want to see those bastards in hell, that's all!' the Berliner roared, his face contorted with fury. 'I want to get that swine Weise in front of me . . . and . . .'

'The others are already doing that,' Vonwegh said quietly.

'And I want to be in there with them,' Gruhnke answered. 'I've waited a whole year for this . . . day and night I've thought of nothing else . . .'

The platoon leader stood in the doorway and watched as four, five B-soldiers, Petrat among them, ranged themselves behind Gruhnke. There was a pause.

Vonwegh's fists flew and hit home. Kordt came to his aid. Plump Muller, the bespectacled embezzler, hesitated and then took Vonwegh's side. Kortetzky, still suffering from the effects of his wound, rushed through from behind as a backup.

At that moment they heard whistles and barked orders. Then, suddenly, there was a loaded silence. Oberst Prinz had brought in his police unit from the edge of the camp, and the uprising was on the retreat. Gruhnke and his allies saw what was happening, and fear replaced the anger in their faces.

'Now's your chance to hand us over,' he snarled.

'Idiot,' Vonwegh countered coolly. 'Now listen carefully,' he said to them all. 'Here there has been no breakdown in discipline . . . the whole platoon has stayed in its quarters . . . no one has tried to join in the mutiny. Is that clear?'

They all shouted agreement, but for the next few seconds they looked at each other uneasily. What use was it their all holding together if some 'listening machine' talked?

Vonwegh understood. 'I know who our informer is,' he said, 'and I am warning him here and now: in my platoon, no one mutinied and no one will be denounced. Understood?'

For a moment they thought he was bluffing, though they guessed he probably suspected someone. None of the men in the first platoon seriously believed that Vonwegh could actually know who the 'listening machine' was – or could be aware of his plans.

'You know who the swine is?' Gruhnke muttered menacingly.

The platoon leader nodded.

'Well, name him then . . .'

While the B-soldiers outside were being driven back to their barracks like cattle, Barrack VIII experienced its first moment of human contact.

Ignoring Gruhnke, Vonwegh said: 'We all want to come through this, don't we?

'Have you a wife?' he asked Muller.

'Yes,' the man answered.

'And you?' he turned to Kordt.

'A mother.'

'Me too,' Kirchwein said.

'My old lady divorced me,' Petrat chipped in.

And Kortetzky asked incredulously from the background, 'Do you really mean that . . . we might get back to our mothers some time?'

'Perhaps,' the platoon leader said quietly. 'But at any rate we want to try, don't we?'

By the time the conversation was over, Vonwegh felt that he had these men firmly back under his control. Outside, it was now deathly quiet. The first 'listening machines' would soon be creeping into the dacha to report on their comrades. But Vonwegh was sure that the informer in his platoon wouldn't be doing his job tonight – he'd had warning enough of the consequences.

Exhausted, Paul Vonwegh threw himself on to his straw mattress. The light was still on, but most of the platoon was already asleep. After a minute or two, however, Gruhnke came over to him.

'I was a bloody fool,' he said. 'It won't happen again, you can depend on it.'

'That's all right,' Vonwegh answered.

Another came later, the boy Kordt.

'Tell me,' he began, blushing, 'have you got a wife or something like that?'

Vonwegh shook his head slowly.

'No one at all?' Kordt asked, disturbed, noticing how the platoon leader stared into the emptiness. Then he crept away. *No one at all.* The words seethed through Paul Vonwegh's mind, echoing, reverberating.

He wanted to live for another human being – instead, he was fighting against a system. Was that a substitute?

Was it possible that there could be a substitute for Karen, the woman he had found, lost, and found again – found again so that he could hold on to her more tightly than anything else in the world . . .

Everything had gone well, they had told themselves when Vonwegh came back that time from the discussion with Karen's cousin. They persuaded each other that it was so, because they wanted to believe it – though perhaps they knew, even then, that there was no hope . . .

Everything had seemed all right for a couple of days. Then the crisis had come.

'I'll be back in a moment,' Karen said. 'I just have to go round the corner . . .' Vonwegh nodded and watched her go. She was so young, so arousing . . . he wanted to rush after her and put his arms round her. Flowers stood on the table, heavy with a melancholy scent, a scent of parting. But it was too late for that. He had dragged Karen into things now. But then her cousin Wulf-Dieter couldn't be an informer, otherwise they would no longer be together . . .

Karen returned. Her face was flushed, but she said nothing. Vonwegh could guess: she had been speaking to her influential cousin, the public prosecutor, from the telephone booth round the corner. As she busied herself in the kitchen, he followed her in and stood there, watching. When she noticed him she turned round with a start.

'Is it difficult for you . . . to sign this statement?' she asked, screwing up her courage and launching straight into things.

He nodded.

'You shouldn't do anything . . . that you don't . . .'

Vonwegh shrugged. Now he realised the cause of his indecision over the past two days. He was too much of a coward to sign this piece of propaganda rubbish – but not brave enough to refuse outright. He wanted to have everything and give nothing away. And that, particularly now, was impossible.

He handed Karen the statement and she read it through; he could see that she understood none of it, except for the fact that it disgusted him.

'Don't sign it,' she said, while all the time her eyes pleaded: do it . . . for my sake . . .

'What did Brillmann say?' Vonwegh asked harshly.

'Everything is all right,' she answered, 'but it would be better, he thought, if you signed this stupid piece of paper before you . . . present yourself.' She avoided his eyes as she added hurriedly: 'So that it looks more as if it was done of your own free will . . .'

He took the pen and signed his name in large letters, with a rough flourish. Karen's eyes were bright. With feminine logic she said:

'Don't send it yet . . . think it over again . . .'

They didn't discuss it further. It was early evening and growing dark when Vonwegh got ready to go out.

'I'm going to post it,' he said.

They hadn't put on the lights, but he could feel Karen's smile even in the darkness. No one can blame me, he thought; anyone would have found it hard to make a choice like that . . .

He passed the first post-box. And the second. When he got to the third he stopped and took the envelope gingerly out of his pocket. On the stamp was the head of the man he had fought so long and whom he would always fight. No. No . . . Vonwegh thrust the letter back in his pocket. The final postponement.

He began to walk again. The air was cool, with a hint of autumn's sadness. He had forgotten the letter by the time he arrived back at the house; he could only think of Karen. Then he looked up and saw that the lights were on in both rooms. Suddenly he felt fear coursing through him, wrenching every nerve in his body into alertness. Approaching the house from the back, he crept close until he could hear the caretaker talking to his wife.

'I knew there was something wrong with those two,' the man was saying. 'Spies . . . just imagine . . .'

It was all Paul Vonwegh needed to hear. Karen had been arrested, and he himself had escaped only by the most fantastic chance. They were waiting for him, using the girl as bait. Wulf-Dieter, the well-connected prosecutor, had revealed himself for what he was: a Nazi swine.

Karen was their pawn. He would have to give himself up, he realised with something approaching relief; his decision had been made for him. Then, as he looked up again, he saw the lights go out – they must have got tired of waiting. Sneaking round to take up position opposite the house, he could see the two green police cars parked in front. A few minutes later he also saw that his suspicions had been confirmed.

Karen looked anxiously up and down the street; she looked

relieved when he was nowhere in sight. Then she got into the car and was quickly driven away.

Vonwegh decided that he would smoke a cigarette, then give himself up at the nearest police station. He trembled with impotent hatred as he thought of Brillmann, the 'go-between'. His first thought was to make for the man's apartment, to get even with the bastard . . . then the fog of anger in his mind cleared, and he began to reflect that it was more important to help Karen than to avenge her. He remembered that her mother was Swedish, and that sparked a new train of thought. He came to a decision.

It was crazy, but the next day Vonwegh, the outlaw, stood in broad daylight outside the Swedish embassy in Berlin. He paused in the entrance, and got no further. Something was stopping him . . .

He felt a hand on his shoulder, shaking him, and gradually he realised that he was not in Berlin but at Dirlewanger's camp, at dawn – in the aftermath of mutiny . . .

It was a dark, miserable morning. Thick walls of fog drifted across the filthy slush of the parade ground. The B-soldiers stumbled out of their quarters at the double, as if eager to make good the damage done by the previous night's uprising. They still believed that Dirlewanger had been put under arrest . . . and their stomachs pitched with fear when they saw the Standartenführer on the parade ground. He stood, raw-boned, pallid, with a look that was emptier than purgatory; the skin of his unhealthy face stretched more tightly than ever over his bones. The death's head lived – and grinned . . .

They cringed at the thought of the horrors ahead as they filed out. Then the unthinkable happened. Dirlewanger stood for a moment, watching balefully, with that thin, insane smile playing on his lips, and then he turned his back and walked away. He was headed for his private landing-strip, where his Fieseler Storch was waiting for him. A few minutes later, the aircraft droned over them, veering away from Lahuisk, with Dirlewanger aboard. A convulsive shudder of relief went through the assembled brigade. Satan was gone from his kingdom. And Weise, chief among the demons, was absent, too; some said he was in bed, drunk; others had heard tell he had gone to the Russkies in Camp II . . .

Then came the next mystery. Oberst Prinz left, along with his staff. There was no explanation, and it appeared that they had left empty-handed. Only a very few of the men knew the truth, that he was taking two vital witnesses with him: Kleinschmidt, to whom he had promised freedom; and Aumeier, alias Haubach, for whom the gallows were waiting. Prinz had got his statements safely under lock and key.

Again, half an hour later the police force that had been called in to restore order withdrew.

Things were becoming uncanny, almost ghostly. None of the instructors spoke. None of the regular staff referred to the previous night's revolt. The camp was afflicted by a leaden paralysis which they all knew to be the calm before the storm.

If S S Standartenführer Dirlewanger ever came back, then his men would experience a new hell, in comparison with which everything that had gone before would seem harmless.

If . . .

Chapter Ten

The Russian winter of 1943 was just seeming to relax its icy grip when there was a sudden resurgence of bitter weather. The mercury in the thermometers plummeted like a torn sail in a storm: eight degrees, ten degrees, fourteen degrees below . . . A savage wind blew across the huge expanses of the Russian plain, from Stalingrad to Kiev. In the hinterland men huddled round their stoves. Whoever could, stayed at home; whoever had to go out was forced to wrap up until they looked like deformed animals, grotesque tortoises under improvised shells of clothing.

The cold could not dampen the news that spread like wildfire, raging from position to position, to the most remote outposts. At first the rumour was only whispered; then murmured; and finally, spoken aloud: on the street, in transport columns, on parade grounds, over telephone lines.

Dirlewanger was dead.

Executed by a court martial.

On the orders of the S S!

At the mid-day meal at headquarters, a high-ranking Wehrmacht officer openly called for the special brigade of murderers, thieves and burglars to be disbanded immediately. There was agreement. Satisfaction temporarily overshadowed even the political differences between the Nazi activists, the opportunists, the party hangers-on and their opponents. The classless society of the occupation was delighted that the parasite in its body had at last gone the way of all flesh.

An avalanche of gossip had already descended on Poland, where Dirlewanger had made his debut and had become a living legend for his cruelty. By this time, the rumours were completely out of hand. Only one man knew the truth, and he was lying low.

Anyone who knew Oberst Prinz or had connections with his staff made desperate attempts to find out what had actually happened at Dirlewanger's camp that day. Everyone tried: the man sitting next to him at dinner, his chess partner, the head of the military hospital, the senior officer of the garrison. But all of them, even the commander-in-chief and the Gauleiter, got no clues.

Incommunicado.

The stubborn police Oberst with the square, shaven head rapidly became unobtainable. There were no exceptions: even dispatch-riders were turned away from his headquarters, and it was no different for higher-ranking visitors. The police Oberst had reached his quarters just before the cold spell set in, and since then he had been driving his men with an old-German thoroughness and single-mindedness; he would brook no interruptions.

Prinz had formed a special commission of eleven police officers from among his most trusted colleauges and had installed them in a next-door building, alongside the witnesses. They were completely shut off from the outside world. Anyone wanting to enter or leave the house had to show a pass signed personally by Oberst Prinz.

After the return from the camp, the interrogations went on without cease. They ran day and night in three shifts, each officer taking a turn for two hours, like a changing of the guard. Every man who was put on the Dirlewanger case was carefully trained and drilled, instructed in every aspect of the affair. The results could almost be calculated with a stop-watch: success rolling off the assembly-line, progress per hour . . . The staff working there were producing evidence that would cry out to heaven, building up a grim picture of crimes that no one had even dreamt of in their wildest nightmares. And for the first time in his life, the gruff old policeman began to feel satisfaction in serving a system he despised. He was going to turn that system's weapons against itself; without needing to come out into the open, he was going to be able to deal Dirlewanger's SS protectors a blow from which they would never recover.

In the evidence that Oberst Prinz would present there were no hypotheses, no suppositions, no 'ifs' or 'buts'. There would be no room for doubt. For him there existed only facts, events, facts, proved several times over – incontrovertible . . .

And there was only one end-result possible: the gallows.

The gallows for Dirlewanger.

Late afternoon. Typewriters rattled like machine-guns in every office. Today was the day when the interim report was to be presented. This was the final spurt, and everyone on Prinz's staff was working like madmen. The telephones were off the hook, the telex machine switched off from the outside world.

In Prinz's sweltering, overheated office the senior members of his team were putting together the report. Even to hardened policemen such as themselves, it made horrific reading; they were protected against the icy weather outside, but nothing could stop the inner cold that came from the report on Dirlewanger.

Oberst Prinz looked up reluctantly from his reading and saw an officer standing in front of him.

'What is it?' he asked wearily.

'Report from Berlin,' the man said. 'Apparently Dirlewanger has been seen there.'

'That's all right by me,' Prinz growled. He gave a brief smile, but the creases round his mouth tightened and his eyes narrowed. Yes, the Standartenführer was trying to gather his forces for a counter-attack; he would mobilise his friends at the Reichssicherheitshauptamt; he would try to defuse the Oberst's report . . .

Prinz's smile became more confident. The dossier he had drawn up on Dirlewanger was foolproof. It was put together with consummate cunning, calculated not just to satisfy justice but also to appeal to Himmler's weird psychology, with a tailor-made emphasis on obedience, the cult of order, and racial purity . . .

Aumeier, Dirlewanger's personal butcher, had served his purpose. Now he was nothing more than a wreck – pathetic, soft and pliable as wax.

His confession had been put on record. His fingerprints had been checked. His identity had been confirmed by the Red Cross sister he had raped in Kiev as well as by a dozen other witnesses. Along with him, in the cellar of the building, Kleinschmidt was quartered. The latter's statements had been skilfully edited, doctored, toned down . . .

A job well done, thought the Oberst. He went to find the files on Aumeier's state of health, about the length of interrogations, about the amount of 'special treatment' used on him by the investigating officers. Nothing was going to be left out. In the school that Prinz had been trained in, nothing ever was.

At 6 p.m. a final discussion with Prinz's colleagues took place. Today the files would be closed. The Luftwaffe had put a special plane at the Oberst's disposal for the following day, ready for his flight to Berlin.

'Get me an appointment with the Reichsführer S S,' Prinz ordered one of his assistants before he went into the meeting.

'For when, Herr Oberst?'

'As soon as possible,' Prinz answered curtly.

Then he shut himself in with his senior colleagues and they began to go through the final report once more, point by point.

The evening's first darkness fell like a huge silent shadow over the camp and settled, a mysterious shroud, on the snow-capped huts and barracks. Detachments of B-soldiers had returned from their duties and had been dismissed to their quarters. The chimney-stacks punched feeble gaps in the merciless cold. From time to time the east wind picked up the smoke and threw it to the ground as if it had been cast by a huge fist, and blew it through the deserted alleyways that smelt of ashes and fear. Slowly the clouds of smoke were driven to the west, to where Dirlewanger had flown – or fled – two days before.

Astonishingly, the revolt had been ignored; no punishments took place. There were no howls from beatings on the parade ground. The standing bunkers were empty. And no B-soldier whispered to his mates of how many men had been hanged today. There was not even a 'show' execution to terrorise the men. And even their rations, which had dramatically improved during Oberst Prinz's visit, did not revert to their old levels of watery soup.

The men marched out to their duties. They cut wood. They carried out orders – orders that were given almost politely, mildly. Their overseers' faces remained rigid, unfathomable, carefully controlled. Bizarrely, so ingrained was the habit, charges and denunciations enjoyed a blossoming unusual even among the Dirlewangers. Men were still looking to cover themselves, establish alibis, curry favour, even though their superiors seemed strangely indifferent. Paul Vonwegh's platoon was the only exception; they had no part in the orgy of recrimination.

The first platoon had been detailed to guard the outer perimeter today. It was the most-sought-after duty – no work, no quota to meet, just keeping half an eye open for partisans, who in any case had long been wiped out in this district. The fact that such a cushy job had been put the way of a particular unit in the brigade two days running was rightly seen by everyone else as a clear sign of favour.

It was now that the B-soldiers realised what they owed to Vonwegh. At the crucial moment, he had stopped the riot with his fists. And now he refused to acknowledge any difference between his helpers and the man who had stood against him that day. Suddenly, every Dirlewanger wanted to be in Vonwegh's first platoon.

Without his even trying, Vonwegh radiated a steely authority. In those days his platoon was almost part of the regular staff.

So it was that Barrack VIII kept out of the weird panic that seemed to afflict everyone else in the camp. In fact, its quarters were an oasis of peace and leisure. On this evening, Kirchwein, Muller and Kordt were playing skat. Gruhnke had disappeared off to Lahuisk to 'organise' some schnapps. Kortetzky, who had now recovered from his wounds, now followed Vonwegh everywhere, a picture of primitive gratitude. Everyone knew that the platoon's heavy would tear apart anyone who tried to threaten his benefactor.

'You've got a bright future here,' Petrat said to Vonwegh, baring his teeth in a feral grin. 'You'll be made an officer, or something like that . . .'

Vonwegh gave a dismissive wave.

'A piss on all officers,' Petrat muttered, 'but I won't grudge you that . . . even if you don't have anything more to do with us afterwards . . .'

'Don't talk rubbish,' the platoon leader said.

Muller pushed away his cards.

'Tomorrow we're getting the first transport of the replacements,' he said. He had been working in the orderly room today, so he had caught all the news.

At least a thousand men were expected in the morning to reinforce the special brigade. The camp was buzzing with rumours: a nephew of Himmler would be among the new 'Dirlewangers'; an Olympic gold medallist; a demoted general; a famous show-jumping champion; and God knows who else . . .

'And,' Muller continued, 'this time there are some really astonishing types among them.' He handed Vonwegh, who was hardly listening, a cigarette and continued in a conspiratorial tone: 'Politicals . . . just imagine . . .'

The platoon leader practically choked on the smoke from his cigarette. The word hit him like a haymarket punch. *Politicals,* he thought, and had to fight to remain calm. He knew the Nazis to be capable of anything, but he had not believed that they would be prepared to use their own opponents as cannon-fodder.

Suddenly they heard hurried footsteps outside and Gruhnke burst in and rushed into the room. His eyes were bloodshot; you could smell the schnapps from across the other side of the room.

'Hey!' he bellowed. 'Comrades, to the victory celebrations!' He pressed half a bottle of vodka into the gorilla's huge, clutching hand. The others stared at him blankly. 'Drink, boys!' the Berliner shouted. 'I have news for you . . . and this is wedding, birthday and christening all in one!'

Seeing how they were all eagerly grabbing at the bottle he had given to Kortetzky, Gruhnke pulled a second one from his coat.

'Here . . .' he said, and gave it to Petrat. 'This is the greatest day of my life . . . Do you know why?'

Vonwegh went over to the Berliner and looked at him searchingly. No chance. He could control a man, but a skinful of schnapps . . .

The Berliner ignored him. 'The swine has had it!' he bellowed. 'Hanged . . . he's dead!'

'Calm down!' the platoon leader thundered at last.

Petrat started grinning. Kirchwein brought down both hands with a thump on the table. The gorilla laughed until tears ran out of his tiny eyes. Kordt looked like a child in front of a Christmas tree. Muller looked as if he was about to utter a prayer of thanksgiving. Even Paul Vonwegh could not hide his curiosity.

'Dead as a doornail!' Gruhnke continued. 'Everyone out there knows . . .'

'You're drunk,' Vonwegh snapped at him.

'You're dead right, mate,' Gruhnke answered with a raucous laugh. 'But Dirlewanger is dead, got it? The bastard's as dead as a pig on a butcher's slab . . . understand . . . ?'

Vonwegh knew he couldn't win against this. Hoping that Gruhnke didn't have a third bottle, he threw himself down on to his straw mattress. What could he do? Wait until they had finished with the vodka, and in the meantime try to stop them going outside . . .

The platoon leader sat watching his men from the background, then saw with relief that Gruhnke had run out of alcohol. Pretending to be taking a nap, Vonwegh carried on keeping a sharp eye on them. No one had left the room so far.

At last they were quiet. And at last the lights went out. They had made it, and he could carry on aiming for his goal. The news of the day had put him on edge, though. Political prisoners, in with this bunch of gangsters? Then he realised, with a grim smile, that maybe he was the precedent: Paul Vonwegh, 'political', who hated the Nazi regime for all the same reasons as the others, but who also had a very personal reason . . .

Karen.

Then . . .

For Vonwegh, the night following her arrest seemed never-ending. During those tortured hours he swung between feeling like committing suicide and like throwing hand grenades, leading a people's uprising that would free Karen . . .

At last reason began to gain the upper hand and he could think again. The first thing he realised was his powerlessness. One part of him told him to disappear and try to make it across the border. That, though, would have denied everything he felt about Karen . . . but what good would it do her if he gave himself up, without even a fight?

He walked around the city, and considered his options. In the east, in front of the Brandenburg Gate, he could see the first silver streak that marked the beginning of day. Vonwegh examined himself. He must shave; he needed a fresh shirt, creases in his trousers . . . he would need all those trivial things if he were to get past the porter at the Swedish embassy. And to get them, he would have risked everything . . .

He managed to take a bath and a shave at the Anhalter station. He was the first at a clothes shop when it opened. Of course, he needed clothing coupons; ridiculously, it was a fact he had forgotten. He tried to bribe the shop assistant with fifty marks. Even more ridiculous. Then, just as he was leaving the shop, the manageress motioned to him and handed him a package while the other assistants weren't looking. No coupons, no money – the desperation in his eyes had done the job for him.

At the embassy, he made it past the door-keeper. Then he managed to get through two female clerks to the embassy's secretary, and from there, without even saying who he was or showing any identity, into a waiting-room. It was there that a quiet man with pale-blond hair and a freckle-smothered face granted him an interview of sorts. While Vonwegh was outlining his case, the Swede did not sit down; he was obviously prepared to leave at any moment, not certain whether he had a criminal or a lunatic in front of him. After a while, the man also decided that he had wasted enough time being polite.

'I still don't understand exactly what you want from us,' he said curtly, in near-perfect German.

'Karen's mother was Swedish . . . born in Uppsala,' Vonwegh said. 'An aunt of hers still lives in Malmö . . .'

'But the lady in question is a German citizen. What could we do?'

'I just wanted to make you aware of Karen's situation,' Vonwegh said lamely. 'In an hour I am going to give myself up . . . voluntarily. There won't be much I can do after that.' His face was pleading. 'There has to be someone who will know about her, and perhaps . . .'

'Sit down,' the Swede said, more kindly now.

He offered his visitor an English cigarette. An English cigarette, in the capital of England's deadliest enemy; in a neutral oasis at the heart of a country that lived behind barbed wire.

'Can I take that as binding . . . your promise to give yourself up?'

'In one hour,' Vonwegh repeated.

For the first time the attaché smiled, faintly, without disturbing the bland equanimity of his features.

'Shall we say . . .' he replied '. . . thirty minutes after you leave this building?'

Paul Vonwegh nodded. Then he was taken to a small, windowless room which resembled a cell. He was given coffee and cigarettes, and once more they gave him a chance to leave before his fate was sealed. He refused.

By mid-day he was beginning to fear that they had forgotten him. They're covering themselves, he thought, making sure I wasn't followed. They have to do that before they start to make soundings; the Swede Vonwegh had spoken to looked as though he knew how these underground deals worked.

He also knew something about Aquavit. Around four in the afternoon, Vonwegh was sent for. The attaché he had seen that morning pointed to a glass on his desk.

'Skol,' he said, and poured him some of the spirit. 'Yes,' he went on after they had tasted the Aquavit, 'so far it all seems to add up. No warrant of arrest has been issued. It seems she is with the security police, who are using her as some kind of . . . hostage. For you,' he added, refilling the glasses.

Paul Vonwegh nodded agreement. It was just as he had thought.

'Anyway, you were informed on,' the attaché explained, 'and by her own cousin.' He thought for a moment. 'Brillman is his name, or something like that.'

'He was supposed to be liasing between . . .'

The Swede shook his head sadly.

'He had intended to, but he got cold feet about it.' He paused. 'We have prepared the ground for some business – a sort of exchange deal. If you present yourself in the Prinz-Albrecht-Strasse, they say that they will set your lady friend free.'

Vonwegh shuddered with relief.

'And you think that it will work?'

'If you keep your side of the bargain,' the official replied. 'Sometimes they do . . . and then again . . .' He shrugged his shoulders. 'You wanted us to keep an eye on her, and we will do so. I can't promise anything beyond that . . . and you have never been here, is that clear?'

Vonwegh nodded.

'If you say anything about this visit, you will put the woman in even greater danger . . . and I,' again he smiled that strangely immobile smile, 'will lose my job.'

Vonwegh wondered if he should offer the man his hand. Anticipating him, the Swede stretched out his, his eyes tough and unsentimental. As they shook, he looked hard at Vonwegh.

'If I were not a realist,' he murmured, 'then I might wish you all the best . . .'

'Thanks anyway,' Vonwegh said shortly.

He would have liked to say more, but he knew that the man from the Swedish embassy understood. Just as he was leaving, the Swede handed him a packet of cigarettes, German ones this time. Yes, this man knew something of life in the underground . . .

It took Paul Vonwegh seven minutes to reach the Prinz-Albrecht-Strasse, the headquarters of the Gestapo. There too he had to pass through three underlings before his enemies realised what prize had fallen into their hands . . .

Suddenly the platoon leader was awake. A noise. Soft, suppressed. On planks. A man was creeping towards the door from the left. A shadow, moving. No one else seemed to notice. Then, with a final, almost imperceptible groan of the planks, the man was outside.

Vonwegh had prepared himself well for this. Dressing quickly and silently, he was outside in seconds, running in a wide arc towards his aim: towards Dirlewanger's 'castle', the dacha.

He hid behind a stack of wood, so close to the camp headquarters that he could see the castle gendarmes' eyes. No one appeared for a moment, and Vonwegh began to have doubts. Had it just been his nerves? Or had someone really left Barrack VIII? But Vonwegh followed his instinct. Now was his chance to be certain; he had to catch this man, to get rid of him or use him in some way. But above all, he had to get him in the act, this man who was sneaking here to inform on Gruhnke for the second time.

Then the platoon leader heard steps. The nearer the man got to the castle, the less cautious he was having to be. It would not be easy; Vonwegh would have to jump him before the castle gendarmes saw him. The approaching B-soldier, the informer, stood still for a moment, looked around, and then went on, as if in some zombie-like trance, towards the castle.

As he came level with Vonwegh, the platoon leader's hands

snapped round his neck like pincers, cutting short the cry that was coming alive in his throat, dragging the man behind the woodpile. It was all happening in a weird silence, like a violent ballet without music. There was only a soft shuffling noise, as if someone were pulling a sack a short distance.

One of the bodyguards at the entrance to the dacha looked quickly in their direction, saw nothing, shrugged and lit a cigarette. Vonwegh's hands were still pressing against the traitor's neck as he bent over to examine his captive and saw that he had been right all along. He recognised the man who had once given away his secret during an attack, the man whom fear had made an informer.

It was Kirchwein, the epileptic.

It was a cold, dark night. You couldn't see further than ten paces in front of your face. The wind blew great clouds of fog over the landscape, then released them to settle, to float to the ground and lie like sinister grey quilts. The town slept dreamlessly in the blackness, its strong points guarded all night long.

The only sound was the crunch of the sentries' heels on the frost-bitten ground. The soldiers made no attempt at conversation. Cold forced them to breathe through their noses; the frost brought tears to their eyes; woollen mufflers crammed under their steel helmets made them deaf. They communicated in their own sign language. Anyway, it was all routine. 'Idiots' theatre' the conscripts called it, 'occupational therapy'.

It was long after midnight. Prinz's special commission had completed its work some hours before. The files were packed, the aircraft was ready to take off. The Oberst was due to make his formal report to the Reichsführer S S on the afternoon of the next day.

Three a.m. Were those shadows surging silently towards the darkened police headquarters? A sentry stopped for a moment and stared into the night. He yawned.

'Hey!' he called out to his comrade on the other side of the perimeter. The man signalled to him with one hand. Everything OK, the gesture said. As ever.

Guard duty in Russia. Cold, lonely, and tedious. You chopped the time up in your head – hours, minutes, seconds . . . you imagined yourself at home and wondered whether there was still the same food to eat, you checked the time and cursed the others for lying in their warm beds, you calculated how long it was until you came off duty, and maybe you read your last letter from home over again in your mind . . .

The night became quieter, colder. The wind was picking up now, howling like a whipped animal.

Then the town came awake.

The explosion could be heard for miles around.

In seconds, flames were shooting up from the police complex, clawing blood-red holes in the blackness, eating up the fog.

The men from the emergency units struggled dazedly from their bed still half asleep, and grabbed their weapons. Outside, others were stumbling around, staring towards the outskirts of the town. Barked orders were starting to bring some system to the chaos, but meanwhile, from the town's edge, the sound of small-arms fire pierced the silence. At that moment, the soldiers standing there realised that this was no accident. It was an attack . . .

Chapter Eleven

Men were tripping over each other in crazy panic. From all over the town, units were converging on the red-emblazoned target, choking the streets around the central area with trucks, ambulances, fire-engines.

The plan had been practised a hundred times over, but now that the emergency had actually happened, they all ended up blocking each other's way – the fire-brigade slowed down the military police, the infantry barred the road to motorised units . . . by a few minutes after the attack, an even half-way orderly approach to the fire-fighting task had become beyond the army's capabilities.

The local army commander was an old soldier who was no authority on traffic matters. In such cases he used to rely on police Oberst Prinz to organise things – the same man who was now crushed under the ruins of his own headquarters.

It was hard to say who made it to the scene first. As the first teams stumbled in from nearby units, still half-asleep, they realised that the attack had been directed exclusively at the police complex. It brought a grim smile to their faces, despite themselves. What a joke! It was the worst joke of the partisan war!

When the men reached the burning building they stood in front of it for a moment, awe-stricken. Any malicious pleasure they had felt vanished as completely as if it had never been. Now they could feel the flames, and hear the screams rising, then suddenly breaking off; screams which turned into agonised howls, then oozed away like water in the sand . . .

All attempts to get into the building were beaten back by the searing heat – heat in a night when the temperature outside was minus seventeen degrees. And then the flames reached greedily for the next house, licking round it, then shooting upwards in grotesque shapes, blazing mockingly and viciously like witches' eyes, spitting out random showers of white-hot sparks that rained down on the helpless watchers.

No one among the helpers felt the sting of those sparks. Smoke stung their weeping eyes; the taste of burning wood filled their mouths; some raged silently at their impotence. Then abruptly they all stopped and listened. There was nothing more to be heard from the building; no screams, no shrieks of anguish. Nothing. It was all over now, and only their own fury was left.

Wet canvases had been spread out on the roofs of the neighbouring buildings. Because of their dampness they had frozen solid just as quickly as they were now being turned to ashes by the fire. Winter fires are as treacherous as they are difficult to fight, and happen mainly because of overheating during cold spells. Here, however, as the experts from the fire brigade could tell the moment they managed to get close enough to the building to get a good look, there had to be another explanation.

As a guerilla strike, there had never been anything like it. Even with their fiendish talent for behind-the-lines warfare, the Russians would never normally have tried something on this scale. This attack hadn't been carried out by some band of fearless *muzhiks*, or by young communists, however fanatical, but by trained specialists, probably dropped behind the German lines by parachute. And they must have possessed plans of the police headquarters . . .

The experts had realised all this right at the beginning; but it was not until they were already picking their way through the glowing heap of ruins, looking for evidence that might shed some light on the cause of those events on that merciless winter night, that some sort of order was finally restored to the centre of the town.

The panic had subsided. Now all the important streets and buildings were under military guard, and house searches had begun. Even a stray dog couldn't have escaped; the trap was slammed shut. Two hours after the explosion, the police complex was surrounded by a wide cordon. No one could enter or leave the area. At the same time, police officials from another unit took over the task of investigating the cause of the explosion. The full horror of the attack was now becoming apparent; it was gradually becoming clear that police Oberst Prinz's entire staff had been killed – twelve men, including the Oberst himself, the auxiliary guards, a sergeant, and five men, plus two detainees who were later identified as B-soldiers from Dirlewanger's special brigade.

Finally it was realised that a bomb of enormous explosive power had been planted in the cellar. The culprits must have been in the heavily-guarded building for at least half an hour without being seen. How did they get in? How did they get past the sentries? Did they bribe them? Or had the sentries deserted?

Hours later they found the guards. In an outhouse, dead. They had been stabbed and stripped of their uniforms.

Thus the riddle was solved. The partisans had obviously overpowered the sentries and killed them; then they had put on their uniforms and used them to get close to the other soldiers; after murdering them, too, they had broken into the building, set up the bomb, and left before the explosion. Only a couple of the conspirators had stayed behind to keep check on things.

While the freezing town was being turned into a hunting ground – where the hunters were shooting at each other – and the first suspects were being taken in foı interrogation, a patrol on the outskirts, fourteen kilometres from the scene of the crime, had its first brush with the enemy.

A pair of sentries heard steps and voices behind a wall of fog, voices which sounded strangely muffled. They heard what sounded like commands. At first the two soldiers thought it was a German platoon that had taken the wrong path on a night exercise.

Then the voices came closer, and the sentries realised that the voices were Russians, Ivans, who had no business to be around here at night. One of the Germans called out to the intruders, vague shadows in the fog, and was answered by a burst of fire. The sentry opened up with his machine-pistol into the night, and was joined by his companion.

The sound of firing alerted the nearby combat units. A soldier almost fell over the body of a Russian and called to the man next to him. Then, just in time, he saw the hand-grenade and managed to hurl himself into cover. The partisan had obviously been killed and his corpse booby-trapped by his own comrades.

The crazy pursuit finally dispersed in the fog and the confusion. But the incident was reported to Minsk and became the centre of a full-scale dragnet. The ripples of the explosion at Prinz's headquarters spread wider and wider, involving the whole neighbouring area – until they even reached the headquarters of the Dirlewanger brigade which, like every other German unit in the district, rushed to join the hunt.

Determined and ruthless, the pursuit spread over great expanses of the Russian steppe . . .

The heavy truck skidded to the right on the icy road and went into a seemingly endless slide towards the ditch. Panicking, the driver wrenched at the wheel and pressed the accelerator pedal, only to find that he had pressed too hard, sending the lorry veering wildly over the other side of the road to end up in an ice-patch.

The leaderless Dirlewanger brigade was in the vanguard of the German units as they stormed forward into unknown territory. The first platoon found itself part of a motorised unit for the first time in its history; a sign of favour which had raised Paul Vonwegh to the status of a demi-god in his men's estimation. For Dirlewangers not to have to footslog was incredible . . .

As the truck got under way again after the near-disaster, Gruhnke stared morosely at the floor, groaning and clutching his head at every jolt of the hard suspension. It was partly the effects of yesterday's vodka, but it also had something to do with his realisation of what he might have brought down on his thick skull by yesterday's drunken orgy. He had thrown his comrades into a frenzy of joy, with the schnapps and with the rumour that Dirlewanger was dead. But if he was wrong about the Standartenführer . . .

Kortetzky crouched next to the platoon leader, his tiny button-eyes fixed on Vonwegh like an adoring dog.

Muller and Kordt were trying to doze. Kirchwein sat on Vonwegh's right, leaning against Petrat. Whenever his glance met Vonwegh's, he gave an involuntary shudder and his eyes took on a pleading look. The unhealthy skin of his face had taken on the pale-green colour of fear, as if he were about to suffer another of his attacks.

Vonwegh had caught him, the traitor and informer, directly in front of Dirlewanger's dacha, right in the act, and had dragged him away, half-strangling him. It had taken some minutes before he had been able to get the epileptic to talk; Kirchwein had seemed in a daze, like a man after an accident, but finally he had forced him back to consciousness of the world around him. He had groaned as he recognised Vonwegh and everything came back to him.

'You . . .' he whined.

The platoon leader jerked him to his feet.

'I haven't . . .' Kirchwein tried to say.

'Tomorrow . . .' Vonwegh hissed. 'For the moment, keep your mouth shut.' He stared into the man's face, at the features contorted with fear, read the desperation there, and nodded. 'No,' he continued, 'I won't tell the others.'

Somewhere there was the sound of a whistle. Brakes squealed, and the truck slid sideways again, throwing the cursing B-soldiers against each other.

Contact with their next-door unit had been lost. They would have to get out and wait until it was re-established, stamping up and down and beating their arms to keep warm. Paul Vonwegh seemed to acknowledge Kirchwein's existence for the first time. He nodded to the epileptic and the two of them went unnoticed round to the other side of the truck, away from the rest of the platoon.

'You wanted to grass on Gruhnke last night,' Vonwegh said harshly. 'Am I right?'

The epileptic said nothing; he was desperately trying to think of a way out.

'I couldn't help it . . .' he answered at last, his feverish bright eyes darting from side to side. 'They forced me . . .'

'Who were you going to report to?'

'To . . . to Sergeant Weise.'

'He's not there,' the platoon leader said.

'Then to the clerk-sergeant. They both . . . if I didn't . . . at least once a week . . .'

Vonwegh nodded. That was their style all right, he thought – even their crude minds knew the old adage: divide and rule.

'Please . . .' Kirchwein whimpered. 'Don't . . . don't say anything to the others . . .'

'All right,' Vonwegh answered curtly, 'I'll give you a chance.'

Kirchwein's face was filled with pathetic gratitude.

'But in future you will report everything to me, understand?'

'Yes,' the epileptic said, a shade too eagerly. 'But I must . . . Sergeant Weise and Müller-Würzbach . . .'

'I'll decide what you pass on to them,' the platoon leader said, and suddenly the conversation was over. Leaving Kirchwein standing, he strode off to join the others, and around the corners of his mouth there was the faint twitch of a smile.

They had been waiting for half an hour. Today the special brigade was not as isolated as it usually was during action; in this sort of situation it was impossible to keep the B-soldiers from coming into contact with regular Wehrmacht units. Stopped along with them now was a company of sappers just back from the front – soldiers who were fed up with kicking their heels behind the lines and who didn't have to worry about keeping their mouths shut. They were cursing along with the rest of them.

'What's going on then?' Gruhnke asked a lance-corporal.

'How the hell should I know?' the man growled. 'Some sort of partisan raid in Minsk or somewhere . . .'

'What?' Paul Vonwegh asked.

'Told you, I don't know. But I heard the buggers blew up an entire police headquarters.'

A police headquarters? In Minsk? As if a knife were being

twisted in his guts, Paul Vonwegh knew instinctively that police Oberst Prinz was involved.

Vonwegh had long since stopped having any illusions about the enemy he was fighting; it was safer to expect the worst. And suddenly he had a fatal feeling that he had underestimated Standartenführer Oskar Dirlewanger.

The ripples from the killings at Minsk had reached the capital of the Reich; and soon they had penetrated to its sick centre, to the Prinz-Albrecht-Strasse, where the diseased brain of Nazi power was housed.

It was lunch time, but no one went out to eat. The big, spacious building was alive with a tension that could almost be physically felt, from the offices at the top to the archives and the grim cellars in the basement. But the building was silent as its inmates went about their business; as if the deadly Gestapo machine were running on rubber wheels . . .

Then the suppressed tension was released, and all hell broke loose. Doors slammed, messengers flew about, telephones rang, telex-machines chattered, couriers were dispatched, official vehicles got ready. All departments were suddenly in permanent conference.

The first report from Minsk had come in an hour or so before and had been received with a certain perverse pleasure; it would give a good excuse to toughen up policy in the East. Gross negligence in military circles, they thought in the Prinz-Albrecht-Strasse, and at first, as is usual with disasters, they were interested mainly in the numbers of those killed, not their names. Then the casuălty-list came through the decoding machine: Police Oberst Prinz and all his staff . . .

Prinz. Wasn't that the outsider who seemed so much in favour with Himmler? Confirmed. Himmler's headquarters had ordered a formal report. The Reichsführer S S was demanding to be kept up to date on progress.

In the Prinz-Albrecht-Strasse, too, Dirlewanger had his friends and his enemies, his protectors and his accusers, perhaps in equal proportion. Both sides were immediately seized by the same suspicion: had the Standartenführer organised the attack? This could mean more than a little local trouble . . .

The man who stumped along the corridor now was ignored in the general excitement. He was thin, too thin. His S S uniform hung loosely from his body, as if it had been stolen from someone else. The braided epaulettes with the two stars showed him to be a colonel in the Waffen-S S, a Standartenführer.

He stopped, made to turn right, then went on unhurriedly, as if he had thought better of it. His eyes were deep set in their dark sockets, as if they had been forced into his face. Greyish skin was stretched tightly over a grotesque bone-structure that gave his head the look of a death's head mask. Only one thing still lived in his hooded eyes: greed – greed to live, greed to eat, greed for women . . .

At that stage of the war, the most outrageous people seemed to be entitled to wear uniforms, but this Standartenführer was a freak even among the freaks who peopled the ranks of the S S. He was the purest, most unholy embodiment of the Nazi 'master race' in its vilest form.

This man was taking the final steps to his goal. He was heading for a meeting with his protector. If the Gruppenführer couldn't cover for him, then he was as good as dead. They couldn't prove anything directly now; the only question was whether anyone *wanted* to prove anything against him. Dirlewanger walked on a few paces, apparently unconcerned and relaxed. But his brain was working feverishly, because this was his personal moment of decision.

He entered an ante-chamber, and for the first time in years he had to wait outside – in the corridor.

The hunt for the Minsk killers was broken off as suddenly as it had begun. Had the men been caught, or was further searching considered useless? No one knew.

Dirlewanger's brigade was marched back to barracks. By the late afternoon they were lined up, waiting to be dismissed. But they were not dismissed. Instead they were left standing on the parade-ground in formation. Forgotten. Or . . .

Suddenly Sergeant Weise re-appeared, complete with his entourage. They strutted arrogantly past the cowering B-soldiers like harbingers of evil. Gradually the special brigade began to suspect what every one of them had feared: the way was being paved for Satan's return.

Gruhnke whispered something to Kordt; the sergeant noticed it and made them stand to attention until their fingertips were numb. When they were allowed to relax again, they moved their hands slowly and uncertainly, like arthritic cripples, as if they feared their fingers might drop off.

One of them fainted. He was carried out of the ranks and laid on the snow while water was poured over him.

'He'll rest for ten minutes – whether he likes it or not . . .' Weise ordered, with a feral smile that exposed yellowed, pointed teeth.

The newcomers were lined up opposite the first platoon. They were poor benighted innocents who had volunteered to get out of prison, mixed with political detainees who had been drafted. Most of them still looked as though they thought they'd won first prize in a lottery.

Paul Vonwegh smiled sadly. He knew the road these men travelled – and like his it had come via Prinz-Albrecht-Strasse.

When he had gone there, after his visit to the Swedish embassy, it had been an anti-climax. At first it had seemed as if they were going to send him away to spare themselves the bother of the paperwork. There had been a few half-hearted questions, a shrug of the shoulders; then it turned out that the man from Spain, the fool and idealist, was in the right place but with the wrong section.

At last they had him. They took away his tie and shoelaces, and they beat him up in a cellar to welcome him. It wasn't too bad. Afterwards they tipped a bucket of water over his head, put a cigarette between his lips and began to interrogate him.

Paul Vonwegh told them no more than they already knew. They nodded, as if it was all they expected. They had pale faces and empty eyes.

Then a man came and lectured him; the usual mixture of

slushy patriotism and Nazi jargon . . . and finally they asked him to sign.

They promised Vonwegh a life of freedom if he would sign the document they presented to him as a true account of his experiences . . . oh, and pass on to them a few more bits of information about his former comrades . . . Perhaps they would have kept their word, but it never got that far.

Paul Vonwegh was marched off to a pitch-dark cell. He got virtually no food. The beatings took on a new thoroughness. He took it all in silence, as well as he could.

The fellows who tortured him took it in turns. Vonwegh didn't know their names, just how well their fists could hurt. Eventually a man had come who at first treated him with kid gloves. He was a newcomer to the Prinz-Albrecht-Strasse, but Vonwegh already knew his soft, puffy, effeminate face. It was the man who had sold his own cousin to the Gestapo as the price for his own entry into a cushy job in the Reichssicherheitshauptamt – Wulf-Dieter Brillmann, the 'go-between'.

Brillmann seemed to have a guilty conscience at their first meeting.

'*Heil Hitler*!' he rasped.

Vonwegh was silent. Then the man came up close to him, looked at him hard, and then, without warning, hit him with the flat of his hand straight in the neck. Still Vonwegh didn't move, but bile rose in his throat. Eventually he couldn't stop himself from throwing up. Brillmann waited until he had finished, then handed him a sheet of writing-paper.

'Here,' he said, his soft features wrinkled in disgust. He sat down and lit a cigarette. So far as violence went, Brillmann was still a beginner; but he was obviously beginning to enjoy it more all the time.

'You think I wouldn't have stuck to our agreement,' Brillmann said with a shake of his head. 'It was your fault, Vonwegh.' He laughed coldly. 'You waited too long, and I couldn't allow myself to be suspected of favouritism to a traitor . . .'

Vonwegh had to force himself not to lose control.

'What has happened to Karen?' he asked through gritted teeth.

Brillmann smiled and shrugged his shoulders.

'Haven't you got even a spark of decency left?' Vonwegh asked.

The newly-minted Gestapo man studied his finger nails.

'Do you know something?' he said at last. 'I've had enough of you, Vonwegh.' He wrote his name on a document. 'I'm having you transferred to Buchenwald . . . They'll teach you love of your fatherland in a concentration camp. Heil Hitler!'

Just as Brillmann was about to leave, Vonwegh asked him one more question.

'Where is Karen?' he said.

'Where traitors belong,' Brillmann had answered, and that had been the last Vonwegh saw of him.

Since then, Vonwegh had seen the man's face in front of him day and night; he had kept that picture of Brillmann's slack features, the eyes that took on a bright gleam at the sight of another's suffering. Yes, he had become the centre of Vonwegh's private universe of revenge – the spur that kept him alive. If he could survive, he could settle with Brillmann . . . The Nazi system was just an idea, but the 'go-between' who had betrayed him and Karen was living and tangible.

The platoon leader was still standing in the first rank of the B-soldiers. How many lonely nights had he spent imagining his hands round Brillmann's neck? Whenever he thought of him, the fury came, the conditioned response. He knew Brillmann's face so well by now that he could have drawn it with his eyes shut . . . the slack lips, twitching silently like a fish's mouth, and the fish's eyes, with the carefully-groomed and parted short hair, the moustache that was so repulsively blond . . . a face just like that of the man opposite him now, the second on the left in the ranks of the newcomers.

Paul Vonwegh looked more sharply at the man he had just noticed.

The similarity was uncanny.

'Half-circle!' Sergeant Weise yelled.

They closed ranks. The newcomers came closer, so close that now you could see their faces clearly. And at that moment Vonwegh stepped out of line for the first time since he had joined Dirlewanger's brigade. He came to a sudden stop, as though he had been nailed to the spot, so that the others, cursing, had to hop around him.

The platoon leader had just realised that the man he had seen among the reinforcements bore more than a fleeting resemblance to the 'go-between'. He not only looked like, but was Wulf-Dieter Brillmann.

Chapter Twelve

Paul Vonwegh took a while to recover from the shock. He stood there for several moments, in the other man's way, like a statue – and then he was off, following his comrades into the semi-circle they were in the process of forming. Sergeant Weise had noticed Vonwegh stumble and stop, was amused and overlooked it. Now the platoon leader was standing straight in line, thoroughly correct.

By now Vonwegh had a grip on himself once more. A glance to the side and there was no doubt about it: the newcomer was Wulf-Dieter Brillmann, the man who had betrayed him; Karen's cousin, who had delivered her to the Gestapo, the public prosecutor who had been responsible for delivering Vonwegh to this hell on earth, who had sentenced him to the hunger, the beatings-up, the 'standing bunker', the humiliation, torture and murder. Now, for some reason, this man was a member of the Dirlewanger brigade . . . B-soldier Brillmann . . .

Vonwegh suddenly began to feel pleasure. Now he could consider what to do about the face. But no, he would do the real thinking later on . . . more slowly, deliberately . . .

'You idle bastards!' Weise was roaring. 'You shits!' Then his voice became ominously quiet. 'Do you know why you're here?'

'No, sergeant,' they chorussed.

'You don't deserve anything . . no mercy. I wouldn't touch you with a barge pole. You're a bunch of mutineers . . . deserters . . . defeatists . . . thieves, whoremongers . . .' His voice rose to a roaring crescendo, then subsided. But he had not yet finished. He was just waiting out a meaningful pause.

The newcomers were still grinning at this bizarre exhibition. They thought the speech was witty, humorous. They didn't know Weise yet . . .

The second from the left, Brillmann, was not smiling. His face expressed the worthy seriousness of the model pupil, following his teacher's every word.

Paul Vonwegh followed everything with narrow eyes. Brillmann was still the trier, the ambitious one, he thought with grim amusement, Well, let him try here, and see how far it gets him.

'So. Let me let you into a secret . . .' the sergeant continued thickly. His eyes glowed with hate, or alcohol, or with both . . . 'I have to tell you . . .' he was playing it for all it was worth, savouring every second 'some good news. And the good news is that Standartenführer Dirlewanger is now on his way here. He will be landing soon . . .'

The men stood numb with shock, silent, their spines prickling with fear. And yet they still hoped. Why was Weise telling them this? It couldn't be true. Dirlewanger had been executed . . .

'Now. We want to greet him in the right fashion, don't we?' Weise continued with a leer. 'Let's practise that now. Welcome back . . .' he said, staring along the front rank of the men. Then he said quietly, 'Gentlemen, I ask you not to whisper this . . . *Achtung*!' he bawled, and motioned them with his hand to shout out a welcome.

'Welcome back!' the hundreds of B-soldiers yelled back at the sergeant, their voices choked with fear.

'You feeble bastards!' Weise raged. 'That's like a bloody bunch of nanny goats.' He raised his hand a second time.

'Welcome back!' they shouted, desperately fighting against the muffling panic.

'What the hell do you think you are?' Weise shouted angrily. 'A church choir? Or a bunch of frightened virgins?' He went up to the first row, his eyes narrowing. 'Or is it lack of enthusiasm, eh? I'll give you all one last chance . . .'

Again he signalled and they roared. And again. And again . . .

After about half an hour, Müller-Würzbach took over from Weise. Mouths twitched. Eyes flickered with pain and fatigue. 'Welcome back . . .' the barrack walls echoed with the words, like loose stones falling in a valley, crushing everything in their path.

And they practised the words while they crept through the snow. They repeated them with gas masks on. They groaned them while they were lying down, kneeling or standing. They blasted them out in hateful resignation; in desperate, repellent self-loathing. And when they were finally allowed to stop repeating those words of 'Welcome', their heads felt as if they were filled with angry insects, eating away at their brains . . .

Then they were ordered to form ranks again. If anyone whispered, snorted, or even thought a little too hard, the order came: 'Attention!'

Evening was coming now. They stared upwards to the west. They heard noises, saw specks in the distance. Dirlewanger 'landed' a hundred times . . . and each time it was only their terror.

Then there was a roar in the sky and a shadow hung over the camp. It became larger, more visible, clearer.

This time, a Fieseler Storch was preparing to land, making a last run over the assembled men, waggling its wings like a fighter pilot after a victorious flight. Then it landed smoothly. A man got out and walked over from the airstrip. He wore a leather coat over his uniform, and his hat was slightly tilted back on his head.

He walked quickly towards them, with that crooked smile, pistols in his belt, everything hanging so loosely on that thin body . . .

And now the B-soldiers roared without needing to be primed; they yelled until their lungs threatened to burst: 'Welcome back, Standartenführer!'

Weise saluted. Dirlewanger shook his hand firmly, and they exchanged a knowing glance. Then the sergeant gestured at the assembled men, as if he were telling Dirlewanger to do whatever he was intending to do now, at once . . .

The Standartenführer nodded and turned to the B-soldiers.

'Men!' he shouted. 'I have come from Berlin, and I bring

you personal greetings from the Reichsführer S S.'

He was lying, cleverly and without compunction like the crook he was, Vonwegh thought. For a few seconds, he imagined his own hands round Brillmann's throat . . . It was all he could think of; forget Dirlewanger, nothing really mattered except one thing . . .

'My NCOs have reported a mutiny to me,' the Standartenführer was saying. 'But of course there aren't any mutinies in my brigade.' He smiled broadly. 'And because this is so, there will be a trial tomorrow – three men from every platoon . . .'

He grinned and went quickly along the ranks, looking searchingly at every single man, seeing how they cowered and cringed, how they tried to disappear into the ground, or ingratiate themselves. Then he stopped and met Vonwegh's gaze.

Weise, at Dirlewanger's side, whispered something to the Standartenführer. Dirlewanger nodded, then clapped the platoon leader on the shoulder and looked him straight in the eye.

'Well done,' the Standartenführer praised him. 'Barrack VIII is exempted from reporting tomorrow morning.' Then he turned to all the men and smiled slowly. 'Trust breeds trust!' he bawled. 'How many men have you?' he asked Vonwegh.

'Forty-six,' the platoon leader said.

'Good,' he turned to the staff-sergeant. 'A wristwatch for every man, and a chicken. Do we have enough?'

'Yes, Standartenführer,' Müller-Würzbach replied, eager and servile as ever.

'Every man gets his just reward,' Dirlewanger commented. Then, turning back to Vonwegh, he said: 'I'll talk to you later. Report to the castle this evening.'

The Standartenführer stalked off to the dacha. Weise made as if to follow, then waited while Müller-Würzbach allocated the newcomers to their platoons. He lit a cigarette, then noticed where Vonwegh's gaze was directed and walked up behind the platoon leader unnoticed.

'Now then, you . . .' he said.

Vonwegh sprang to attention, but the sergeant simply gave a casual nod. 'Stand easy, man. It's just that you look like a hungry wolf.' He pointed to Brillmann. 'Do you know him?'

'Yes, sergeant,' Vonwegh answered.

'An old score?'

'Yes, sergeant.'

'All right. Then I'll give him to you,' the sergeant laughed. 'Call it a reward for good behaviour.'

Vonwegh watched as Weise went and spoke to the staff-sergeant, who made a note in his pad.

'Welcome back,' he thought, and his mouth twitched silently as he thought of the irony of the words they had practised all afternoon long. Welcome back, Herr Brillmann.

The victory celebrations that evening in the castle were relatively subdued. Maybe this time Dirlewanger had not come out of things entirely unscathed. He didn't seem quite so sure of himself. Someone, it turned out, had told Himmler about Oberst Prinz's death. Just the simple fact, but there was potential trouble there. At dinner the Standartenführer sat once more at the head of the table, enjoying his favourite songs and food. He asked about the women. 'Shall I have them brought in?' asked Müller-Wurzbach. Dirlewanger considered for a moment. 'Later,' he said. Then to the others: 'Take care. We'll have to go easy for a while . . . with everything. This business with Prinz's death hasn't done us any good, you know.' He grinned crookedly.

Sergeant Weise nodded when he saw that smile. He understood.

'Right then,' Dirlewanger continued. 'Everything by the book for the time being. No "accidental" deaths. Physical punishment only according to regulations. Otherwise . . .' He turned to the sergeant, 'There's always some kind of come-back after these things.'

This time, everyone nodded agreement.

'They've established that it was the partisans who killed Prinz?' the Standartenführer asked Müller-Würzbach.

'Yes,' said the clerk-sergeant, straight-faced. 'There were

two attacks on the railway line in grid square thirteen. The raiders just disappeared afterwards . . .'

'Like the Minsk business,' Dirlewanger laughed.

In Minsk it had been decided that the attack on the police complex had definitely been the work of partisans. They had, the authorities now thought, worked to a meticulously prepared plan. A crucial part of the whole affair had been the use of German speakers; after the explosion, it was believed, they had mingled with sapper units and then simply faded away in the confusion as the pursuers arrived.

'That's all very well,' said Dirlewanger, 'but it shows us up in a bad light. I mean, that partisans could get away with something like that.' He looked at Weise. 'Now I could do with a schnapps, and then,' he stuck out his chin and stroked it lightly with his bony fingers, 'a victory – a proper one, eh?'

'That will be arranged, Standartenführer,' said the sergeant.

The first platoon were back in Barrack VIII at last, after a crazy day, but one that had been good – for them, at least. They were going to get watches, or at any rate some chickens. More important was the commendation from Dirlewanger, which would provide security of a sort for a while.

In a corner, a group of them discussed the latest arrivals, particularly the four new ones in their own platoon.

Paul Vonwegh observed them from the window and smiled. 'Just don't push them too hard,' he said. Then he called the gorilla over. 'Clear me a space so that I can have a word with each of the new boys,' he said. He pointed to Brillmann. 'And keep that bastard until last.'

The others watched Vonwegh in amazement. They'd never seen him like this before; he was usually as flat as a gramophone record, this Vonwegh, never a sign of pleasure, or of depression, of hope or fear.

There was always a chance for some light relief when newcomers arrived, who had no idea of how Dirlewanger ran things. The platoon leader stood half-hidden behind a locker as the first reported to him. 'Ernst Kuberg at your service,' the man said. 'I was sentenced for being a so-called confidence man.'

'Right,' said Vonwegh with a sour smile. 'You'll need all the confidence you can muster.' Then he dismissed him. Everyone seemed to like Kuberg; he strolled around the place like a famous conductor who has been forced by circumstances to direct a village brass band.

'Exner,' the second said stiffly. A real chocolate soldier, this one.

'General?' Vonwegh asked sarcastically.

'B-soldier.'

'And before that?'

'Untersturmführer in the S S.'

'What was it? Rape?' asked the platoon leader, impassive as ever.

'Theft of army stores,' the man said with a hint of outrage.

Vonwegh dismissed him with a nod.

'B-soldier Braun,' the third introduced himself.

'Volunteer?'

'No. Drafted from Oranienburg concentration camp.'

'Political?'

'Socialist,' the man replied curtly.

The two of them examined each other distastefully, almost sadly.

'Are you wealthy?' Vonwegh asked.

'Yes.'

'Good. That'll do for now . . .'

The last one stood smartly to attention and held it, or at least tried to. 'B-soldier Brillma . . .' he stammered, and the final syllable stuck in his gullet. His eyelids twitched; he began to breathe heavily, like a tired boxer going into a clinch. He began to sway and sag as recognition dawned . . .

'Well, aren't you going to stand up straight?' Vonwegh asked quietly.

Wulf-Dieter shuddered.

'Give him a hand, Kortetzky,' Vonwegh said.

The gorilla grinned, baring his teeth. He may have been primitive, but he understood. In a moment he had stepped up behind Brillmann and delivered a vicious, flat-handed blow across the man's back.

Brillmann staggered forward, almost fell, pulled himself up and stood, bony shoulders back, stomach forward. This time Kortetzky 'straightened' him with a thump in the guts.

Vonwegh did not wait for the man to recover his breath. He leaned forward and looked into Brillmann's contorted face, as if he were about to spit in it.

'I am Paul Vonwegh,' he said. 'I'm the platoon leader here. Released on probation from Buchenwald concentration camp, where I was taught what it means to love the Fatherland.' His face was absolutely impassive, his voice a soft hiss. 'And where have you come from?' he asked, chewing off the words one by one.

'From Berlin . . .' Brillmann said miserably.

'Profession?'

'Civil servant,' Wulf-Dieter muttered quickly.

'And before that?' Vonwegh's voice was quiet and merciless.

'Public prosecutor,' Brillmann mumbled.

'Speak clearly,' Vonwegh said loudly. 'Your comrades,' he pronounced the word with relish, 'would like to hear it all.'

'Public prosecutor,' repeated Brillmann with slightly more volume.

They all understood then. You could have sharpened a knife on the look that Petrat, the murderer, flashed at him. Kortetzky just grinned, but even that was more than enough.

Vonwegh could feel his skin prickling and tingling with excitement. Slowly, he thought, take it slowly – nothing too crude, nothing exaggerated, just take it easy, enjoy it . . . For three years they flayed me, beat me, kicked me. I could have forgiven them that. But finally they got Karen. Perhaps I could have let Brillmann off, even for that. But Karen is his cousin, flesh and blood, and she is the woman I love. And for that he's going to choke, and die . . .

He wouldn't, he thought, do it the way they did in the cellars at the Prinz-Albrecht-Strasse. Nothing like that. No: something more elegant, more refined. No beating, no kicks in the head. I'll knead you like dough, my dear fellow, Vonwegh mused bitterly; and in the end you'll beg me to torture you physically, anything rather than what I'm doing to your mind – oh so gently.

'Why are you here?' Vonwegh asked him softly.

'Cowardice in the face of the enemy.' Brillmann all but gagged on the answer.

Vonwegh raised an eyebrow.

'An enemy? In the Prinz-Albrecht-Strasse?'

'No,' the other said wretchedly. 'At the front.'

'And how long were you at the front for, Herr Public Prosecutor?'

'A week.'

'One week?' the platoon leader repeated slowly, turning to the other men in the room, his face impassive but his aim clear. He knew that he had thrown Brillmann to these lions to devour, and he was beginning to feel the emptiness that came from exhaustion.

'You'll be given the chance to make up for it,' he said. Then he grinned at the others and said affably: 'We'll bring him up to scratch, won't we, comrades?'

From the eyes of every man in the room, he could see that Wulf-Dieter would be 'brought up to scratch' – and that he might not survive the experience . . .

'Right – ten minutes' basic drill to start with,' Vonwegh said finally to Brillmann, 'and then report back to me.' He pointed through the window. 'Outside.'

Vonwegh suddenly realised that he was close to the end of his self-control. He wanted air, and light, and to be alone with the old wounds. But then he saw Karen's tender, painful smile, and that hurt him more than the dark cells, the deprivation and the beatings for which he had to thank Wulf-Dieter Brillmann. Then, when he had come back from interrogations, when they had led him back to his cell, the thought of her had made things bearable; in his imagination she had stroked his forehead and nursed his battered body. Even now, standing in the open air, the memory of that time suffocated him. He paced backward and forward, up and down, fifty paces one way, fifty paces back. How long was ten minutes? Suddenly he realised why his mind was so confused, his will so weak. He knew that in a few minutes he would find out what had happened to Karen, would know the answer to a question that had obsessed him for two years, and which still tormented him. The glimmer of hope among the ashes of despair. There were still six minutes to go. Vonwegh gradually felt his self-control returning. He went to the door of the barracks and tore it open.

'Come here, Brillmann,' he called.

He said nothing as the man staggered up to him. Brillmann looked exhausted. His breathing was laboured, his face a picture of misery and submission.

'Right,' the platoon leader began. 'I want to know about her.'

'Nothing happened to her, nothing at all,' Brillmann cut in hastily, his eyes darting around, like a cornered dog.

'But I want to know exactly.'

Brillmann gave a last desperate look, then began to speak.

'She was only with us for eight or nine days.'

Vonwegh stared at him fixedly.

'I mean . . . with the Gestapo,' added Brillmann quickly.

'And then?'

'She was handed over to the regular authorities.'

The regular authorities, thought Vonwegh bitterly. He knew all about those 'regular authorities', and their 'justice' in the era of national socialism.

'She was detained for two months pending further investigations,' the man continued haltingly. 'In normal detention – she was allowed reading matter, writing materials, cigarettes . . .'

'Get to the point.'

Brillmann took a deep breath. For a moment he straightened his back, then slumped again.

'I have to say . . .' he faltered '. . . how sorry I am . . .'

'Oh no!' Vonwegh said, fighting to keep his hard-won self-mastery. 'You're sorry! How wonderful, how kind of you!' His voice was grating, as if it were being crushed in a vice. 'So that makes everything all right. Our little chat has settled things . . .'

'You're going to finish me off . . .' Brillmann mumbled, as if to himself.

'Is that what you think?' Vonwegh asked. His steely grey eyes seemed to take on a clear colour, like pale fire. 'Well, you're right,' he said eventually, quietly, so quietly, as if he were talking through a mask. 'I'll finish you off all right.' His voice grew louder. 'But it will be in my way . . . and when I choose.' He smiled, and his face did not change as he continued:

'What happed to Karen?'

'Four months' imprisonment for aiding and abetting,' Wulf-Dieter recited, as if it were some formula he had learned by heart. 'Suspended.'

And Paul Vonwegh knew for certain that he was lying.

Chapter Thirteen

Outside it was cold and cheerless. But in the dacha they were full of the joys of spring. Behind the ring of castle-gendarmes, there was raucous laughter; Dirlewanger was already half-drunk and had unbuttoned his uniform.

In the study in the castle Paul Vonwegh waited. He had been ordered to report to the dacha, then forgotten.

'I have an idea, chief,' Sergeant Weise was saying.

'You're always having ideas,' the Standartenführer said thickly. 'Just keep having them, my son.'

'We still have two Russian girls in the detention block,' Weise continued eagerly, 'and they know where the partisans are hiding, sure as hell . . .'

'Well?' Dirlewanger asked, already becoming bored with the subject.

'They won't talk,' Weise continued. The leer on his face left no doubt that he had tried everything so far to make them 'talk'. 'I thought . . .' his face took on a new cunning 'that Maria could get something out of them – your Ukrainian girl, Standartenführer.'

'They'd never fall for that,' Dirlewanger replied listlessly.

'No?' Weise said slyly. Then he began to unveil his plan in all its devious glory.

Maria was one of the girls taken as booty in February; her relatives had been murdered and her village burned down by Dirlewanger's men. And then the Standartenführer had picked her out for his pleasure. He had used force – he preferred it that way – and Maria hated him. But at the same time, something mysterious and incomprehensible had happened: the simple habit of submission had re-asserted itself, the humility of the Slav peasant girl who knows and desires to know only one man in her life, be he good or bad, rich or poor, decent or a devil like Dirlewanger. Maria remained silent, submissive. She served her master – though she hated him still . . .

Sergeant Weise proposed to beat her just as a show and then to throw her into the detention block with the other Russian girls.

'If we gave her a proper thrashing, they'd think she was one of them and they'd trust her. It just has to be convincing . . .'

'Hm . . .' the Standartenführer considered. Then he noticed that Müller-Würzbach had sidled up to him. 'What is it?' Dirlewanger asked irritably.

'You ordered the leader of the first platoon to come here, Standartenführer,' Müller-Würzbach said.

A minute later Paul Vonwegh stood tall and correct before the drunken Standartenführer.

'Sit down,' Dirlewanger muttered, pointing to a chair. He shoved a glass of schnapps across the table in Vonwegh's direction. 'So you're the paragon of virtue, eh?'

The platoon leader made no reply.

'Why?' Dirlewanger asked.

'I was obeying orders,' the B-soldier answered.

'That doesn't impress me,' the Standartenführer sneered. 'Come on . . . the real reason . . . why?'

Vonwegh said nothing. Gradually the rest of the room subsided into silence as well, and it turned into a contest. The chief's mood was touch and go as his yellow, hooded eyes bore into Vonwegh's. Dirlewanger's gaze was thoughtful, wary.

'Where the hell have I seen you before?' he asked suddenly.

Somehow the platoon leader kept a cool head. In the decisive moment, he was totally without nerves, without feelings.

'In Spain,' Vonwegh replied calmly.

'What?' Dirlewanger said in complete astonishment. 'You were down there?' He stood up in his excitement.

Vonwegh got up automatically and stood to attention. It was quiet in the room, uncannily quiet – like a casino where the wheel is spinning and everything is staked on one bet: red or black . . .

'For God's sake,' Dirlewanger bawled. 'Where the hell were you then . . . ?'

'On the other side,' Paul Vonwegh answered baldly, loud and clear.

The Standartenführer was so drunk that it took a while for Vonwegh's words to sink in. He just stood staring at the platoon leader, swaying, with eyes whose pupils were like blotting-pads soaked in red ink.

Vonwegh was still standing to attention, but there was no servility in his stance. From the outside, no one could have guessed that his nerves were strained to the limit.

Slowly Dirlewanger came closer to him.

'What did you say?' he growled. 'You were down there in Spain . . . with the Reds?'

'Yes, Standartenführer.'

'And you're prepared to admit it to me?'

Weise and co. had made their way over and formed a semi-circle around Paul Vonwegh; it was as if a ring had closed round his fate.

'Yes, Standartenführer.'

'Stop giving me that idiotic "Yes, Standartenführer",' Dirlewanger exploded. 'Tell me why you're admitting it!'

'I am admitting it because the staff-sergeant can find out anyway from my personal file,' the platoon leader answered, without moving a muscle, without change of expression.

'Fair enough. Maybe you're not so stupid . . .' Dirlewanger conceded. He turned to Müller-Würzbach. 'Have we got any more like this one?' he asked.

'No, Standartenführer,' Müller-Würzbach answered dutifully.

'You of all people,' Dirlewanger said, his attention back on Vonwegh '. . . a Red swine . . . behaving like a model soldier . . .' He took another swig of schnapps and fiddled with the empty glass, as if he were playing with the platoon leader's fate. 'Now talk . . .' he said harshly.

'I want to live, Standartenführer,' Paul Vonwegh answered, coldly and without emotion. 'I want to eat, breathe and come through . . . and one day I want to get out of all this shit.'

'Hm . . .' Dirlewanger reflected. 'And where did you learn that piece of wisdom?'

'In Buchenwald concentration camp,' Vonwegh said. 'I was re-educated . . .' He said it matter-of-factly, but the irony came through in his voice.

Dirlewanger seemed to be thinking, coming to a decision. For a moment his face wrinkled and became pinched. Then it relaxed and he let out a deep belly-laugh.

'You can congratulate yourself, Vonwegh, on your humour and my generosity,' he said with a laugh that was as dry as parchment. 'What I can't understand is how a fellow like you could hang around with that Red riff-raff . . . What were you, in fact? Socialist or Communist?'

'Republican,' the platoon leader answered. 'Liberal.'

'Oh no,' Dirlewanger grinned. 'An intellectual . . . one of those gutless wonders. But a fellow like you . . .' he repeated, with genuine puzzlement '. . . you don't look like a pansy.' He went back to his seat, sat down and took a hefty swig from his schnapps bottle. 'Stand at ease,' he said patronisingly to Vonwegh, 'or, better still, come over here. I get nostalgic when I hear anything about Spain. Man, the girls . . .' He turned to Sergeant Weise and clicked his tongue. 'The girls were really something,' he repeated, 'not like these Russian hags.'

And then the Standartenführer began to reminisce, delighting his entourage with tales of his time in the sun. To Paul Vonwegh, his table companion, Dirlewanger's obscene interpretation of the Spanish tragedy brought rising nausea. He had to sit and drink the Standartenführer's vodka while Dirlewanger went through those 'glorious' years, leaving out no details, wholly in his element. And his element was blood. Again Dirlewanger stood under the burning Spanish sky, advancing over corpses, standing civilians against the wall, ordering bombardments, burnings, pillage, filling his pockets and the whorehouses as a member of the so-called 'Condor

Legion'. Condor was the name of a vulture – never was such a useless division given a more descriptive name.

Suddenly, at the height of the drinking and the chatter, Dirlewanger leapt to his feet.

'Stand to attention!' he bawled at Vonwegh.

It was quiet again as Vonwegh straightened and stared fixedly ahead.

'I hereby appoint you,' Dirlewanger roared, 'to the rank of S S lance-corporal. You will spend your probation under my direction with the permanent staff.' He laughed throatily. 'After all, we are old Spanish comrades-in-arms . . .'

The platoon leader's face remained impassive.

'So . . .' the Standartenführer carried on. 'And now we'll have another drink.'

Paul Vonwegh clamped his jaws tight together to fight back the nausea. He had taken another step towards his goal, but it sickened him. He could feel the clouds of alcohol wafting through his tired brain as he stared at the man who had appointed himself to be his patron – a twitching death's head, a murderous wreck, a living insult to heaven . . .

Paul Vonwegh reached for his glass and squeezed his fingers round it until the knuckles turned white. All he could see was Dirlewanger's face, swaying in his vision.

'Lucky for you that you can drink,' Dirlewanger was muttering. 'I can see already, Vonwegh, you'll go a long way with me . . .'

Despite the alcoholic fog, Vonwegh knew that he was skating on the wafer-thin ice of this man's favour. One laugh misjudged, one order misinterpreted, one look at the wrong time, and he was done for. Here I go, Vonwegh thought; I am making my career with the killer brigade. And he stood up to be sick.

The lights were out. The men in Barrack VIII had plunged into the desperate, restless sleep of slaves. Petrat was gasping as if his neck were already where it belonged: in the noose. Kordt was muttering incomprehensibly to himself. Kuberg, the newcomer, was dreaming of escape. Kortetzky, the gorilla, was already taking imaginary bites out of the extra rations they were going to get tomorrow.

Vonwegh was not there. He had been ordered to report to the castle. For once, they were not afraid for him; he was obviously due for some praise, and that would do them all some good. Muller was thinking of his home for the first time in weeks. And even Kirchwein, the epileptic, seemed calm and unafraid.

One man in Barrack VIII felt like smashing down the walls: Wulf-Dieter Brillmann, Karen's cousin and Vonwegh's betrayer. A few weeks ago he had been a power in the Reichssicherheitshauptamt; today, a cruel coincidence had played him into the hands of his mortal enemy.

I must forestall that swine Vonwegh, Brillmann thought feverishly as he lay on his mattress, unable to sleep; I must do something, quickly, before he gets a chance to finish me off. And before he finds out what really happened to Karen . . . Brillmann cursed himself for his carelessness.

His downfall had begun in a trivial, even absurd way; an evening with friends, where everyone had too much to drink, the women included. One girl in particular had given him the eye and there had been a fight – that was the 'master race' off duty.

Bad luck, too.

It turned out that Wulf-Dieter Brillmann had made a play for someone else's wife, and the wronged husband had kicked up a fuss about it in official quarters. Even then, things need not have been too bad. Brillmann had friends and protectors in the Reichssicherheitshauptamt – Heydrich liked him, and he had already attracted favourable attention from Himmler . . .

'Go to the front for a few weeks,' his Gruppenführer had advised him. 'By the time you get back, the whole thing will have been forgotten. We'll recall you . . . and anyway you could do with a bit of tinsel on your uniform if you're going to spend the winter in Berlin . . .'

They had smiled and shaken on it. Each understood the principle: eight days' leave and then Brillmann would be sent to the front for the usual tour of duty. He had ended up in a Waffen-S S infantry unit, though, and that had been his second piece of bad luck, because it turned out that the company commander was a tough, experienced combat officer who had an aversion to 'armchair warriors' like Brillmann.

'Want a chance to prove yourself?' he had asked with ominous chumminess when Brillmann reported.

'Yes, Hauptsturmführer, of course. I have been assigned to you for six weeks.'

'Then we must get a move on if you're going to see something of the war,' the man had said, grinning at his victim's discomfiture. 'I'll send you on a reconnaissance patrol with three others this evening. You've got a good chance of making it – it's very foggy out there . . .'

The patrol set off at eleven o'clock that night, with the other three cursing about being sent on a 'suicide mission'. They were to be guided into no man's land, and from there it was up to them. Their task was to estimate the enemy's fighting strength and, if possible, to bring back a Russian prisoner for interrogation. It had started off quite well, with the four of them running one behind the other into the dense fog. After a while, they were away from their own lines, still pushing into the swirling nothingness, and Brillmann began to shudder with a fear that got worse with every step. All at once he was at the rear, and a moment later he had hit the ground and lost contact with the others. It was so easy, he thought: all he had to do was make it back to the German lines . . .

He had got back safely. An hour later, he had reported to his company commander that he had got separated from the other three in the fog. The Hauptsturmführer had held a brief court martial, had telephoned the Divisional Commander, a man who was also not overfond of gentlemen from the Reichssicherheitshauptamt, and that was how Brillmann had ended up as one of the Dirlewanger gang.

Brillmann could console himself with the thought that in a

few days the Prinz-Albrecht-Strasse would take steps to get him out of this hole. Before that, though, Vonwegh could have killed him . . . He began to weep silently with self-pity and drum his fist against the hard straw of the mattress. He had to do something. Eventually, after half a night of agonising mental torment, he came to a decision.

Brillmann got up and dressed without being noticed. Then he crept to the dooı and opened it hesitantly. It was then that Kortetzky's eyes came open; as Brillmann moved out through the door, the gorilla got up and followed him.

Brillmann had almost made it to the castle when Kortetzky jumped him and tried to drag him back. In the struggle, his victim kicked up such a noise that the castle-gendarmes approached. Kortetzky vanished just in time, but Brillmann was caught.

He wanted to see the Standartenführer, he said. Urgently. As the castle-gendarmes dragged him towards the dacha, he kept babbling about having important information. Finally he ended up facing Sergeant Weise.

'I am a government adviser in the Reichssicherheitshauptamt,' Brillmann began, trying to put conviction into his voice.

'You were, sonny, you were . . .' said Weise, obviously totally unimpressed. The sergeant lit a cigarette.

'I'll be one again in six weeks, s-sergeant . . .'

Weise nodded lazily.

'If you survive them,' he retorted matter-of-factly.

'I'm a convinced National Socialist!' Brillmann's voice was getting desperate now.

'You won't win a medal for that round here,' the sergeant replied, patting the Nazi emblem on his own chest. 'We're all Nazis.'

'Vonwegh is a Bolshevik, a Communist,' Brillmann gibbered frantically. 'He fought against the Führer in Spain . . . he was put in a concentration camp by me . . he can't possibly take over a command here . . .'

Weise grinned.

'You're obviously a strategist,' he said. 'Got something to teach us, eh?'

'Vonwegh will use any opportunity to undermine the war effort,' Brillmann went on, trembling with frustration and growing fear.

'Why don't you tell him that yourself?' the sergeant asked after a moment.

He grinned again when he saw how Brillmann drooped, shrunk in on himself like a cripple. Weise told him to wait, left him standing there, and fetched Vonwegh from Dirlewanger's table. When he came back with him, he pointed to the figure of Brillmann and said:

'He seems to have something against you, Lance-Corporal. Can you make any sense of it?'

Vonwegh went calmly up to Brillmann.

'You wished to make a complaint about me?' he said flatly.

'No,' Brillmann mumbled. 'I really didn't want to . . .'

'Then why come here?'

'I . . . I was afraid. Because of the business . . . because of Karen.'

'In what way . . . why Karen?'

'Well . . . because I . . .'

'Because . . . ?'

'Because I reported her to the Gestapo.' The words came out in a rush.

'And who is Karen?' The voice went on, merciless, seeming to come from a long way off, like the sound of Doom.

'My . . . you know . . .' Brillmann yelped '. . . my cousin . . .'

'Ah, I see,' the platoon leader said, and studied his fingernails for a long moment while Brillmann sweated.

'You denounced your cousin. Why, in fact?' he asked finally.

'Because I . . . because . . .' Brillmann began, then stopped in mid-sentence and stood staring down at the ground, speechless.

Vonwegh waited for a few moments in the silence, drinking in the man's agony and humiliation.

'Go back to the barracks,' he said at last, 'and think about why. And think about it hard. Good-night,' he concluded softly, and the sound was like a striking snake.

Weise watched the man go, thunderstruck, then turned to Vonwegh.

'God almighty,' he said admiringly. 'That's a new method. You'll fit in well here . . . we might learn a few tricks from you . . .'

The killer brigade was arrayed in full glory on the parade ground. On their left stood the scapegoats for the mutiny. They had been selected during the previous night: three from each platoon, with the exception of Vonwegh's.

The whimpering and screaming of Maria, the young Russian girl, gave a foretaste of what was to come for all of them. She was being driven and beaten, half-naked, backward and forward across the exercise area behind them. As she stumbled around, castle-gendarmes were beating her with hide whips, kicking her, then pulling her to her feet again for another run down their gauntlet of pain. The assembled B-soldiers listened dumbly to Maria's torment, not knowing the cruel reasoning behind it; even the most hardened among them felt some slight twinge of humanity, perhaps of shame . . .

The blows, of course, were genuine, but the scene was a set-up. Shortly afterwards, Maria was locked up in the cell with the two other Russian girls, where her task was to ferret out information about partisan movements. In her abasement, in the strange love–hate relationship she had with Dirlewanger, Maria was prepared to commit that kind of betrayal.

And shortly afterwards the men on the parade-ground had another sensation thrust upon them. Paul Vonwegh was nowhere to be found among the rank and file; he marched out and stood to one side of the formation in the uniform of an NCO, secretly feeling like a clown at a funeral.

The special brigade were not sent out on wood-gathering details today, but were retained for an emergency. If Maria's efforts in the cell with the two Russian girls showed any results, there would be a 'partisan operation' later.

After they had been dismissed, Kuberg remained at Vonwegh's side.

'Congratulations,' he said with his urbane, man-of-the-world smile. 'If I am not imposing on you . . . I wonder if we could have a few words . . .'

'Go ahead,' the platoon leader said.

'Well,' Kuberg went on, 'the problem is that I don't really like it here very much. This unit doesn't . . .' he searched for a way of expressing his distaste '. . . you know, I am used to the international scene – Nice, Deauville, Monte Carlo – but this place here . . .'

'No good for business, eh?' Vonwegh finished for him, and had to laugh at this character in spite of himself.

'Thank you,' Kuberg said, unabashed, 'that is precisely the problem. For that reason, I should very much appreciate some advice . . . Herr Vonwegh.'

'Please, continue.'

'You see, I wish to escape. Perhaps you could recommend a suitable escape route . . .'

'I regret,' Vonwegh replied with equal politeness, 'that I am unable to be of service in such matters.' Then he became deadly serious. The joke was over. 'You idiot,' he growled. 'One word of this and you're a dead man . . . finished, understand?'

'Could be,' Kuberg answered smugly, 'but I know you won't pass on what I said . . . not you. In my profession one becomes something of a psychologist, and you are not the type to . . . grass.'

Vonwegh thought for a moment, then shrugged.

'There's a chance,' he said. He listed all the security points to Kuberg and said he could use the information as he wanted to. Finally he said: 'Don't try to escape from here so long as you're serving under me.' He smiled broadly. 'When you've made your travelling plans, I'll make sure you're transferred to another command, is that clear?'

'Don't worry. I'll make sure not to embarrass you in any

way, Herr Vonwegh,' the con man said. 'And thank you very much.'

The platoon leader watched him stroll off back towards the barracks. He shook his head in wry amusement. So now they had their own court jester . . .

Then he went to the dacha to collect the special rations he was now entitled to, skilfully hiding a few extra crusts of bread for his men while he was in the stores. But more important for him in his new position as an NCO was another privilege: they now allowed him to write letters. Perhaps one would get through unopened . . . He wrote the same letter to five different acquaintances. Each contained the same request: to enquire at the Swedish embassy about Karen's fate.

By early afternoon he had finished writing.

Then he had to pack his things together and move them over to the castle. He took his time over it, feeling the atmosphere in the camp; it was oppressive, another lull before another storm.

Nothing moved. Paul Vonwegh was one of the few who knew why the Standartenführer had behaved with such mildness in his treatment of the selected 'mutineers'. His victims had been sentenced only to strict detention, and in the special brigade that was almost no punishment at all. Astonishingly, there were to be no show executions, no floggings.

Dirlewanger, of course, had other worries. The police investigating the attack on the police complex in Minsk had produced a preliminary report of their findings. On the one hand, Prinz's successors were inclined to see the attack as a carefully-planned mission by Russian partisans; but their conclusions left open the possibility that the deed had been carried out by Germans with Russian aid. That pointed to Dirlewanger, who had been the party most interested in removing Prinz from the scene. The Standartenführer was free again, but he wasn't out of the woods yet. Until he was, he would go by the book . . .

*

Maria proved herself as an informer. She managed to pump the two girls she was imprisoned with and bring back exactly the information Dirlewanger needed at that moment – a report of partisans massing in an area where the special brigade thought they had exterminated all resistance.

Dirlewanger sent through an advance warning to Berlin, then sent his ragged cohorts out on the march without waiting for a reply from the capital. Cunningly, he sent two units off in the wrong direction to camouflage his main drive. The main body advanced swiftly under cover of darkness and made their first contact with the enemy just after dawn, when part of Dirlewanger's advance guard was surprised and badly shot up by partisan scouts. Ignoring the safety of his men, Dirlewanger ordered pursuit at all costs and at maximum speed, underestimating the number, tactical skill and weaponry of his opponents.

The killer brigade marched until they dropped, but they were marching into a vacuum. They had long since reached the partisans' camp, only to find it deserted; and they were pushed onwards, engaged constantly by harrying groups of the enemy on their right. Paul Vonwegh was in command there, and he quickly got a good idea of the partisans' tactics: they were obviously drawing Dirlewanger into an ambush.

Vonwegh sent a messenger to the rear and proposed that his platoon wait for the other units to catch up and reinforce them. The first courier was killed by the Russians. The second came back with an unmistakable order from Dirlewanger: 'Thrust forward!'

The B-soldiers stumbled on through the featureless wastes, into the foggy night, over swamps and mushy grassland, constantly harassed by unseen partisan snipers. With every step they took, Vonwegh was more convinced that they were walking into a carefully-set trap.

Corporal Belle led a group on the right-hand flank which included Gruhnke, Exner, Kirchwein, Petrat and a few others. In the dawn light Paul Vonwegh heard shots; Belle's group had reached a hamlet.

When it was fully light, the platoon found itself under concentrated Russian fire. Quickly finding cover, the B-soldiers surveyed the scene: there was a hill ahead of them, with Russian sharpshooters occupying the top and behind the snipers the main mass of partisans. In fact, the Russians had neatly succeeded in cutting them off from Belle's unit, at the same time inflicting a loss of fifteen or so men on the Germans and also threatening their rear. The enemy had thought things out very carefully indeed.

The first platoon was finished – unless they got reinforcements from Dirlewanger.

Paul Vonwegh was staring instinctively over to the right while his men, like cattle round the leader of the herd, gathered at his side.

'Spread out!' he roared – bunched like this, they were sitting targets.

Seconds later, splinters from several exploding shells flew past them. The partisans had started using light grenade-throwers.

'Move!' Vonwegh yelled.

Even to get into a tenable position, they would have to risk a lot. And when you offered yourself to the Ivans, they didn't miss the chance . . .

'Together!' Vonwegh ordered, 'One! Two! . . .'

They jumped out of the sparse cover on the count of three. They had only to go six or seven steps, but even after that there were many who did not survive. When the platoon reached a flat gulley that provided surface cover, Paul Vonwegh realised that he had lost almost half of his men.

Jump, fall, roll, jump . . . Fire came from the left and from ahead. They managed 100 metres, 200. Ten or fifteen men were left as they rushed to the right, frantic, trembling, with aching lungs and hearts that felt like lead. They made it a few more paces, then hurled themselves to the ground to take stock of the situation.

A Russian machine-gun was positioned between them and Belle. And there was neither sight nor sound of the corporal.

'Cowardly swine . . .' Kortetzky cursed.

Near him, half-crazed with fear, lay Brillmann. With one leap, Vonwegh was with them, narrowly dodging the cross-fire from the Russian machine-gun. He handed the gorilla two hand grenades.

'Move . . . there's four or five men up there – get them . . .' He pointed to the machine-gun emplacement. 'Before the rest of the Ivans come . . . we'll give you covering fire.'

Vonwegh smiled bitterly. Two men against a machine-gun. Covering fire – that was splendid, marvellous, and so generous, Heil Hitler!

He watched Kortetzky go, then looked at Brillmann's chalk-white face. Nothing to do but wait, twiddle their thumbs, and hope.

There was a short pause; nothing to be heard from the right; perhaps the Russians had sealed off the circle and were preparing to close in, Vonwegh thought. Anyway, he had no idea how the hell they were going to get out of this hole. He reached for a piece of wood, stuck his helmet on top of it and poked it up over the edge of the ditch. A burst of fire from the Russian machine-gun practically knocked the helmet out of his reach. Vonwegh nodded grimly to himself: this was no ditch, it was a burial plot . . . and of all things he was stuck here with the swine Brillmann . . .

'You too, in a minute,' he said, without looking at the man beside him.

'No,' Brillmann gasped. 'I know what you want to do. You'll send me out there . . . I won't let you . . .'

'You'll go if I tell you to,' the platoon leader said simply. He listened for a moment. If the gorilla had the brains, he would have tried getting at the machine-gun nest from behind.

'On your left!' he called out to Muller. Through his field-glasses he could make out partisans beginning to crawl towards their position.

The fat man swiftly took aim and fired off a few rounds in the direction of the Russians. It was a pretty feeble response, but might just hold them off for the vital minute or two.

'If I chose to order you to make a breakthrough to our right, it would be the end for you,' Vonwegh said, still staring straight ahead in the direction of the enemy. 'But you would have to do it.' He heard Brillmann's laboured breathing and finally turned to him with a clear, hard gaze. 'If you refused, you see, I could shoot you, quite justifiably – I'd be mentioned in dispatches for devotion to discipline.' He lay there, meeting the man's horrified eyes, savouring his terror, then quite suddenly he said: 'What happened to Karen? Tell me . . .'

The man began to whimper, his face contorted like a child caught by a stern parent at some wrong-doing.

'I've already . . .'

'Where is she?' Vonwegh cut in mercilessly.

'Released from normal judicial processes and then . . . then . . .'

'Then what?'

Brillmann seemed to be choking on his words, knowing they could be his death sentence.

'She . . . she . . . went to a concentration camp. I couldn't do anything . . .'

Just then, grenades exploded to their right. Kortetzky was there, firing from the hip, with him two other B-soldiers, knocking the Russian machine-gun position to kingdom come . . .

Chapter Fourteen

The skin on Vonwegh's back felt like corrugated iron. He launched himself forward, driven by the will that sustained him. He dashed ten paces, twenty, with the others following close behind him, hell for leather, driven by the most effective goad a man can know – greed for life, fear of death . . .

They made it over forty metres, and still no response from the Ivans.

Ahead on the left, a man outstripped the platoon leader; Vonwegh had a fleeting thought that it was Kordt, the student. They pressed on for a few more paces. It seemed that the partisans had been thrown into total confusion by Kortetzky's grenade-attack on the machine-gun nest; the shock had given the first platoon a respite, the chance to make some ground, but how much no one could tell.

Suddenly there was crossfire zipping across their ranks. The man on the left rolled forward twice, then lay kicking feebly. Vonwegh crouched beside him. It wasn't Kordt after all, the platoon leader saw with relief as he looked at the dying man.

He hugged the damp ground, wriggling his way over towards a tree stump to his left that would give some cover. Done. Now Vonwegh could half-raise his body, relax . . . the ground became like an eiderdown . . . he was quite small and a long way away . . . and Karen was at his side, smiling, pressing her mouth against his . . . Vonwegh shook himself out of his dangerous fantasy. What were memories . . . ?

The Russians had realised that the Dirlewangers were attempting a breakout; now they were plastering their route with concentrated mortar fire. Metal fragments whizzed past Vonwegh's head, like furious flying insects.

'Forward one at a time!' he yelled, without turning round.

He went first, zig-zagging; three paces, then he threw himself down and rolled, drawing the enemy's fire away from those who were to follow. Somehow he was there, in the middle of this battle, but at the same time he was miles, half a continent away, with Karen . . .

She was in a concentration camp. Karen in a concentration camp, in the 'care' of those SS bitches he had seen in Buchenwald. They were worse than the men – even the most hardened guard was scared of them with their rat's tail hair, flat shoes, flat breasts . . . neuters, rejected by the world, who revenged themselves on normal women every time they wielded the whips they loved so much. Karen would suffer more than most, because those bitches did not have her soft, blonde hair, her fine features, or her full lips; because they could not love, believe, hope, cry, or laugh. Yes, they would beat, kick, torment a woman like her . . .

Vonwegh pressed his hand against the butt of his machine-pistol until the knuckles were white and the veins throbbed with effort. My fault . . . he thought, turning, looking for B-soldier Brillmann, the 'go-between'. No – that bastard's fault . . .

The partisans' rate of fire was rising to a deadly crescendo. They would have to break out further, or be pinned down here and picked off one by one. The platoon leader calculated the odds coolly: if they were quick, and if one stayed to cover the others, half a dozen of them might make it through – maybe more than that, maybe none at all.

He saw Kordt go, with Muller following him, saw the fat man keel over and the glasses go flying as he bumped over the high ground. Vonwegh stayed crouched where he was, waiting for Brillmann, eaten up by envy for the Russian bullet that could take Karen's cousin out of his clutches for ever.

And now he went forward at the same time as the man, providing cover for Brillmann to the left with his own body. In a weird way he had thrown in his lot with the 'go-between'; with every step he risked his life so that the man might live to experience his revenge . . . They both crawled over the same corpse; they lay together in the same shell-hole; the same pain stabbed at their lungs as they stormed on towards safety.

There was fire from the left. It was Kortetzky, covering them, holding off the advancing Russians – no orders, just pure comradely decency. As Vonwegh dragged Brillmann forward, he thought how much more humanity an old criminal can show compared with a Nazi public prosecutor.

Suddenly, Vonwegh realised that they were running into trouble.

'Halt!' he shouted.

Two hundred metres ahead of them stood a small hill. Beyond it lay cover and safety, but in between were only a few tiny hollows; their lives would depend on how much protection they afforded, and the situation didn't look too hopeful. Vonwegh glanced around him. Twelve of them had reached the last ditch before the open ground, and the Russians, seeing their chance, had laid a sweeping barrage of fire in front of them. They were pinned down again.

Vonwegh calculated once more, with the cynicism of the model soldier: if they all went forward at once, perhaps half, at least a third of them would get through.

'Forward on the count of three!' he ordered his men. 'One . . . two . . .'

Just two hours before Vonwegh's remaining men made their life-or-death dash for safety, the right vanguard under Belle had reached the small hamlet they had been aiming for. The place was just a group of four or five Russian farmhouses with low roofs; quiet and peaceful, so peaceful that it had to be a trap.

Corporal Belle surveyed the pastoral scene through his field-glasses. A few Ivans were there; either they had slept through the partisans' warning or they had been kept there to lure the Germans in. As he looked, a horse-drawn sleigh loaded with wood appeared from behind one of the buildings, driven by a bearded *muzhik*.

'Give me your carbine,' said the corporal to the man next

to him. He took the rifle, aimed carefully and shot the Russian straight through the head. As the farmer slumped over the reins, his horse bolted wildly and the sleigh veered off again behind the building, scattering wood in its crazy progress.

Belle grinned with wolfish satisfaction.

'Accidents will happen,' he joked, pulling a face. The B-soldiers around him smiled dutifully.

'Not much going on there,' he said then, jerking his thumb towards the hamlet. 'Get going! Spread out!'

They sealed off the hamlet, moving in at a run in a semicircle, with what weapons they possessed at the ready. Belle positioned himself in the middle, at the fore; he had realised that this was no trap, and the thought of the booty awaiting him had made him daring. As the men fanned out he ran on eagerly ahead of them . . . A shot rang out. The B-soldiers threw themselves to the ground, peering ahead, and waited. Nothing moved. Hesitantly, they got to their feet and began to move forward again. But one of their number had not got up: Corporal Belle.

Gruhnke, Petrat, and Braun, the political, bent over him. 'Clean as a whistle,' Petrat muttered. 'The bastard's finished.'

Who could have killed Belle? It could have been any of them; there was no shortage of hate, or the opportunity . . .

Exner, the chocolate soldier, assumed the command. He wasted no time on Belle's fate; perhaps he wasn't yet versed in the finer points of life with the killer brigade. They advanced again.

The Russian civilians had seen the Dirlewangers approaching and were running from their homes in blind panic. An old man, two women, and one child. Exner killed them all with one burst of fire from Belle's machine-pistol. He decided to ignore the fate of Vonwegh's platoon; Exner wanted to prove he could make it alone, to make a reputation for himself – the sooner he bathed himself in glory and blood, the sooner he would be out of this shit-heap . . . And so they pressed on into the village to loot the houses.

Then, a few minutes later, guards on the outside of the

village gave the alarm. Before Exner had managed to collect his men and get them into position, it became clear that the unit they had seen approaching was the remnant of Vonwegh's platoon. Five men, that was all. Five men.

Who had got through? the men in the village asked themselves as they stared, straining to recognise faces among the tiny, battered band who stumbled towards them. Gruhnke, who had the sharpest eyes, said: 'He's with them'. They all knew he meant Vonwegh, and every man there looked relieved; all, that was, except Exner, who looked across at Grunhke with a kind of puzzled anger.

The five came slowly, heads hanging with exhaustion, carrying two men with them: Kordt, who had been badly wounded, and Muller, white-faced and delirious. By the platoon leader's side hobbled Brillmann, who looked as if he was in a trance. Kortetzky, a grinning, ghost-like figure, brought up at the rear. He had managed, God alone knew how, to get out of yet another fix.

Exner strode up to Vonwegh, ready to report. The platoon leader nodded listlessly, then stopped. Feeling the eyes of his men on him, he drew himself up straight.

'Why did you break off contact with me?' he asked coldly.

'Because we . . .' Exner pointed to the houses '. . . I mean, first we had to . . .'

'Loot,' Vonwegh cut him off. 'And because of that, we got slaughtered – almost the whole platoon . . .'

'Yes, but . . .'

'Shut up,' said Vonwegh, his voice flat and dangerous, 'and come with me.'

The ex-S S officer stayed at the platoon leader's side like a shadow as Vonwegh strode into the village.

They reached the first farmstead, where the dead lay sprawled just as they had fallen. Only the corporal's body, which they had brought here from where he had fallen, was laid out with some measure of order and respect.

'Belle got his,' Exner said hastily.

'So I see,' Vonwegh said indifferently. 'And these here?' He indicated the bodies of four women, two men and a child of perhaps ten years old.

'Russian scum,' Exner sneered.

'Did they shoot at you?'

'No,' Exner answered, puzzled and irritated at the same time. What on earth could this idiot be getting at? They were only Ivans . . .

Paul Vonwegh said nothing, just carried on walking, coolly and quietly, while Exner tried to hang back. The platoon leader motioned him to his side, then nodded as he took in the signs of looting, went on slowly, and finally opened the door to a small room and went in. In the room was a rough wooden cradle. Vonwegh bent over it and saw tucked up in it a child, not more than two years old, lying peacefully on its back with its pale blue eyes open to the world. Between the eyes lay a neat bullet-hole.

Vonwegh turned away and looked at Exner, his face a complete blank.

'Did you do this?' he asked.

'Of course.'

'A partisan, too?'

Exner shrugged.

'Russian scum.'

Vonwegh turned away. 'Make a list of the loot,' he said coldly. 'Anyone found in three minutes' time with even a flint in his pocket will be shot.'

He left Exner standing and went outside. He was feeling shattered, sick; but he forced himself to think of their next move. He had to secure their position and care for the wounded. How many casualties? He bent over the two wounded men: Kordt had a chance, but he was not so sure about Muller. Seeing Kirchwein nearby, Vonwegh took the epileptic to one side.

'Who killed the Russians?' he said quickly.

'Exner,' Kirchwein said. 'Every one of them. Belle was shot from behind . . .'

'Shut up,' Vonwegh cut in. 'You will only answer questions, understand?'

'Yes,' Kirchwein answered, taken aback at the new face of his platoon leader. Shaking his head, he went off to join the others.

Kuberg, the man who had already been nicknamed 'the Baron' after only a week with the platoon, stood staring distantly into space, apart from the rest of them, with Braun, the political, beside him. They weren't made of the stuff to take this kind of action, Vonwegh noted with satisfaction. He strode over to Kuberg and, mimicking his affected style of speech, said: 'Well, Herr Baron, can it be that our little party is not to your taste?' The man stared at him for a second, then turned and vomited. As he went on his way, the platoon leader reflected on the way in which humanity showed itself in the reactions of the stomach . . .

As he walked around the village, Exner approached with his list of booty. Vonwegh stuffed it in his pocket, as carelessly as if it had been a handkerchief. Ignoring Exner then, he went over to Brillmann, who was leaning against the wall of a house, breathing in painful gasps, his face white with fear and nausea. One look from Vonwegh and the man jumped forward; he stood swaying, in a daze, his head jutting forward like a turtle's, his back hollow.

'Stand at ease,' said Vonwegh curtly, 'I have a task for you. I want you to go into the first house there, in which you will find a dead child in a cradle. Fetch it and bring it out to put with the other dead.'

Brillmann lurched like a tree hit by a blast of wind.

'I can't do it . . .' he mumbled. 'Please . . .'

'Are you refusing to obey an order?'

'No, corporal,' the man whined.

'Get on with it, then.'

He followed Brillmann slowly as he went into the house. Gruhnke stood next to him, apparently by chance, his eyes on Exner.

'He shot the child,' he hissed between clenched teeth. 'I'll get that bastard some day . . .'

Paul Vonwegh smiled sadly.

'But first you will go into the house,' he said softly to him, 'and check up on the progress of' he drawled the words 'our lawyer friend.'

Gruhnke nodded and set off while Vonwegh waited by the door. As he stood, a guard came up to tell him that Dirlewanger was on his way towards the hamlet. Then there were screams from inside the house.

A couple of minutes later, Brillmann appeared, pale and sweating, a wrapped bundle under his arm.

Vonwegh stopped him.

'Brillmann,' he said, 'will I always have to send a nursemaid in after you?'

'No, corporal.'

Vonwegh pointed to the bundle.

'You didn't like the order, then?'

'No,' answered Brillmann, his eyes filled with loathing.

The platoon leader nodded.

'Do you know what this is?' he said, staring at the bundle.

The informer made no reply.

'Well, it's called Applied National Socialism,' Vonwegh continued. 'Repeat that after me.'

'Applied National Socialism,' Brillmann said, tonelessly, like a talking doll.

'What are you playing at?' Dirlewanger's voice burst into the conversation, like a hidden snake striking; the Standartenführer had arrived at last, to see their glorious 'conquest'.

Vonwegh turned the question skilfully.

'A bloodless theoretician, Standartenführer,' he said, pointing to the bewildered Brillmann. 'I was just in the process of furthering the practical side of his education.' Then he reported factually: 'Thirty-four men dead, and two wounded.'

Dirlewanger's eyebrows rose.

'How come only two?' he asked.

'The partisans got the others, Standartenführer.'

'Spilt milk,' Dirlewanger said. 'Don't worry. You'll soon get replacements.'

He walked briskly over to stand by the pile of dead Russians. As if by chance, Exner was standing nearby, waiting his cue.

'Hm . . .' said the chief of the killer brigade. 'I can see you've learned fast.'

'Yes indeed, Standartenführer,' Vonwegh said evenly.

'I killed . . .' Exner tried to butt in, eager to cash in on Dirlewanger's favour.

The platoon leader half turned and hit him in the face with the flat of his hand, sending him reeling backwards.

'You will only talk to your superiors when asked,' he said coldly.

Dirlewanger's yellow smoker's teeth were exposed in an approving grin.

'Excellent. Carry on,' he said. 'Take your remnants of past glory back to camp.'

He and his entourage thrust purposefully on. No time for idle chatter: He had to give the Reichsführer concrete results.

It was homecoming for the first platoon – in so far as thirteen men could be called a platoon and a shabby barrack-room could be called a home.

Vonwegh managed to ward off Müller-Würzbach's attempts to find work for his men to do, and so they were able to put their feet up and play a few hands of cards.

The platoon leader himself was waiting for news. It had been fourteen days since the last field post had gone from Lahuisk, and he wondered how long it would have taken. He imagined that any replies would go from Berlin to Warsaw, then via Minsk to Lahuisk. Or would they go via Kiev? And could partisans have got hold of the mail sack, or ambushed the train, or . . . ? Vonwegh pulled himself together and willed himself to 'switch off'. The important thing for the moment was to work on his plan, keep moving towards his goal. Exner had to go, that much was clear; and then there was the business of Brillmann. The rest of the platoon – even Petrat – were behind him on both those issues.

Vonwegh was sitting in a quiet corner of the barrack-room when, after days of silence, Kuberg sidled up to him and started on his old line again:

'I hope I'm not disturbing you?' the con man asked.

'Not at all, Herr Baron,' Vonwegh replied with a smile.

'I don't want to detain you for long,' Kuberg said with an acknowledging nod, 'but the fact is that I can no longer beat about the bush. I intend to take my leave of this place.'

'I congratulate you on your optimism,' Vonwegh rejoined wryly.

'I have my own methods,' the Baron continued. 'However, I don't wish to make any difficulties for you. Please tell me when it suits you for me to make my escape.'

Vonwegh thought for a moment.

'First of all, I give formal notice that I forbid you to run away,' he said. 'However, if you should decide to contradict my order, then please do so only on a day when Brillmann is on guard duty, understand? Brillmann – no one else.'

'Thank you for your advice, Herr Vonwegh,' Kuberg answered gravely. With that he bowed and left the room.

As the platoon leader watched him go, he noticed Kirchwein wandering up and down in front of the barracks, obviously agitated. Vonwegh moved to the window and motioned for the epileptic to come over.

'What's up?' he asked.

'I have to make a report to Weise,' Kirchwein said bleakly. 'Otherwise he'll . . .'

'Don't talk shit,' Vonwegh rasped.

He looked at the epileptic, then the solution occurred to him.

'Come with me,' he said quietly. 'I've got something for you.'

The two of them walked off in the direction of the kitchen barracks, with Vonwegh talking insistently as they went. At first Kirchwein seemed to hesitate, then he nodded reluctant agreement.

'Is everything clear?' the platoon leader said.

The epileptic nodded energetically.

'OK,' Vonwegh said then. 'Now send me Gruhnke and the gorilla.'

When the two came, they seemed quicker on the uptake. And as B-soldier Exner watched them from the shadows, he had a nasty feeling they were hatching something against him. It was a remarkable thing about Exner: no one liked him, but no one dared do anything against him. The truth was that they all realised that he was made of the stuff that meant success in Dirlewanger's empire. A man like him, a cold fanatic, who killed out of principle, would come to the Standartenführer's notice sooner or later, and when he did he was guaranteed a career. They had all started like Exner – the Weises, the Belles and the others . . .

Vonwegh came back to the barracks with Gruhnke and Kortetzky to find a human tangle on the floor; a whole bunch of men were giving a thorough pounding to some unidentified victim at the bottom of the heap.

'Cut it out!' the platoon leader bawled, and then he realised that it was Brillmann that they were beating up. Maybe, without fully intending to, he had stirred up their hatred of the man too far; this wasn't the way he intended the 'go-between' to get his deserts.

The B-soldiers took no notice until, at a sign from Vonwegh, the gorilla waded in and tore them off their victim with his great spade-like hands. Brillmann lay sprawled on the floor, his face pummelled almost beyond recognition, his eyes closed, in a real or feigned faint.

'On your feet, you pansy,' the platoon leader said contemptuously. 'You don't seem to be too popular, as I suppose you may have noticed.

'I think you have to learn some discipline,' Vonwegh continued. 'Otherwise you'll stand no chance here.' He thought for a moment and then smiled. He didn't take 'Baron' Kuberg too seriously, but nevertheless he would give him a chance.

'From now on,' he ordered, 'you will take night guard. See

if you can at least make a success of that.'

When the brigade returned from an anti-partisan sweep three days later, Vonwegh had laid all his latest set of booby-traps. If things worked out the way he intended, they would all explode silently during the night.

That evening there was a big party in the castle. The whole kitchen staff were mobilised to Dirlewanger's dacha to keep the food and drink flowing. These days the entertainment consisted of fifty-six nubile Russian girls, none of them under thirteen or over twenty. The Standartenführer knew what a host owed to his guests, and he was not a man to stint on quality.

Eventually the orgy began to tail off as the guests became unconscious or incapable, but only one person left before the end: Sergeant Weise, who had an appointment. He had drunk almost as much as he could take when he walked out of the dacha, but when he had talked with B-soldier Kirchwein he sobered up very quickly indeed.

Weise would have liked to have acted immediately; the Standartenführer, though, was in no fit state to be consulted. The sergeant decided it would be best to leave the matter until the morning.

Meanwhile, a man in the uniform of an S S staff-sergeant was seen hurrying through the corridors of the castle. As he left the dacha, the two castle gendarmes in front of the gate noted the stiff correctness of the man and saluted smartly.

'Do you know him?' one asked the other.

'Never seen him before,' his companion said.

Shortly before midnight the man in the sergeant's uniform passed the guard post on the outer perimeter. He was written into the log as staff sergeant '?'. The sentries thought he must be one of Dirlewanger's drinking-companions. The Standartenführer was fond of showing outsiders his little kingdom.

Morning.

'Into line! roll call!'

The officer on duty had them do it again. Then he finally established that there was actually a man missing: Kuberg. He kept quiet about it for half an hour while an on-the-spot search was mounted and then reluctantly reported the disaster to Weise, who had just discovered that his best uniform was missing, stolen from its cupboard in his quarters. Vonwegh was the first to put two and two together. My respects to you, Herr Baron, he thought; I'd never have believed you had it in you . . .

An hour after the discovery of Kuberg's disappearance, every B-soldier knew that the Baron had pulled off the impossible. Most of them thought he couldn't get far, but they were wrong: the Dirlewanger brigade never saw him again. Months later, it was rumoured that he had been arrested and convicted in Berlin, posing as a war-hero . . . and that he had escaped again, this time disguised as a prison guard and for good.

Dirlewanger was dragged out of bed early, which after a night like the previous one was bound to mean bad news for someone. He sent for Vonwegh straight away.

'Filthy trick!' he bellowed, his crow-like features contorted in rage. 'If this story gets around, we'll be the laughing-stock of the army. Have you found out who was responsible?'

'Yes, Standartenführer,' Vonwegh replied impassively. 'B-soldier Brillmann was on guard.'

Dirlewanger nodded. 'Get the man,' he ordered.

Vonwegh had not yet left the castle when he was summoned back into the Standartenführer's presence. The platoon leader smiled to himself as he turned on his heel and headed back into the depths of the dacha: his second booby-trap must have gone off. When he arrived, Weise was with Dirlewanger, and both men looked grim.

'Your platoon again, Vonwegh,' Dirlewanger said baldly. 'Another case of shitting in our own nest. A man in your bunch has been to say that I . . . I killed that bloody fool of a policeman, Oberst Prinz.'

'Yes, Standartenführer,' Vonwegh said, trying to match

Dirlewanger's theatrical look of righteous indignation. 'B-soldier Exner.'

'You knew that?' Dirlewanger exploded. 'Then why the hell didn't you tell me?'

'I have made a report, Standartenführer . . . in writing, through the official channels.'

'Go and check that,' he ordered Weise. A few minutes later the sergeant re-appeared with Vonwegh's report in his hand.

'For God's sake, Vonwegh,' Dirlewanger said quietly. 'Forget about red tape when it comes to things like this. The man could have started a terrible scandal.' Then he carefully read Vonwegh's signed report, which named Kortetzky and Gruhnke as witnesses.

Exner's 'trial' was extremely brief. When it was over, Dirlewanger called the 'standing bunker' Kapos into his office.

'First twenty-five lashes,' he said. As he spoke he blinked his eyes, and something in the way he did it meant the death sentence. 'And I think that our friend Exner may well get an inflammation of the lungs very soon,' he added.

Two weeks later, the former S S Untersturmführer left this life with as little ceremony as the Russian civilians he had massacred with Belle's machine-pistol . . .

Life – if that was what it could be called – continued at the killer brigade's camp. Two months after Exner's death, Himmler was still undecided about what to do with Dirlewanger. The investigation of the Minsk explosion had found rumours of Dirlewanger's involvement, but no concrete proof, and all the time the Russians, victorious at Stalingrad, were pushing west – the front was coming closer to Lahuisk. Every unit was needed to help resist the Soviet steamroller; the partisans were multiplying as they scented victory; Dirlewanger was becoming a valuable man now, and that helped to tip the balance in his favour. His brigade grew, in spite of its horrifying casualty record.

After 20 July 1944 and the attempt on Hitler's life, the barracks threatened to burst at the seams. The Gestapo was pulling in anyone who might conceivably threaten the Third Reich, and now there were more and more political prisoners being drafted along with the criminals. There was a different atmosphere. It was then that Paul Vonwegh was put in charge of a company and met old friends from Buchenwald again.

Chapter Fifteen

By the summer of 1944, the war in the East was totting up a death-toll without precedent in human history. In the sultry, burning hell of that summer, it was as if the Second World War, now drawing to a close, was out to show what it was still capable of. Suddenly the Russians were outside Minsk, and Dirlewanger's base had become part of the immediate war zone.

Hitler had ignored the lesson of Stalingrad, where he had lost 300,000 men through his refusal to allow a retreat. Now, more than a year later, his stubborn order to resist at all costs was speeding up the inevitable collapse of the German armies. Even in this sector of the front, irrational fanaticism was preventing the organisation of a second fortified line of defence which might have held the Russian onsurge. Disintegration was well under way in Minsk now. Stragglers blocked the roads. Supply-lines were cut by the Germans' own combat-groups. Tanks ran out of petrol. Units wandered about without direction. Everyone was looking for a bolt-hole, a way out, some hope to cling to. Most of their comrades had gone; those who were left simply wanted to survive.

Fear affected officers and other ranks alike, turning the army into a classless society. Sappers and infantry, military police and S S, clerks and murderers, heroes and so-called cowards – everyone swam frantically with the tide, and bad luck to those who couldn't keep up, because no one would hang around to help. The retreat was reaching a terrible, destructive climax; the last, bloody act of the Third Reich was about to begin.

The Red Army was preparing for its final push. The men in its ranks now were no longer the same Ivans who had been crushed, massacred or taken prisoner in their thousands in the victorious German advance of '41. The Red Army was tired and had been terribly mauled, but hatred spurred it on: what the Soviet troops had seen as they liberated their homes had given them all the strength they needed. For a year now they had stormed forward, over the unmarked graves of thousands of partisans – the results of what Dirlewanger had reported to Berlin as 'successful missions'. They had passed through burned-out villages, where nothing had been left alive. They had spoken to men and women who could no longer laugh or cry. They had no further need of propaganda or Commissars – and they knew that the most hated S S unit of all, Dirlewanger's Special Brigade, was trapped in Minsk.

Marshall Zhukhov had put a price of a million roubles on Dirlewanger's head, but it was unnecessary. There was not a single Red Army soldier who wanted anything more than to catch the infamous torturer of his people.

As for Dirlewanger himself, he prospered. Promoted to S S Oberführer and decorated for his 'services' against the partisans, he had already taken precautions against being trapped with the remains of his brigade in Minsk. To be fair, his personal courage could never be questioned, sadist and gangster though he might be. He would risk his own neck if need be; it was just that he did not see his B-soldiers as human beings, merely as pawns in the military game, totally expendable cannon-fodder. So it was that he flew from Minsk to the village of Kadi in Western Poland when the Russians began to surround the city. At Kadi he took charge of the replacements for his 'lions'. If his old B-soldiers escaped the inferno at Minsk, then good luck to them; if they stopped a Russian bullet, then that was all right, too. There was, of course, the added advantage that dead B-soldiers couldn't be called on as witnesses to his past atrocities . . .

Meanwhile, the remnants of the brigade fought on in Minsk, trapped by the Russian advance, engulfed and hampered by a swelling tide of refugees, fighting for their worthless, ragged lives. Mown down by murderous enemy firepower, crushed under advancing tanks, recompense was coming to the men who had spread terror through occupied Russia for so many years.

By the second day of the chaotic battle, a third of the brigade was either dead or wounded. The next day they had broken through the Russian ring and were heading hell for leather westward, but the losses had been even more terrible: Paul Vonwegh's No 1 Company was no longer a functioning unit. It was a situation of complete chaos, one that he, the Third Reich's strangest S S NCO, had long dreamed of. Now he might have had his opportunity to rise, to take aim, and to blast the system he hated.

But the time was not ripe. The Russians regarded the Dirlewangers as murdering cut-throats without exception; they could not know that the Nazis had deliberately coupled criminals and sadists with political dissidents like Vonwegh. The fate of any German soldier who fell into Russian hands was a miserable one, but a member of the Dirlewanger brigade would stand no chance of making it even as far as a prison camp; he would be strung up on the nearest tree if he was lucky, and if not his death might take a good deal longer . . .

All the B-soldiers knew what to expect from the Ivans, and they retreated like crazed animals in a wild obstacle-race over the dead and wounded. Death was the time-keeper, and they broke all records.

They reached the edge of the 'Minsk Cauldron' and weighed up their chances, which were miserable, but they fought on. They attacked, they died or got through, or disappeared; they stumbled on, clutching their guts, nursing their raw, bleeding feet, driven by a horror and desperation that even dissolved the hatreds within their ranks and created a weird comradeship that verged on heroism.

After Minsk, they clung on at Lomska and defended it so desperately and so bravely against the Russians that every one of them deserved to be decorated as a hero. But the high-ups could stuff their medals; the Dirlewangers just wanted to stay alive, nothing more or less. They had hung on to life with animal determination, even when they were being whipped or forced into the 'standing bunker'; they had hung on to it with every heartbeat, with every fibre and sinew of their being, and they were not going to give up now . . .

Vonwegh recognised that he was no exception. His bones were not made of rubber, nor his hide of leather, and even the burning hatred inside him couldn't stop his lungs from bursting or his legs from threatening to collapse. There was no idealism now; what kept him going was an instinct for self-preservation that disgusted him but was, he knew, absolutely essential – as if this most sordid and ruthless of human feelings were also the most extreme affirmation of life.

They went on running. They were the first in and the last out of Lomska. Then, as if some dark god had suddenly taken charge of their fate, they had the luck to meet up with a motorised supply column which gave them a ride to the rear, out of the battle zone. Finally they could rest, count and take stock. There were just over thirty of them left alive. More dribbled in from the front. Gradually life resumed its normal pattern; Vonwegh became hard again, and Weise strutted like a black-clad turkey-cock. There were orders, thin food, blows.

A few days afterwards, the B-soldiers who had broken through the Russian encirclement reported to Dirlewanger's headquarters at Kadi. They limped into the camp in complete silence; they had made it, but there was no strength left for cheers. Breaking out of Minsk had been a brilliant military feat, but no one was interested. It had been a tactical and fighting achievement which would not be quoted in any histories or military training manuals. Nobody wanted to know whether these jailbirds were heroes or not, because nobody wanted to have to admit that prison scum could put on uniforms and carry the nation's honour like regular soldiers.

So they arrived, a weird, terrifying sight, exhausted, crippled, emaciated wrecks with no flesh on their faces, no life in their eyes, no guts left, no backbone, unable even to march in decent file. Women ran screaming at the sight of them, and children cried in terror.

Dirlewanger's recruits stood at the edge of the camp and gazed on the remains of his old brigade in silence. A stocky

Saxon cracked a joke, and those around him laughed in weird, cruel relief. Then there was a sudden barked order and they all jerked to attention.

S S Oberführer Dirlewanger had appeared.

He stood in the gateway, obviously displeased that today his old lions were not marching in step, singing, or even acknowledging his presence. He counted them and gazed down their pathetic ranks with a stare that held interest rather than sympathy. He nodded to Vonwegh, clapped the wounded Müller-Würzbach on the shoulder, and shook Weise's hand with genuine pleasure.

'Is that all of you?' he asked tersely.

'Yes, Oberführer,' Weise said.

'They really made a good job of you, didn't they?'

'Yes, Oberführer.'

The recruits were still standing around, their eyes bright with fear.

'Now, you lot!' he rasped, with a sour laugh. 'Now you've had a foretaste of what the Ivans have in store for you.' He waved a bony hand in the direction of the weary remnants from Minsk. 'It's kill or be killed!' Dirlewanger licked his lips, as if in eager anticipation.

Then the Oberführer took a look at the survivors. Petrat was there, and Kortetzky the gorilla: the unit's two heavy-weights, and both of them wounded.

'Now,' he said, 'have a bit of a kip . . . but make it a quick one, lads.' For a moment his voice had been almost kind, but now he raised it again, as if ashamed of his weakness. 'The struggle for Germany's destiny allows no respite!' As he was about to go, he noticed that the fifth man in the second rank had fallen asleep on his feet.

'Idler!' he bawled, his face contorted with rage. 'I'll have your guts! Take that man's name!' he said to Staff-sergeant Müller-Würzbach. With that, the survivors from Minsk realised that they had come home again. Vonwegh stood to one side, his mind fuzzy with exhaustion but oddly under control. All he could think of was the fact that Brillmann had escaped him; he had fallen into Russian hands, and Vonwegh hated them for it.

He began to count up those he had left to him: Braun, the political; young Kordt; Gruhnke, and one or two others. It was not much, but it was something.

Because of Brillmann, Vonwegh realised, he had neglected the most important part of his plan: communication with the Russians. He would have to overcome his men's fear of the enemy before he could make his move; they must be sure that a mutiny on this side wouldn't get them hanged over there. There was still so much to be done, and he had allowed his vendetta with Brillmann to deflect him from his plan. He had wasted his hatred – he should have made his revenge quick and clean, instead of savouring it all for so long. The realisation brought new clarity and determination for Vonwegh. If Brillmann were here now, he would make an end of him and get on with essentials.

Now, back in 'normal' circumstances, Vonwegh was the boss again, the one his men looked up to, who fixed things for them. He turned to survey them and was amazed to see a man with one leg hobbling towards him. He was even more surprised when he realised that it was Muller, the fat man with the glasses; he had been badly wounded weeks before, and Vonwegh had managed to swing it so that he got proper medical treatment in a decent hospital. Now here he was, reporting back again without a leg . . .

'I volunteered,' he told the company leader.

'Have you gone crazy?' Vonwegh bawled at him.

'I'd rather be with you,' Muller said, unabashed, 'than in a concentration camp . . .'

Vonwegh left him standing there. That same day he tried to work a miracle with Dirlewanger: he requested that Muller be released from the killer brigade and sent home.

'Are you out of your mind?' Dirlewanger hissed incredulously when Vonwegh reported to him.

'No, Oberführer,' the company leader said calmly. 'I was thinking that if word gets about . . . it will do wonders for the men's morale.'

'This isn't the Salvation Army,' Dirlewanger snarled. 'That kind of thinking's too clever by half.'

Vonwegh decided to use the language that a pillar of the Third Reich might understand.

'It will be more use than a hundred hangings . . .' he countered.

Vonwegh's ploy worked. Dirlewanger smiled, and Muller was discharged the same day. Vonwegh saw him later, sitting on an upturned box, crying like a child, and kept out of his way. Muller wanted to thank him and refused to leave the camp until he had done so. It was only when Weise, now promoted to S S Obersturmführer, threatened to have his discharge cancelled that the fat man left camp.

Muller's release became a legend. The B-soldiers looked up to Vonwegh as if he were a saint who could work miracles. He let them believe it; he used it, and he waited for his opportunity.

At last four more survivors from Minsk made their appearance: three of them, carrying a fourth whose soft, beardless face was ashen grey and seemed old, though the man was barely out of his twenties. Vonwegh had seen them coming from a long way off. As they reached the gates, he went up to them and bent over the wounded man.

The recognition hit him like a bolt of lightning.

As Vonwegh slowly straightened up, he felt himself shudder. Fate had delivered his enemy back into his hands. The wounded man was B-soldier Brillmann.

The first shots fell in the centre of Warsaw. A German patrol was mown down by well-aimed fire from a nearby building. This in itself was nothing unusual: during the last few months, with the Russians approaching, the Polish Resistance had been stepping up hit-and-run attacks in the capital. What was strange this time was that the attackers did not disappear; today a crowd gathered, and men carrying weapons began to occupy surrounding houses. Starting from that flashpoint, a spirit of wild purpose spread through the city. A few minutes after the patrol was ambushed, the sirens wailed and police units roared through the surrounding streets, only to find barricades in their way and rifle fire being directed against them. The police withdrew, or were caught in the centre of the city to be picked off by the Polish freedom-fighters. It was 1 August 1944, and the Warsaw Rising had begun.

It was the second time that the Polish capital had seen open rebellion against the Nazi occupiers. A year before, the Ghetto had confronted S S formations in a ruthless battle to the death; Jewish men and women due to be shipped off to extermination camps had preferred death in open war to a humiliating end in the gas-chambers. That time, the revolt had been crushed with ruthless brutality, ending in agony and self-sacrificing courage.

Now the moment seemed to have been better chosen. The German Army Group Centre had been convincingly defeated and was in headlong retreat. Warsaw was already close to the main battle front: the Russians were on the far bank of the Vistula, and the first Red Army units had fought their way into the northern Warsaw suburb of Praga. With the Russian approach, more and more German army units had been withdrawn from garrison duty in the city and hurled into the battle, leaving their control of Warsaw dangerously vulnerable. As the first exchanges of the revolt began, it was no longer a question of disturbances among an isolated section of the population; this was a general rebellion, one dictated not by fear and desperation but by the careful strategic planning of General Bor-Komorovski, commander of the 'Polish Home Army'.

The uprising spread from the centre to the outer districts of the city like a forest fire with the wind behind it. Suddenly, from nowhere, appeared an army of fifty thousand guerrilla fighters willing to die for their nation's honour. The Nazis had treated the Poles as sub-human vermin for years, enforcing a bloody policy of deportation and genocide; now the dam had burst, and the lust for freedom was surging through the heart of an oppressed nation.

For the German army, it meant a war on two fronts; just

as they were attempting to construct a viable defensive line, the enemy appeared behind them. The Wehrmacht's high command, appallingly stretched in its resources, was in no position to take sufficient counter-measures against the rebellion. Himmler, who had recently been placed in command of the Reserve Army by Hitler, was left to 'deal with Warsaw' in his own way, and he preferred to entrust the suppression of the revolt to the hands of his proven S S generals, murderers like Bach-Zelewsky and Reinefarth. They in turn called upon men they knew were right for the job: Dirlewanger's and Kaminski's killer brigades. With that decision began what was probably the cruellest episode of the Second World War; practised sadists and gangsters were offered unlimited licence to loot and rape in a proud, beautiful city.

As Oberführer Dirlewanger prepared to move his men into Warsaw, he was well pleased. It was like the black fulfilment of all his wildest fantasies.

Basic training was carried out practically in the firing line, at express speed. The newcomers were drilled until they could hardly stand. The previous day they had been chased around the training area in gas masks until ten at night, then given another two hours' insults and beatings. By the time they fell on to their straw mattresses, many of them had been too weak to undress. Dirlewanger was determined that his dream of direct front-line action would see his men as fighting heroes, and he wanted no mistakes.

Now the whistles were being blown again, piercing the dawn. The B-soldiers staggered up and tumbled out. Fall in! Before they could sort themselves out on the parade-ground they were sent back to reappear in full marching gear. A convoy of trucks with police number-plates arrived in the morning light. The drivers and their mates were silent and sullen-faced.

No. I Company was at the head of the convoy. Vonwegh had managed to keep his original men as a sort of 'personal staff'.

Opposite him now was Brillmann, still suffering from his wounds – obviously longing to escape, but too much of a coward even for that. Petrat, on his left, was looking gloomy. The gorilla was asleep. Young Kordt was there, too; he had become a hard, reliable character.

The company leader's mind was not on his men this morning, however. He had received a letter the day before, his first answer to the many he had sent out so many months ago. From it had he learned that Karen was now free; she had been released from a women's concentration camp, apparently due to the intervention of the Swedish embassy. Her present address was unknown.

Vonwegh was torn between anxiety and relief.

Behind them and in front, the situation was confused. To the rear, the sky was on fire; ahead they could hear the thunder of shellfire. As the B-soldiers looked at each other, fear flickered in their eyes. They sat in silence, unnaturally still, their faces glistening with sweat, waiting for something to happen. Petrat was the first to crack: he suddenly jumped up, tore aside the canvas screen at the back of the truck, then turned and screamed:

'They're going to court-martial us! They're taking us behind the lines to be shot . . . !'

Kordt looked at him with contempt.

'Shut up,' he muttered.

'They're scared, you see,' Petrat said frantically. 'First they order us to kill the Russians . . . then they don't want anything to do with us . . .'

'Rubbish,' Gruhnke said firmly, and Petrat seemed to get a grip on himself. 'The main thing is we're on the right road,' he continued, with a tight smile. 'It's in the direction of home.'

'But slowly,' Kordt chipped in acidly.

'Every little helps.'

The convoy jolted on. Vonwegh and Brillmann met each other's eyes for a moment. The company leader's face was expressionless, but the 'go-between' had an imploring look. Vonwegh spat neatly on the floor between them and craned round to read the names on the streets. They were passing through a working-class district.

'Warsaw,' he said, turning back to the others.

'What the hell are we doing here?' Petrat asked stupidly.

Vonwegh didn't need to answer. The fighting was so close that they could distinguish the sounds of individual weapons: machine-guns, anti-tank guns, mortars and pistols. The convoy halted suddenly. As the B-soldiers leapt out, they found to their shocked surprise that Dirlewanger himself was there to meet them, a contented smirk on his face.

That should have been a warning to them, but the opening stages of their deployment in Warsaw seemed harmless, even comic. They reached Dluga Street in some confusion and took cover, only to find that they had to wait for Dirlewanger to go and fetch the orders of the day from Reinefarth's mobile headquarters.

To their left was a hospital, and it was from the hospital building that their first direct experience of fire came when isolated shots started to get through into the courtyard where they had taken cover. A couple of the First Company crawled over to the wall to take a look and were relieved to find that it was not they who were being fired on. Some S S troops had driven twenty or so nursing sisters from the hospital out into the yard and were standing the white-faced women up against the wall. Their white aprons made the women's faces seem corpse-like in their pallor; some had flung themselves to the ground and were pleading with their captors, while past them hurried nervous-looking young soldiers carrying cans of petrol. An Untersturmführer was bawling at them to speed things up. Shots could be heard from inside the building, too. Then came more soldiers, driving sick and wounded men before them with rifle-butts.

Vonwegh saw what was happening and stepped slowly to one side. He knew what was about to come. He could avoid seeing it, but he could not shut out the sound. First one volley, then another, followed by inhuman shrieks of pain and terror. Some of the sick and wounded were being burned like living torches. Vonwegh noticed that some of Dirlewanger's new recruits were watching, fascinated; he felt nausea in the pit of his stomach and walked on. But there was no escape from the massacre: as he came to a crossroads in the driveway he saw patients lying on stretchers, and at that moment their captors opened up on them.

'Get a move on!' he heard a cold voice say. 'Petrol, a match, then on to the next one . . .'

The cries became fainter, weaker. Weise came up to Vonwegh, stopped for a moment to take a lingering look at the butchery and smiled.

'Taught 'em a lesson, eh?' he said. 'We're really giving those bastards a hard time.'

Vonwegh nodded mechanically, as he knew he must. He felt a searing pain in the back of his head, but outwardly he stayed cool and calm.

Weise, still glancing at the scene in the hospital yard, continued talking absently to Vonwegh, for all the world as if he were trying to conduct a conversation while watching a concert in the park.

'What was I going to tell you?' he said. 'Oh yes . . .' he added quickly, 'there's something you might like to know. This friend of yours . . . Brillmann . . .' Suddenly he had Vonwegh's whole attention; the company leader looked at Weise sharply. 'Well,' the newly-promoted Obersturmführer went on, 'there's been an enquiry from the Reichssicherheitshauptamt about his whereabouts. Apparently they want to recall him now that he's learned his lesson.'

'What?' Vonwegh said, totally taken aback.

Weise smiled unpleasantly.

'You heard me right,' he said. 'If you want to settle your account with the swine, you'd better move fast. There won't be much time.'

Then they both whipped round as they heard the familiar predatory croak of their chief's voice. He was back from headquarters.

'What are you doing hanging about here like idiots?' Dirlewanger screamed, pointing at the hospital yard with his swagger-stick. 'Get in there and lend them a hand!'

The Special Brigade's participation in that bloody massacre of the innocent was their first task in the 'pacification' of Warsaw. And however appalling an atrocity it may have been, it was just a foretaste of the horrors that Reinefarth's combat group were to inflict during the days to come.

Chapter Sixteen

The lust for freedom that coursed through the Polish capital in those first days of August, 1944, was as burning and deadly as a stream of lava, and just as impossible to stop. The eruption may have seemed blind, but there was military organisation behind it. The Poles had been waiting years for this day; for this moment they had hoarded supplies and hidden weapons, had risked their lives and suffered unspeakable tortures.

The Russians were to the north of the city, and the Germans held on to the eastern suburbs. In the rest of Warsaw, everything was a frenzy of national feeling; no one asked who would win, only that for a few hours, days, weeks, they would be free. The streets were barricaded, and the Resistance was busy turning every house into a strongpoint. During that heady, desperate lull, rumours ran wild.

The chief of the Special Brigade had just finished bawling out some of his men, sending them off whining like craven dogs as he so enjoyed to do. He turned to Weise with a grin.

'Those arseholes haven't got enough to do . . . yet,' he said. 'Oh well, maybe tomorrow – Rome wasn't built in a day, and Warsaw won't be knocked down in a day either . . .' He guffawed at his own wit, and Weise joined in dutifully. 'There'll be schnapps arriving soon, and then we can enjoy ourselves,' he added. Noticing Vonwegh, Dirlewanger clapped him affably on the shoulder. 'How's things?' he asked the bemused company leader. 'Loosen up a bit, Vonwegh. You're an intellectual, so you should know how to enjoy the finer things of life.'

'Quite correct, Oberführer,' Vonwegh answered, impassive as usual.

Grunting with satisfaction, Dirlewanger stumped off. He was happier than he had been for a long time. No need to hunt *muzhiks* in the backwoods; no more calls to round up chickens; no more kidnapping children and burning villages . . . he had got what he had always wanted – a direct engagement with the enemy, and the chance for his cut-throats to shower their leader with some real glory.

A couple of B-soldiers dragged up a case of turnip schnapps, and there was a general stampede towards the alcohol.

'Easy . . . easy . . .' Weise bawled good-humouredly, taking his cue from the Oberführer's sunny mood. 'There's plenty for everyone . . . anyone would think that stuff was the be all and end all of your miserable lives.'

Ignoring the scramble for schnapps, Vonwegh walked away from the others. He had gone only a short distance when he saw Braun standing distractedly against a wall near the entrance to the yard. The 'political' was staring fixedly at the spot where a boy had finally collapsed as a human torch after they had poured petrol over him and left him to die slowly.

Vonwegh touched the man's arm and tried to draw him away.

'Don't think about it,' he said gently. 'There'll be worse to come.'

Braun still did not react.

'You have to try to stop it getting to you,' the company commander continued. 'But look . . . and wait . . . and remember.'

No reaction.

Then suddenly: 'No. I can't do that.'

'Snap out of it,' Vonwegh said insistently. 'There's no point . . .'

'I can't go on with this gang of killers!' Braun shouted suddenly, sweating and breathing heavily like a man in a fever. 'We're all guilty – all of us!'

Before Vonwegh could try to quieten the man, they heard Dirlewanger calling them together from the other side of the yard.

'Come and listen to this!' he was yelling. 'Gather round!'

Braun's eyes grew to great saucers of despair, and he had to support himself against the wall.

'What's going on over here, Vonwegh?' Dirlewanger bawled, taking a few steps in their direction. 'Oh no, the man's not going to puke, is he? Give him a drink . . . anyone else going to have a breakdown?'

Nobody moved.

'Well, hear this,' the Oberführer said, forgetting Braun in his boundless delight. 'I tell you, this is a red letter day. Are we lucky?'

'Yes, Oberführer,' the B-soldiers mumbled in unison.

Dirlewanger threw them a satisfied leer and dragged a piece of paper out of his uniform pocket.

'Active service orders,' he announced importantly. 'From Reichsführer Himmler, personally. Written in his own handwriting.' He raised his voice as he read from the document: 'You can do what you please with the Poles. Nothing is forbidden!' He snorted in triumph and put the orders away again.

'Well, that sounds about right, doesn't it? Music to all your ears, eh? Something to work for at last – so long as you get results, anything goes. And what you can get, you keep . . .'

'Yes sir,' they all chorused, with the enthusiasm of true thieves.

Sneering, Dirlewanger ran his eyes over his 'lions'. Most of them had already made good headway with the schnapps. He let them enjoy a few minutes more of pathetic celebration, then chased them into the city, heading for the centre and their appointment with 'glory'. He drove them mercilessly, taunting, needling, turning them into rapacious wolves. But wolves hunt in packs and kill by instinct: Dirlewanger had to use alcohol to get his killers into fighting trim . . .

As they marched at the double towards the battleground, Petrat wore that nervous grin of his. Kortetzky loped like the half-ape he was, still never quite understanding what all this was for. Brillmann hung on to Dirlewanger's every word like a model pupil. Vonwegh watched him and resolved that he would be going with the next batch into the next world. The 'go-between' had been sent for by security headquarters, but he was not going to be deflected from his revenge now. The security boys could have him, but they would get him dead...

Vonwegh's mind was full of revenge, but his eyes searched for Braun. The 'political' didn't seem to be anywhere near.

'What you have to do,' Dirlewanger was shouting, 'is to take things gradually, but make sure you finish the job. No one is to be spared. Best to use the butt and save ammunition, understand?'

'Yes, Oberführer,' they yelled back.

'Anyone who doesn't follow that order gets stood up against a wall for wasting government property,' he grinned. 'In one hour we go forward to take over the vanguard,' he added. 'We'll be tearing straight into them – the straight road is the shortest! Our brigade is the most successful unit here... so . . .' he tipped the peak of his cap to them '. . . grand celebration in Warsaw town hall tomorrow night!'

With a wave of his hand, Dirlewanger dismissed his troops. 'Company commanders to me,' he growled. Then he saw a column of Polish civilians passing, escorted by S S troops.

'Röttenführer!' he called to the officer commanding the escort. 'Where are they going?'

'To be shot, Oberführer.'

Dirlewanger nodded approvingly. The civilians straggled on. In the rear was a woman with a young child. The child in her arms was smiling, oblivious of the guards threatening them with their rifle butts; it obviously thought this was all a game . . . They had half a kilometre to go to the park where the firing squad was based. Anyone caught was shot, irrespective of age or sex – eight hundred victims a day was the lowest figure accepted from the execution platoon . . .

'Now then, Vonwegh,' Dirlewanger said, returning his attention to the company commanders and taking a hefty swig from a hip-flask of schnapps. 'You will take the left wing and give covering fire.' He turned to Weise. 'You take the right, and remember: don't miss a single house . . .'

A dispatch-runner from an infantry unit was asking where

he could find the force commander. Müller-Würzbach shrugged. Reinefarth was riding up and down the front line in his mobile operational headquarters: where could you start looking?

'What's going on?' Dirlewanger asked when he saw the two men talking.

The runner snapped to attention and rattled off his enquiry.

'What do you want General Reinefarth for?' the Oberführer asked.

'There's an anti-tank gun,' the runner answered, still panting from his dash across the battle-zone. 'It's got us pinned down, and we need artillery support.'

'Pansies!' Dirlewanger exploded with contempt. 'Shitting your pants over a few Polacks with a pop-gun!'

Ignoring the astonished infantryman, he called over to his own section commanders:

'Cigarettes out . . . get ready to move!'

Then he looked back at the runner.

'Do you know anything about my brigade?'

'No,' the man said, more bemused by the minute.

'I thought not,' Dirlewanger snorted. 'Well, I'm going to give you a demonstration. Artillery, you say?' He turned to Vonwegh and Weise. 'Take the flanks – we're going straight down the middle!'

Just then, a shot rang out nearby. Everyone else thought it was an attack and dived for cover, but Vonwegh had his own ideas. He ran at a stoop towards the house the sound had come from. In the passage lay the body of a man, its face covered in blood and almost unrecognisable. Almost. Vonwegh took one glance and it was enough; there was nothing he could do. The dying face he had seen was oddly gentle and peaceful, in spite of the gaping, ugly wound in the forehead.

Braun, the 'political', had ended it all . . .

Defensive positions in Warsaw were street barricades, cellars, ruins, tombs, holes in the ground. This was not the kind of situation they wrote about in the military textbooks. It was impossible to speak of 'flanks', useless to consider giving effective covering fire. The front was where the firing was – and they were firing from every possible direction, from every hole, from behind every shattered wall.

But the killer brigade stormed in regardless, led by Satan himself and inspired by schnapps. They didn't have far to go before they made contact with the enemy; half-way down the next street, the B-soldiers ran into a group of infantrymen who had been forced back by witheringly accurate Polish fire.

'Our turn now!' Dirlewanger said triumphantly, and set to making his dispositions.

Weise had already started working his way down the houses on the right, while Vonwegh was combing through the buildings on the other side of the street. Without waiting for them to report, Dirlewanger pointed straight ahead and his men, properly armed for the first time in the brigade's history, tore on into battle, in packs, eyes bloodshot and brains fuddled by drink, with fear incarnate stalking behind them. Thirty metres . . . forty . . . the Poles let them come. Then the first concentrated volley sent them sprawling on to the paving stones. Many didn't get up again. Seeing the survivors crawling frantically towards cover, Dirlewanger grabbed a machine-pistol from someone and levelled it along the street, swinging the weapon from the hip and bawling like a maddened angel of death:

'No retreat! Get on with it, you cowardly bastards!'

The B-soldiers got to their feet like puppets and went forward again, straight into another barrage from the Poles. Then the others came, the second wave, stumbling over the corpses. Dirlewanger drove them on, like cattle through a minefield, taunting, shrieking, threatening, to gain a few blood-soaked metres of Warsaw ruins. The Poles didn't waste a single round; they recognised the crazy attempt at breakthrough for the piece of lunacy it was and brought up reinforcements. It was more like a pigeon-shoot than a battle against soldiers . . .

Dirlewanger called for reinforcements. On the right, Weise had encircled a deserted ruin. Contact with Vonwegh had been lost. The Oberführer shrugged and prepared to send the next batch into action. An engineer officer who had been separated from his unit saw it all and made a desperate attempt to call the brigade chief to his senses.

'This is madness,' he told Dirlewanger. 'We've called for armoured support. Can't you wait for half an hour?'

'Bugger off if you haven't got the stomach for it!' Dirlewanger snarled.

From his position in the hallway of a shattered house, he slowly raised his right arm to signal to the waiting men.

'On the command "Go", move!' he bawled. He turned to his adjutant. 'Give me another drink.'

The Oberführer took the flask, drank in great gulps, then spat out what was left. 'Now we'll show what we're made of,' he said. Waving his machine-pistol at any of his men who were not quick enough to jump up, he counted and cursed. There were too few, and he would have to wait for reinforcements after all. Even he could not make bricks without straw.

It was then that he noticed the engineer still standing there, a contemptuous smile on his face, and Dirlewanger's whole attitude changed again. He shook a finger at the Wehrmacht officer:

'Now watch this, Captain,' he spluttered. 'I'm going to show you something you'll never learn in any military academy. You're going to see how my lions fight. If the rest of the Wehrmacht had guts like theirs, we wouldn't be retreating on all fronts,' he added venomously, hurling his cigarette end into the blood-clogged gutter. 'And now we'll have five bottles of schnapps on it that we'll have knocked that anti-tank position flat in ten minutes.'

With one bound, Dirlewanger was among his men, urging them into action. In the first ten metres he had lost his bet as murderous fire from the anti-tank gun and the massed rifles of the defenders cut a swath through his brigade. Out of his mind with fury and schnapps, Dirlewanger tried to force what was left of his unit on again with kicks and blows, scuttling among them in full view. He had to dive for the paving-stones himself at one point under fire, but still he remained unhurt. It was almost uncanny how that storm of fire kept on and on, but never touched the monster who stood in the middle of the street, a sitting target; as if fate were saving him for the hangman . . .

Still Dirlewanger would not give up. He drove his men on yet again, against incredible odds – maybe because he was a deadlier enemy than all the Poles put together. An insane, sneering smile contorted his hawklike face as he yelled and cursed. Whatever happened, he would not be the loser: either his bunch of cut-throats would destroy the enemy as he had ordered, or some German executioner would be saved a lot of trouble. Either way it was no more than these men deserved.

'Go!' he bawled, and ran forward again.

The defenders were taking careful aim, as if they were on a rifle range. Every shot found a victim; they could have handled two or three times the numbers without any trouble. To make it over the remaining ground up to the skilfully-constructed Polish position would have cost at least another two hundred lives. It was a price Dirlewanger would have paid without compunction for the piece of 'glory' he lusted after. His cannon-fodder was delivered free of charge, by dignified judges in white linen and black robes who carried out their instructions, however criminal and shameful, and asked no questions . . . men whose conscience would come alive only many years later – ready to shelter behind the idea of 'justice' when it came to dealing with Nazi murderers.

Direct hit from the anti-tank gun. Four men blown to pieces.

'Keep going!' the Oberführer screamed at a man who had no face left. Two red holes stared at him out of a black mass of torn, burnt flesh, and out of the face that was no longer a face tears washed tracks in the dirt. The B-soldier was weeping. The man who tasted Dirlewanger's kicks, who now cowered in the road like a dog, was Petrat – the first platoon's hard man, the murderer with the death sentence over him . . . a complete animal, and now a whipped cur. He had curled himself into a ball and was pressing his mangled face into the paving-stones, ignoring the shots coming from all around him, rolling slightly with each touch of Dirlewanger's boot. The tears were still pouring from him. Occasionally he would glance up quickly, but still all he saw around was death: flames surrounding him, flashes in front of him, death and destruction pouring from every rat hole, like a medieval nightmare of hell's torment. Then, just as Dirlewanger's boot caught him in the small of the back, Petrat seemed to gain a last lease of manic strength. He reared up, and Dirlewanger's next kick hit him on the back of the head, making him bite half-through his tongue.

'Filthy swine!' Petrat gurgled. There was a crazed hate on his ruined face as he lurched to his feet like a goaded bull, his only desire to kill, to hit out, to avenge . . . Stretching out his hand to take Dirlewanger by the throat, he looked in shocked amazement at his knuckles, perforated by a Polish bullet; he couldn't believe it – this couldn't be happening to him, Petrat, the indestructible, the hard man . . . The East Prussian's retarded mind finally snapped under the strain. Everything suddenly seemed flaming red in those tiny swollen eyes, in that shattered casing of flesh and bone: red bursts of fire, red flashes; every inch of ground was swimming in red; his hand was red; and so was his fear, his hatred, the skinny, malevolent figure in front of him. That redness was the last eruption of the fire he had carried around him all his life – the world had disappeared behind a curtain of red, and he would never see it any other way . . .

Insane with bloodlust, Petrat rushed at Dirlewanger, crazily eager to have something to grasp at, something with which to appease the fatal force of that redness before it finished him off. Bursts from the machine-pistol sent him careering back, arms and legs splayed. As he lay kicking out the last seconds of his life on the blood-soaked pavement, others joined in. But by this time Petrat could not see anything any more. He couldn't see that his own comrades were shooting him down like a rabid dog . . .

*

While the main part of the brigade was in action, the left flank remained ghostly quiet. But Paul Vonwegh refused to take it for granted. He had split his men up into commando groups to make a house-to-house search, keeping Kordt, the gorilla and Brillmann with him. He could trust the young ex-student, and he knew that Kortetzky was devoted to him. As for Brillmann, he wasn't going to let him out of his sight for a second.

Vonwegh's group had already combed through four buildings, which seemed to have been left deliberately as a kind of *cordon sanitaire* by the Poles. Still nothing stirred. Vonwegh and his men seemed to have struck lucky again; as for the company commander himself, he would have welcomed some action, because silence gave room for his conscience to operate, and that was the last thing he wanted . . .

An eery silence, with only the faint sound of fighting from the main street in the background. Music off.

Suddenly, there was a cacophony of shots from their right. Vonwegh's men returned the fire and moved forward at a stoop towards the house where the shots had come from. A minute later, he heard inhuman screams from women and children – a different kind of music, the theme tune of '44. 'My' men, he thought, and for a moment he felt like following Braun, the political. It would be so easy . . . Sharply, Vonwegh pulled himself together.

'Find out what's going on,' he ordered the gorilla, and immediately the man had left he knew he had made a mistake.

Brillmann shot him a sidelong glance, then lowered his eyes. Vonwegh seemed to glimpse a secret knowledge in that soft face. He nodded to himself: you will not get back, my friend, he thought, and at the same time a deep weariness, a sense of bitter failure came over him like a fog.

The surprise attack that followed came suddenly. The house they had stormed turned out to be a carefully-laid trap, and soon they were being fired on from every direction. Kordt was checking to their left as they dashed for safety. Vonwegh, followed by Brillmann, ran towards the shelter of a nearby shed, tore the door open, checked quickly inside, hearing more shots, more screams. Then, when he jerked round, Brillmann was nowhere in sight. With a shudder of realisation, Vonwegh saw that he had taken one risk too many; at that moment he was alone, terribly alone, and it was then that he saw the world break up into a fiery kaleidoscope, disintegrating as if in slow motion, as the beam cracked down on his head and he knew it was over, dissolving into darkness . . .

S S Oberführer Dr Oskar Dirlewanger, having just realised that his breakthrough attempt had failed for the fifteenth time, was seriously considering retreat. To his left, Vonwegh's men were engaged in house-to-house fighting. On the other side of the street, Weise, the bloodhound, was using his time as he alone saw fit. As Dirlewanger surveyed the slaughtered cattle he had once called his 'lions', he fumed and spat with rage, but even he knew that they would have to wait for artillery support whether he wanted to or not. The order was given for the remaining men to regroup under cover.

'What's Weise up to?' Dirlewanger bawled impatiently.

'Carrying out a mopping-up operation,' his adjutant said.

'Sounds good,' the chief muttered with an edge of sarcasm. 'And where's Vonwegh hiding himself?'

'Vanished into thin air.'

'Then find him,' Dirlewanger barked sullenly. He motioned to his faithful castle-gendarmes. 'Come along,' he said. 'Let's visit good old Weise . . .'

He grinned his hawklike grin and stumped off, making for the right. For a moment he was out of cover, and a couple of shots howled past his head. Dirlewanger nodded contemptuously and walked on.

He reached the entrance hall of a house on the right side of the street, following the signposts of screams and shots. Weise, it seemed, was in his element . . .

As it turned out, Weise had joined up with Kaminski's brigade, a bunch of thugs combed from the Russian underworld whose atrocities finally were to become so notorious that even S S General von dem Back-Zelewski, Himmler's plenipotentiary in charge of suppressing Warsaw, later had to bring their commander before a firing-squad.

In Wolka Street the Poles were driven ruthlessly from their homes in the tenement blocks. About five hundred people, begging for their lives, were herded off the roadway and into Sowinski Park, where they were separated by sex. The first salvos hurled them against the iron railings. Among the victims was the Szlachter family from number 129: a father, a mother, and four children.

The next burst of fire threw the mother to the ground. She lay among the dying and the dead, holding the hand of her youngest daughter, who was still just alive. Murderers in S S uniforms without insignia trampled over the corpses, checking and finishing off those who showed any sign of movement. The woman risked a fearful glance and saw one of the S S men kick someone lying near her; another went up to a pram and shot her neighbour Jakubckzy's twins, who were only a few months old. All around her as she lay were the groans and whimperings of the dying. Nearby under a statue, the entire population of the municipal flats in Elekcyjna Street was liquidated by S S firing-parties. Some hours later there came an S S soldier who gave her daughter the *coup-de-grâce*.

By the evening, as Mrs Szlachtera crawled slowly away, only corpses lay in the park. She found neither her husband nor her son, and never was to know their final fate, but she saw the corpses of her other two daughters. The broken woman was the sole survivor of her family – and the only human being to live through the bloodbath of the Sowinski Park.

Having completed their work in the park, Weise and Kaminski moved on to the Ursus factory, also on Wolka Street. What happened there was described under oath by Mrs Zofiaz Staworzynska, a survivor, in these bleak words:

'Since 1941 I have been living in Warsaw at number 18 Wawelberg Street, in flat twenty. On the 5th August 1944 at about 1 p.m., S S troops accompanied by Ukrainians appeared in the courtyard and ordered all the occupants of the block to leave immediately. There was a terrible crush, which soon turned into sheer panic. Everybody, even the children, had to hold their hands above their heads like captured criminals. I left the house, along with my eleven-year-old daughter, Alina, along with others from our block – about 150 people altogether, I suppose. Then we were lined up in front of the factory, family by family. The gate stood open, and as I came closer I could see great mounds of corpses piled up in the factory yard and hear the sound of shots and screams. Nearby were other groups of civilians, and it was clear what the Germans had in store for us. Soldiers in uniform were herding groups of Poles into the yard, and after an hour our turn came.

'I went with my daughter and two other children, who had hung on to me for protection. Once in the factory yard, we stumbled over bodies which were lying around the area in all sorts of grotesque and horrible positions. We saw S S men and Ukrainians firing shots into the backs of people's necks with their pistols. I asked one of the men, who was stroking my daughter's hair – she had beautiful hair – if they would set us free. He turned to his comrade, but the other man would not agree. He just pointed at us and said, "Polish bastards".'

'My daughter gripped my hand and we went towards the wall. While we were on our way, more shots were fired at us. The first hit me in the neck; I fell and was hit three more times, once in the hand and twice near the heart. My daughter collapsed by my side. Shortly afterwards I heard another shot, and after that my daughter did not move any more.

'In the meantime, more groups of Poles were being brought in; how many, I cannot say. I heard awful shouts and screams, people imploring the Germans, wailing, and shots. How long that went on for I do not know, because I was hardly conscious. In the pauses between the executions, S S soldiers would walk around the heaps of corpses, finishing off the wounded . . . it was in that way they killed my daughter and a person lying in front of me . . . and then they would rob the corpses of their valuables. When they clambered over me, with their heavy boots, they broke my left hand, the wounded one, and my right hip. They pulled a ring off my finger. In the evening it became quiet again . . .'

That is the evidence, from a woman who survived and lives today, indistinguishable from millions of others except by the inner scars that will never heal. The truth of that evidence is proved by photographs. Her sober words, dry as eyes that can cry no more, have reverberated throughout the world. As for the atrocities committed by Reinefarth's combat group, whose nucleus was composed of the Dirlewanger and Kaminski brigades, the storm of rage and shame that went up all over the world went unheeded only in the S S General's native country. After the war, Reinefarth was installed as mayor of his home town and a parliamentary deputy, a pillar of the new West German society. Perhaps it had something to do with the fact that the Public Prosectuor in charge of the case against him refused to hear a single Polish witness . . .

Paul Vonwegh came to quite slowly, almost hesitantly, like a drunkard who has passed out and is trying to struggle back to consciousness. His eyes took a while to accustom themselves to the half-light; the pain in the back of his head hammered brutal morse-signals into his mind. Vonwegh had no idea how long he had lain there, or what had happened: there had been an explosion behind his eyes, knowledge of a blow, and that was all.

His senses clouded over again. A couple of minutes, or maybe a couple of hours later, he was wrenched back to life by nearby firing.

Still feeling as if a pneumatic drill were grinding away inside his skull, Vonwegh tried to raise himself, then had to fall back again. But he was tough; his extraordinary energy was beginning to return.

What was the time? The company commander tried to look at his watch, which was on his left wrist, and realised that he couldn't move his arm. He had been wounded in his left side, just below the shoulder. Reaching over with his right hand, he groped down the left of his body with the cool objectivity of a scientist.

Was that the only wound? Why just one shoulder? A grenade must have been tossed into the building, bringing the beam crashing down from the ceiling on to him. The beam had knocked him out, but it had also protected him from the impact of flying debris. The wound had thus been confined to his left side. But he was surprised he didn't feel anything; whether it was bruising or something worse, his left shoulder felt numb, almost dead.

Footsteps? No: the shots were further off. Vonwegh thought he heard women crying desperately for help, but maybe he was deceiving himself. He ought to sleep; his mind was feeling very strange, tossing up strange images that were not part of this hell . . .

The pictures disappeared from his mind, and the pain roared back into him like an inferno. The footsteps were quite clear, no mistake, no illusion. And Vonwegh simply could not move. Who could it be? Someone looking for plunder, perhaps? Or Poles looking to finish off wounded Germans? It wasn't the gorilla, he thought; Kortetzky's steps were heavier, steadier. It couldn't be Kordt, either; he usually walked at a brisk pace. It could have been the laboured movement of Kirchwein, the epileptic, of someone exhausted, or of someone moving carefully, wanting to kill . . .

With the pain, Vonwegh's vision seemed to sharpen, and he saw that the room was much lighter than he had thought. He saw a pair of legs, a belt buckle, a chest and shoulders, a face . . .

B-soldier Brillmann hadn't seen Vonwegh yet. He was carrying a submachine-gun slung over one shoulder, peering around the building, inspecting the place where the roof was still standing. The man lit a cigarette, then tried to straddle a concrete block to sit, found it too uncomfortable, and stood up again with an irritated sigh. It was then that he noticed the trail of blood. Brillmann came closer and recognised the company commander.

Slowly his soft, boyish face filled with a cold joy. He hesitated for a moment, saw that Vonwegh was in a hopeless position, then listened intently and glanced around to make sure that they were alone.

'This is a surprise,' he said, pulling over a nearby packing case and seating himself alongside the trapped Vonegh. 'Just the right place for you, Herr Vonwegh, don't you think?'

The company commander closed his eyes. The end, he thought; it's all over, and it's my own fault. This bastard wasn't going to play games.

'I can guess what you're thinking,' Brillmann said, blowing a careful smoke-ring. 'You should have done it, Herr Vonwegh. You had a hundred chances, but you were too proud, too sure of yourself . . . you wanted to subject me to some mental torture first. You are a fool, Vonwegh,' he hissed. 'You'll never learn the way the world really works.'

Vonwegh was far away. He kept his eyes on Brillmann, but his face was pale and expressionless. No one could have guessed the physical agony he was going through.

'You wanted to use the criminals to finish me off . . . oh yes, that's the way you planned it, Vonwegh . . . Lately your strategy was based on the assumption that the guerrilla was more honourable than I . . .'

He's seen it, thought Vonwegh. Brillmann had been cleverer than he thought, at every turn of the screw.

'You're a dreamer, Vonwegh,' the other man went on, 'a typical German idealist. That's why you went to Spain – and lost. That's why you thought you could educate the criminals in Dirlewanger's gang.' Brillmann paused, grinning maliciously, and nodded his head in the direction of the street. 'Listen to the screams,' he said. 'Petrat, your friend the murderer, was shot down like a dog when he went berserk out there. Kortetzky, your gorilla, is much too busy looting to bother about you.'

Suddenly they both heard footsteps. Brillmann jumped to his feet, took a couple of steps, looked outside, waited for a moment and then came back.

'No need to worry,' he said. 'Our little chat still has a while to run.' Brillmann paused for thought, trying to remember where he had got to in his speech. 'Yes, those were the people you trusted, Vonwegh,' he continued then. 'If you had helped get me out of all this, it would have been child's play for me, with my connections, to get you a discharge.' He rubbed his hands together and stood up. 'But you wanted your little personal revenge, didn't you?'

Brillmann gave a twisted smile and came nearer. With reluctant admiration, Vonwegh realised that there wasn't a hint of schnapps on the man's breath.

'That would have been the only possibility, if you had helped me,' he continued, his voice thick with suppressed emotion. 'But then there's the other thing. You see, you have never undertsood that I'm not a National Socialist. No, I'm not a Nazi, but I'm not a fool either.' The man's face was calm and satisfied now. 'I know that the war is lost,' Brillmann went on, 'and that soon we're all going to be accountable for our actions.' He bent low over Vonwegh and lit another cigarette, savouring his knowledge that the wounded man was smoking every drag of it in his mind.

'In that way,' Brillmann said thoughtfully, 'it's been quite a good thing to have been sent to a punishment brigade. I have now been persecuted by the Nazis just as much as you have, Vonwegh. I'm a martyr, too . . .'

For a moment there was uncertainty in Brillmann's eyes. Still the company commander refused to answer.

'Still too proud to speak to me?' he hissed. 'Come on, Herr company commander, that's not very comradely . . .' Then Brillmann's look hardened, as if he realised that the time had come, that he had spent too long on enjoying the moment. 'I think it's time to end our little chat, anyway,' he said, unshouldering the submachine-gun, 'and on my terms.' He came to within point-blank range of the wounded man's face and levelled the gun.

Now, as his life shrank to the distance between him and the weapon in his enemy's hand, Vonwegh felt a relief, a surrender, a gladness that the struggle was almost over. An almost pleasant drowsiness came over him; his features relaxed and he felt light-headed, almost merry. The mask of superiority that he had worn for so long began to fall away. In that last moment, he would conquer, and above all he would keep his eyes open and face his enemy when the time came.

Then, with a sudden sharp shock, the peace disappeared. Karen . . . the word erupted out of the burning ache in his head, hammered through his temples, sweeping like a sheet of fire into his consciousness. Karen . . . her fate was the one unsolved question, and it was that thought which gave Vonwegh new strength, forced him back into the struggle when death would have come as a deliverer . . .

As always, the news came through clandestine channels, perhaps from some weird collective consciousness. And as always, the rumour had an anonymous author and a mass circulation. Whichever way, it spread like a fever: Warsaw was in revolt, and the German army had been driven out of the Polish capital. To the female prisoners at Ravensbrück concentration camp, it meant that the war's end was drawing closer.

The women had stood for hours on the inspection-ground, waiting for the beatings, or the 'investigation', or some new trick to torture them. Their life had no meaning, only the system had an existence of its own; they were no longer individuals, just a mass of numbers to be tormented and slaughtered when the system decided.

It was drizzling that day, but they ignored the rain. The season in the calendars was summer, but for these sexless wrecks who had once been women it was always autumn, late autumn, and their world was grey.

A number was called out: 3013. A four-digit number. To those who could still find the energy to work it out, that meant someone who had been nearly two years here.

From the first rank a pathetically thin figure moved forward, but no one felt pity. They were all horrifyingly wasted through malnutrition, and anyway what room was there for emotions in this place? Who could tell apart pity and contempt, fear and hope, good and evil . . . ?

No one looked at number 3013 as she stood there. Apathy had destroyed human curiosity in this place; there was no future, no end, no new beginning for these women. Ravensbrück was here, now. That was all that mattered.

You could still tell that number 3013 was young, even pretty, despite everything they had done to her. She was subjected to the same enormities as the others, lived under the same conditions, was no older than most of them, but somehow everything seemed to have glanced off her. She had an inner power that resisted the physical reality of Ravensbrück, that kept her womanly and feminine.

Number 3013 had reported to the orderly room many times before. At the beginning as a newcomer, with a mixture of fear and hope; hoping for help, and terrified of the beating she knew might be waiting for her there. Like all the others, she had hoped and starved, cried and hated; she had gone through all the levels of this hell, from rebellion to despair, from rage to resignation. But she had never sunk into the killing lethargy that afflicted so many of her fellow-prisoners, the self-anaesthesia that turned them into shambling automatons.

Number 3013 was different. She lived in an illusion, but it was one that gave her strength. She had an ideal, and it was stronger than despair. Number 3013 had come into the women's camp on account of a man. On account of Paul Vonwegh.

Karen's head had been shaved; she had been given a number and put among the grey masses. She had overcome her shock at this place quickly, and she had understood something that she had never been aware of before – that in the past she had been jealous of a force in Paul Vonwegh, one that shaped his being and character. As a woman, she had found it hard to come to terms with it, for at times it seemed more important to him than she did. Now Karen had joined his fight, for at last she understood the force in him: it was what put him on the other side, against women having to carry four-digit numbers, and the fight was so that women might once again have a name, a face, a wish, or a dream.

Karen was far away from the man she loved, but, curiously, she felt closer to him than ever before. In some mysterious way she felt a secret radiation coming from him, though she had no idea whether he was alive or dead. Perhaps that was what made her so similar to him, immune to the filth, the fear and the hunger. The guards gave 3013 a wide berth; even the lice seemed to spare her. Karen went along with those around her, but somehow she was always alone. Inside, she would be with Paul forever.

Now number 3013 had reached the orderly room and stood before the creature who was responsible for the paperwork of death. With this woman, a twitch of the eyelid, a heavy intake of breath, a word too many, or an ill-timed smile could mean torture, deportation to a field brothel, or transfer to the vivisection laboratory. This crone, who in normal times wouldn't have been put in charge of a public convenience, held the power to inflict the most appalling degradations that could be inflicted on a woman, mentally or physically. And she enjoyed showing that power – by maiming women's bodies, or by throwing them as a reward to the kapos in the criminal concentration camp. Karen had managed to avoid both these fates until now. Had her time come? She could not know, but as she looked into the pale, piggy eyes of the woman behind the desk she knew how to hide her uneasiness. Her features remained as expressionless as those of Vonwegh whenever he faced Dirlewanger.

'Here,' snarled the guard. 'Sign this.' She shoved a form across the desk to number 3013, and Karen noticed that it had all been filled in except for the name at the bottom. 'Pledge of Silence' stood in crude, turgid letters above a declaration that was typical of the system, which swore number 3013 to keep secret all procedures of the camp. Karen thought slowly, clearly, rationally, and with a shock realised that it meant discharge, freedom.

Many would have thought it a miracle, but Karen was long past believing in miracles. She knew that some invisible hand had intervened behind the scenes, and she hoped that Paul might be involved, too.

Still 3013 showed no reaction. The guard watched carefully with her obscene, lifeless eyes, like a voyeur. She said nothing, but her face held a volume of words, most of them hateful. Perhaps the woman really did wish to redeem herself in some small way – but more likely she regretted not having sent Karen to the S S doctors when she had the chance.

Karen signed.

'There,' said the guard, pointing to an adjoining room.

In the room were two men and a woman. They spoke matter-of-factly, with the usual bureaucratic jargon. Karen was given a rail ticket, some money, civilian clothes and an instruction to report at regular intervals to the police in Berlin. They asked her whether she had 'reformed', and she answered 'yes' without hesitation. These people could not know it, but her answer had not even had to be a lie.

Things went quickly from then on; there was no feeling of transition. Karen took it all without emotion, letting everything happen and wash over her with an almost inhuman discipline. As they walked her to the main entrance she was cool and controlled, like a marble Venus. To her astonishment, a car stood waiting for her at the gate. She realised that she was to be driven as far as the station, so that she could not have the chance to speak to anyone in the local town. It was a fine way to go: when they set a slave free, it meant first-class treatment all the way. But then maybe it didn't cost them too much in petrol – after all, such events were few and far between . . .

As they reached the main gate, Karen was suddenly aware of the full weight of her body, pulling her down like lead. The light of the real world dazzled her, as if she had just come out of a dark tunnel. She felt nausea rise from deep within her and had to hold on to the gatepost for support; she swayed like a drunk while the clean air filled her lungs. Freedom robbed her of her senses, and all she could feel was a profound and terrible fear.

They pushed Karen into the car as if she were a rag doll, and the driver sped away. As they drove she did not dare look out of the window. She just lay back in the car and cried, because she was free, she had a rail ticket to Berlin, and she had not the slightest idea what she was going to do . . .

Time stood still, like a stagnant pool of water. Paul Vonwegh didn't know how long their eye-to-eye duel lasted as they faced each other in the fashion of fighting dogs, sizing each other up. Then, suddenly, the dark gaping muzzle of the gun disappeared from Vonwegh's view. For a moment the puzzled platoon commander thought his eyes were playing tricks on him, then he realised that it was fear that had caused the gun to waver out of his vision. B-soldier Brillmann killed better in theory than in practice.

Vonwegh had not yet realised the full extent of Brillmann's terror, however. All he saw was a man standing in front of him, hands clutching the gun butt and trigger, desperately trying once again to fire. Nothing stirred outside now; the suburb of Wola had subsided into the stillness of the graveyard.

Now, thought Vonwegh; he felt a course of mental energy welling up inside him, preparing to take the shock; he drew himself up, although he could not move his legs, and stared straight into Brillmann's face. The killer cringed before Vonwegh's gaze, though the company commander was helpless. If B-soldier Brillmann pulled the trigger now, no cock would crow for Paul Vonwegh, no dog would bark an accusation to the world . . . but still he did not fire, though he must have known that he had to, or die himself . . .

Brillmann's hands were clammy with the sweat of fear and indecision; his index finger was so stiff, almost brittle, that he was afraid it would break. Under any other circumstances, his situation would have been ridiculous, but here and now it was uncanny. Fate, the thought was racing through Brillmann's brain – a leftover from that fine humanistic education of his; he was like the slave from the tribe of the Cimbri who let his sword drop because he could not bring himself to kill the old Consul Marius . . . Christ, it was laughable – even now, all that stuff was coming back to haunt him . . .

Footsteps were filling the silence. Paul Vonwegh heard them first, and his hope rose like a geyser. Now Brillmann heard them too. He raised himself as if in slow motion, walked a few terrified steps, and aimed his weapon towards the entrance of the ruin. This would have been the moment to make his play, to knock the machine-gun out of his grasp and finish Brillmann off, but Vonwegh suddenly felt his left shoulder pull at him like a great lead weight, deadening his body and his will.

There were more footsteps: four, five men. Soon they could hear their voices, and the voices came nearer. For a moment it seemed that the men outside were discussing whether to bother to come into the ruin. Brillmann stood like a man under a spell, then managed to shake himself out of his torpor and threw himself on Vonwegh to clap a hand over the wounded man's mouth.

Vonwegh summoned up his final reserves of strength and will. As Brillmann's fingers closed over his mouth, he clamped his jaws tight shut. With a scream of agony, Brillmann whipped his hand away, and in the moment this gave him Vonwegh yelled as loud as he could:

'Gorilla! Kirchwein! Kordt!'

Had they heard? There was no time for thought. Now Brillmann had his weapon back in his hands; his finger was curling savagely round the trigger; in his pain and fury, he was going to be able to manage that final shot . . .

But at that moment they were already there: Kordt at the head, then Kortetzky, wearing that docile grin of his, behind them the others. Brillmann stood paralysed once more, unable to believe what had happened. He watched dully while they dug him out, saw how the mountain of rubble on his shoulder began to disappear. After a minute or two, his enemy would be free once more – free to stand in judgement, to condemn quickly and without ceremony . . . Brillmann staggered to his feet, and a rattling sound came from his throat, as if he were trying to gag out his own terror. The gorilla glanced at him, then gave him a vicious punch in the small of the back.

'Don't just stand there,' he growled. 'Give us a hand shifting this lot.'

And Brillmann, ever the obedient model pupil, joined his clammy hands to the work that would mean certain death for him . . .

Chapter Seventeen

The night which fell on the tormented city knew no peace, no dignity, no sleep, and no mercy. Flames licked across the face of Warsaw, destroying the jewel of Poland, turning hope to ashes. But Warsaw would fight on, to the death.

Where was the Red Army?

This fateful question ghosted through the shattered city, from garret to garret, from cellar to cellar, like a cruel prayer. Had General Bor-Komorovski ordered the attack too early? Were the forward Soviet units in the northern district of Praha too weak to come to the aid of the Resistance? Or had the ancient hostility between Poland and Russia dampened the Soviets' desire to risk their lives for the sake of rebellious Warsaw? Rumours were already beginning to spread that Stalin had ordered the Red Army to stay its hand until the Germans had knocked the spirit out of the Polish nationalists. After all, today's resistance fighters could become tomorrow's partisans when he was master of a 'liberated' Poland . . .

During that night, with its deceptive calm, no one asked too many questions. The wounded were cared for, munitions were replenished, emplacements were cleared and new ones set up. The Resistance radioed desperately for help from the Allies. The free world held its breath – and did nothing.

For Dirlewanger's brigade, the front line was also their headquarters. Only now did they tot up the casualty lists, and they were frightening. But the supply of reserves held steady. Sergeant Müller-Würzbach, who had been sent out to the western edge of the city to keep supplies flowing, had just sent in a couple of hundred newly-pressed B-soldiers, untrained recruits without uniforms or arms. They would do.

'They come straight from the jails and the camps,' the adjutant commented edgily when he saw them arrive, 'and they don't know one end of a gun from the other. Shouldn't we . . . ?'

'Rubbish,' interrupted Dirlewanger. 'They can use their rifle-butts well enough . . .' he added, with a peal of laughter that was as dry as parchment.

Dirlewanger's humour tonight was strictly of the bitter variety. For him, the darkness seemed to go on forever. Even his evening bottle of schnapps had done nothing to cheer him up or relieve the strained impatience that wracked him. Earlier during the night he had sent a scouting party out to weigh up the chances of mounting a surprise attack, but the patrol had reported that it would be no good trying to break though. The Poles had set up powerful searchlights which would turn any battle into a massacre.

Dirlewanger cursed and waited. Artillery support was out of the question. The Luftwaffe existed mainly on paper. Somewhere in the vicinity were a couple of obsolete German tanks, and the special brigade had been assured of their help, but they had not turned up.

Outside Dirlewanger's makeshift headquarters there was a lull in the noise of battle. In that moment, the Oberführer thought he heard a woman's voice, a cry for help. It had become such a commonplace sound of war that Dirlewanger hardly bothered to listen to it any more. So a couple of tearaways had attacked a Polish bitch . . . Any other army in the world would have shoved the culprits up against a wall straight away, but here criminals were in charge; rape was a unit of currency, part of the B-soldiers' pay.

The Oberführer yawned and decided it was time to stretch his legs. On impulse he decided to take a stroll over to the ruins from which the screams had come. He had been right – a couple of his men were wrestling with a whimpering, half-naked woman among the rubble. Dirlewanger chased them off with a few well-directed kicks and regarded their victim.

Though horror disfigured her face, she was young and pretty. Her name was Johanna Krynski, a doctor, and she had been hiding in a cellar when Dirlewanger's 'rats' had discovered her. She did not yet recognise the face of her saviour.

'Thank you,' she said in almost accent-free German.

Dirlewanger raised an eyebrow and looked at her with increased interest.

'You speak German?' he said.

'Yes,' the Polish woman answered. 'I studied medicine in Leipzig and Munich . . . before all this.'

The Oberführer became hospitable.

'Coffee?' he said graciously.

She answered with a bemused but grateful nod. Slowly the fear was beginning to fade from her face. And so Dirlewanger escorted her back to his command post, where his retinue clicked their heels and grinned. With Dirlewanger's luck, they thought, the panzer reinforcements should turn up just as he was settling in to a nice little interlude with his new acquisition . . .

Inside, Dirlewanger offered the young doctor a seat with a punctiliousness that was almost courtly. Was it just his whim, or was there something, a nobility and dignity in this young woman that he could not resist? He conducted himself with such perfect politeness that afterwards she could hardly believe that in the middle of that terrible night she had been the guest of the infamous Dr Oskar Dirlewanger.

He offered her a cigarette.

'My apologies,' he said quietly. 'Was it bad?'

Johanna stared at the floor. She was slowly reviving.

'I just don't understand,' she answered finally. 'I am Polish, but I've never had anything against the Germans . . . I've always defended them, even in wartime . . .'

'Excellent,' the Oberführer said with a smile.

'War is never a good thing,' Johanna continued, gaining confidence, 'and you hear of atrocities on both sides – a lot of it is probably propaganda – but what has happened here . . . it's inconceivable . . .'

Dirlewanger said nothing, and so she carried on.

'The things your people are doing here . . . I mean, Germany is a civilised country . . .'

'What you have seen here,' the Oberführer cut in, as if he were a teacher correcting a small child, and there was pride in his voice, 'is nothing compared to what we did in Russia.'

The young doctor stared open-mouthed at him, shocked and confused.

'It is necessary,' Dirlewanger explained matter-of-factly, 'if we are to win the final victory.' He threw away his cigarette butt and sighed. 'We must exterminate all the racially worthless elements, you see.'

The Polish woman just sat in silence, feeling this madman's words etching their way into her consciousness. In spite of all she had seen and experienced, she still could not believe that anyone could . . .

Dirlewanger stood up. He had had enough of his little chat with Johanna. He motioned to one of his retinue.

'Take this woman to safety,' he ordered, 'and do it personally.' Then he added, still in the same flat, almost indifferent voice: 'If anything happens to her, I will have you shot.'

The man clicked his heels and the Polish woman moved closer to Dirlewanger in order to thank him again. The Oberführer bowed courteously; it was then that she saw his face properly for the first time and froze with fear. But she knew that she had been saved, and that knowledge was more important than anything else at that moment. As Johanna Krynski reflected later, when she was an important witness before a war crimes tribunal, she would have shaken hands with the devil himself to escape from this hell. And on second thoughts, that was precisely what she had done . . .

Having dismissed his guest, Dirlewanger summoned his section commanders.

'I've had enough of this hanging around,' he began. 'We attack at seven on the dot, whether the panzers arrive or not.'

'Yes, Oberführer,' they said stiffly.

'The strategy is the same,' he continued. 'Vonwegh's group takes the left, Weise's the right. They go in first, to provide those blasted Poles with some distractions while we break through in the centre. Understood?'

'Understood, Oberführer,' they chorused, knowing that they would never really understand, well aware that this insanity was comprehensible only to a warped mind like Dirlewanger's.

From then on, it was a matter of watching and waiting. They stood among the ruins, their eyes watering from the smoke that the wind blew across from the burning buildings all around them. The sky was growing light, but there was a strange greyness, an opaqueness about it, as if God had blindfolded himself so that he did not have to see the horror of a Warsaw dawn.

At just before seven, the B-soldiers heard a rumbling noise shatter their pre-battle trance. A tank had arrived. Even Dirlewanger smiled with genuine delight.

'So,' he said, 'and now we can begin . . .' he waved one hand in the direction of the Polish anti-tank emplacement '. . . to blow that shit heap to sweet kingdom come.'

It did not seem to disturb him that the panzer was just an old Mk 4, and he was still grinning broadly in anticipation when the turret opened. A young lieutenant with a face grown old in battle delivered a sloppy salute and placed himself at Dirlewanger's disposal.

'You've come in the nick of time,' the Oberführer said to him. 'Right in front of you is the anti-tank emplacement. You'll pulverise it while we give support from behind . . .'

The tank officer stared at him for a moment, then raised his eyes to heaven.

'Do you think I'm crazy?' he said wearily.

Dirlewanger's face was suddenly contorted with fury.

'Lieutenant!' he roared back. 'You will carry out my order!'

'I have no intention of doing so,' the officer answered calmly. 'If it was just a straightforward massacre you wanted, that would be fair enough,' he smiled sourly, 'but I've got my orders, too, and what you are asking is wasting Wehrmacht property, it's sabotage.'

'I'll have you hauled before a court martial!' Dirlewanger raged.

The lieutenant shrugged his shoulders indifferently. After all he had experienced, a drunken S S pig no longer scared him. He had a whole cluster of medals pinned to his chest, and he wore them with as complete a disregard as his louse-ridden shirt.

'You don't understand this business, Herr Colonel,' the tank officer said, lighting a cigarette, deliberately demonstrating his contempt for the rank of a political S S soldier like Dirlewanger. 'They would blow us out of the street before we managed to get close enough. To try and go straight in would be idiocy. I've learned my lesson,' he said with real bitterness. 'I've not climbed out of the same kind of shit three times just to go back again and do the same thing . . .'

Dirlewanger was swaying wildly in a fit of uncontrolled anger. He was just wondering whether 'emergency disciplinary regulations' would allow him to have this lieutenant, a regular soldier, shot on the spot when he suddenly had an idea, a Dirlewanger special.

When he spoke, his voice was icy calm.

'All right, lieutenant,' he said quietly, 'I will arrange cover for you.' He turned to his adjutant. 'Off you go!' he shouted. 'Don't hang around here, you lazy bastards. Go and get me some Polacks . . . whatever you can lay your hands on . . . women and children . . . the more the better . . . !'

The lieutenant sat in his turret, not bothering to hide his disgust. Dirlewanger glanced in his direction with a satisfied grin.

'You'll get your cover, you can rely on me,' the Oberführer barked. Then he had his attention on his minions again. 'Get started! Half an hour and we're in business!'

Then he dispatched two runners to inform the two commanders on the flanks, Vonwegh and Weise, that they were to begin their attacks at precisely 7.28 – just one minute before the one he would lead himself.

Vonwegh's group seemed more surprised than their commander that he had not been killed. He had severe bruising of the left shoulder, which made him a clear candidate for hospital treatment, but he refused. Why? Maybe just to keep himself and his men from the worst. While he had been almost buried alive, most of them had lost all sense of discipline. The gorilla was playing with a stick hand-grenade as if it were a child's doll. Gruhnke, blind drunk, was wandering around showing everyone the three wrist-watches that he had lifted during the previous day's fighting. Only young Kordt's hands were clean and empty.

One of their group, as they waited to go into the attack, sat pale and sick with fear. The terrified man was Wulf-Dieter Brillmann, and it wasn't the Poles he was afraid of but the vengeance of Paul Vonwegh. Since the others had found him and Vonwegh in the ruined building, he had been through a torment of waiting and wondering that seemed worse than any punishment itself.

As it happened, Vonwegh had simply let things ride. It wasn't even a conscious decision on the company commander's part; their situation had been too hectic – and too public – in the last few hours for him to be able to give serious thought to Brillmann. And Vonwegh still had no clear idea what he intended to do with the man. All he felt when he looked at that craven, puffy face was a nameless gratitude that this cousin of Karen's bore absolutely no resemblance to the woman he loved.

Just before seven in the morning, Dirlewanger's battle-order reached him. He acknowledged receipt and sent the dispatch-runner back; then he posted guards and got his men into order. Vonwegh was functioning once more as the perfect soldier – and his men were back under his command, though he had forbidden looting, which the brigade leadership itself had expressly encouraged.

Suddenly there was a shout from one of the sentries and a second dispatch-runner appeared, this time sent by Müller-Würzbach from their supply depot on the edge of the city.

He stopped for breath and stood to attention before Vonwegh.

'B-soldier Brillmann is to stand by immediately,' the courier said, 'for transfer to the Reichssicherheitshauptamt.'

The whole group around Vonwegh heard the man's words, and there was a collective intake of breath.

'Very good,' Vonwegh answered calmly and dismissed the messenger. The man hesitated, as if wanting to take the transferee with him, but Vonwegh gestured for him to leave.

They all watched him go.

It was then that Brillmann collapsed, holding his stomach as if he meant to be sick. Kortetzky looked puzzled, and Vonwegh whispered a quick explanation: send me back there with him, and he'd never make it alive . . .

The gorilla understood, and so did Gruhnke, who stood behind Brillmann's back, miming the actions of a hangman. Even Kordt shot a look of withering hate at him – the coward who was going back to be a big shot again.

'Did you hear all that, Brillmann?' Paul Vonwegh asked coldly.

'Yes!' The man stood to attention, with some difficulty.

The company commander gazed at the man for a long time, in silence, his face frighteningly devoid of all expression. Nobody there could see what was going on in his mind; nobody realised the struggle he was going through, alone; nobody recognised the temptation which gnawed at him; nobody detected the hatred which lived in every pore of his being.

'Yes,' Vonwegh said at last. 'This could be where we say our good-bye . . ' He stepped forward and stood right in front of Brillmann. He saw the man wilt, savoured his misery, saw how the man's whole personality evaporated in horror.

'You were going to kill me,' Vonwegh said. 'You tried, but you failed. I think you'll agree that it's my turn now . . .'

'Y-yes,' Brillmann stammered.

'Don't you see . . . my methods are more certain than yours . . .'

'No!' the man howled, and finally he broke down, collapsing like a badly-manipulated puppet. Then he scrambled to his knees and begged there, arms spread wide. Even here, no one had ever cringed like that before. The others surrounded the pathetic figure, closing a circle around him. Vonwegh simply nodded to himself, as if it were all just as he had expected.

'You made some very interesting statements during our chat yesterday,' Vonwegh continued, ignoring the man's whining. 'For instance, you said – not incorrectly – that your service with the special brigade might provide you with an alibi for later on. Isn't that right? Didn't you say that the war is lost?'

'N-no . . . I mean, yes . . .' Brillmann gasped, almost choking on his words. Kortetzky booted him in the spine, and the man sprawled forward on to his face in the rubble.

'That's enough of that, gorilla,' Vonwegh said sharply. 'We're all interested in surviving – all of us, no matter what we've done.' He turned his eyes back to the whimpering Brillmann. 'On your feet, you grovelling coward,' he hissed.

Brillmann hesitated, then the rough hands of the others hauled him to his feet. He was swaying like a scarecrow in the wind, but he managed to stand to attention – fear and habit were stronger even than his overwhelming physical nausea.

'Some of us here are murderers, some are "politicals",' Vonwegh continued, his voice gathering in strength. He had come to a decision; he had finally won the struggle with himself and felt free. 'Nevertheless, we'll not have it said of us that we're no better than shits like him,' he pointed to Brillmann, 'understood?'

'No,' Brillmann stammered thickly.

'My methods,' Vonwegh said. 'Scram . . . get out of here.'

Everyone, even Brillmann, looked at him in complete disbelief.

'Yes,' Vonwegh said indifferently. 'Go back to the torture-cellars . . . have some fun . . . kill some more defenceless people. Keep Gestapo headquarters going for a couple of months more. And think of me when you're standing on the gallows somewhere. Now get out of my sight – I don't intend to do the hangman's job for him.'

Brillmann understood. Expressionless, eyes wide, he began to run towards the exit from the ruined house.

'Stop!' Vonwegh called.

Brillmann obeyed like an automaton. So it had been a deception after all, a trap. This could be the end . . .

Vonwegh's face was set in a distant smile.

'Don't you think you should say good-bye to your comrades?' he said.

'Yes . . . of course . . .'

Slowly he did the rounds. The gorilla kicked him again, this time in the stomach. Kordt just turned his back on him and left him standing. Kirchwein barely touched Brillmann's outstretched hand, as if it were a live wire. The others' attitudes varied from weary indifference to hostility.

Finally Brillmann stood in front of Vonwegh, his face drenched with sweat, his eyes empty, waiting for the final outrage.

'Thank you,' Vonwegh said simply. 'You may now report to the sergeant for transfer.' With that he turned his back and got on with preparing for the morning attack.

Kortetzky had to be restrained from sneaking off after Brillmann. Gruhnke swore at the man's back as he left. Only Kordt understood the truth: that Paul Vonwegh had finally won his battle – both with himself and with Wulf-Dieter Brillmann . . .

During her first days of freedom, Karen felt like a tightrope-walker performing without a safety-net; at any moment, she feared, her fragile balance would collapse and she would plummet into an abyss of despair. She walked through the city she had grown up in without any feeling of home, or of belonging there. Even the people seemed to be talking some strange alien babble that she only half-understood. She sensed a hysteria growing within her, and knew that this was going to be harder to conquer than all the dangers and all the camps.

As she walked through Berlin, she felt that everyone was staring at her. She passed young soldiers on leave, seeing them smile at their girl-friends, and all the time she kept asking herself desperately: how can they still find pleasure, how can they still laugh? She saw swastika flags streaming in the wind, and she felt an almost irresistible urge to tear them down.

Slowly and by a titanic effort of will, she got through her hysteria. Soon she could begin to laugh at herself, to take pleasure in everyday things. Her experiences in Ravensbrück had made her 'political', but she remained a woman above all else.

Karen had to report to the police regularly, but otherwise her life was what passed for 'normal' in the Germany of those days. She had been provided with a room in an apartment building where the windows had been filled in with cardboard. All the glass had been shattered by enemy bombing-raids and there was not enough being produced to replace the old windows. The aerial war over Berlin was reaching its final climax.

Karen had taken time to find her feet again, but now, as she looked at herself with cool objectivity in the mirror in her room, she could feel satisfied with her return to life. She reached for her make-up box. Lipstick, which she could now use again after two years, was still an exciting experience.

The only thing that worried her was loneliness. She had no one to turn to, which made her cling even more tenaciously to her memories of Paul, though she still had no news of him. She wondered if she dare look up some old friends of his; perhaps they could make some discreet enquiries about him . . .

She was still thinking of Paul Vonwegh when the doorbell rang. The man who came into the flat spoke German with a slight Scandinavian accent, and he brought with him an impressive-looking document.

'Please sign here,' he said, and Karen's heart leapt. It was an application for an entry permit to Sweden. Only now did she realise what invisible hand had freed her from the concentration camp.

'Do I have a chance of being allowed to leave?' she asked once the formalities were over.

'Perhaps . . .' the official said with a shrug. 'It's impossible to tell with the authorities here. They're totally unpredictable. But at least we are trying . . .'

Karen nodded, then looked puzzled.

'Why are you bothering about me?'

The man smiled almost sadly.

'First of all, you have a Swedish mother. And then . . . well, shortly after your arrest someone drew our attention to you.'

'Paul Vonwegh?' she asked excitedly.

The man confirmed it.

'Do you have any idea what's happened to him?'

'Yes . . .' the official replied slowly. 'He was also arrested and transferred to a concentration camp. From there he was sent to an S S penal unit.'

'When did you last hear from him?' Karen butted in impatiently. All she could think was: he's alive . . . he's still alive . . .

'Not long ago,' the Swede said. He was avoiding looking her in the eye.

'Is something wrong?'

'Well, yes . . . or rather, something is strange. He is with a penal brigade, where "politicals" like him usually don't stand a chance . . .'

'And?' Karen pressed him.

'He has got himself promoted to a regular corporal . . . which doesn't sound right at all . . .'

At first, Karen failed to realise what the official was getting at. She simply felt an overwhelming relief that Paul had hauled himself out of the mire.

'So has he got a field post number?' she asked eagerly.

'Yes,' the Swede said stolidly. 'But I cannot give it to you.'

'Why not? Please . . .' she implored.

'It would be unwise for you to write to him at the moment,' the man explained, nervously fiddling with his hat. 'Things are . . . delicate . . . and you could endanger both yourself and him . . .'

'But Paul wouldn't . . .' Karen shook her head energetically.

'Let's make a deal,' the official said with a sigh. 'If your visa for Sweden is granted, then I will get you Herr Vonwegh's field post number. You can write to him from Sweden, but not from here.'

'All right,' the girl replied with sad reluctance. 'If you think it's best.'

The Swede smiled and clapped her on the shoulder.

'Keep your chin up,' he said.

It was only when the man had left that Karen really began to understand the opportunity that the Swedes were offering her. While they were actually talking, she had been able to think only of one thing: Paul was alive, alive . . .

The joyful knowledge filled her like sweet ambrosia. For a moment she could forget the past – and not have to think of their future . . .

The young tank lieutenant with the old face climbed into the turret of his Mark IV with a look of disgust and sadness as he caught his final glimpse of the world that the masters of the Third Reich had created.

All around the panzer were ranged groups of Polish civilians, women and children, old men and boys, driven by Dirlewanger's thugs out of their hiding-places into the hell of Wolka Street. The Poles' faces were distorted with fear; many of them were still begging and weeping. They knew that something bad was being planned for them, but just how bad they had yet to experience . . .

Dirlewanger looked impatiently at his watch, then proudly studied his latest atrocity. He walked round the tank, picked out a woman who held a child in her arms and forced her to climb up and perch on the turret. The final touch. As for the woman, if the Oberführer had been interested he might have found out that she was called Grzes and that she had been happily married for years to a man who was now fighting with the Resistance. But no one, and least of all Dirlewanger, wanted to know about the private lives of sub-humans.

Seventy or eighty Poles altogether. Dirlewanger completed his inspection and gave a satisfied grunt and a grin to his minions. Ready.

7.28. The units on their flanks let loose; Vonwegh's on the

left, Weise's to the right. The Polish freedom-fighters, realising that they were under attack, returned fire. Meanwhile, Dirlewanger raised one arm. Sixty seconds to go: the Oberführer is the starter, and he makes the rules. If anyone doesn't make it to the winning post, it's all the same to him . . .

'Move!' Dirlewanger roared out the signal.

The ancient panzer ploughed forward, stopped, then started a second time. The civilians gathered wearily round it and prepared to walk forward. Mrs Grzes and her child clung frantically to the turret, while the other civilians gathered in thick clusters to the left and right. Slowly the great steel coffin rolled forward. And behind them all, wild-eyed, mostly still drunk, came the B-soldiers, in their midst the skinny, hawklike harbinger of death they called their commander.

The Polish defenders let them come forty, fifty metres. There was a burst of fire, then sudden silence. The enemy had seen who they were shooting at. They had realised that it was their own wives and children who were being used as shields. Then the shots came again, but sparsely; there were many who still could not bring themselves to it.

The tank lumbered steadily onward, wheeling round and coming closer to the anti-tank gun, which lay well-camouflaged and in an almost impregnable position on the corner of Ciepla and Grzybowska Streets. Behind its sights was a gun-aimer who had become a legend in the first days of the uprising, whose nerves of steel and unassailable calm under pressure had brought him an astonishing tally of German armour. His name was Grzes.

The gunner next to him supplied a range-reading on the approaching panzer.

'Let 'em come on a bit,' Grzes muttered to him grimly.

The emplacement's commander was following the German advance through his field glasses. He could see everything, and he was biting his lip until it ran with his own blood, resisting the urge to scream and shout and throw everything to the winds; for a moment he had a crazy thought of turning his gun against his own head rather than . . . but the officer pulled himself together.

'Ready!' he ordered the gun-crew. Grzes drew a bead on the oncoming tank. Then he hesitated as he saw the women and children in his sights. The German Mark IV rumbled another thirty metres.

'Fire!' the officer yelled.

Grzes knew that he had to obey or let the tank roll over them. He whispered a brief, desperate prayer for forgiveness and lined his eye along the gunsight, his hand on the firing-button. It was then that he recognised the figures on the turret as those of his wife and child . . .

Chapter Eighteen

The man on the anti-tank gun, the Pole called Grzes, formerly a student, now a soldier, stood frozen like the statue of a martyr, his arms hanging limply by his side as if they were the sails of a windmill, waiting for the breeze to catch them. All he could see through his wide, disbelieving eyes was the coming of death. The tank's tracks rasped against the uneven, rubble-strewn ground; its engine coughed and roared; the steel monster was only an old Mark IV, long since obsolete, but it was still capable of flattening a gun-emplacement which didn't defend itself.

Still 300 metres away. Or was it less now? But Grzes seemed to have gone deaf and blind. Only his heart was alive – beating, hammering, thundering its protest at this final outrage on humanity, against the innocent people being driven to their deaths by a gang of murderers. Dirlewanger was using civilians as a living barrier to shield the tank, the essential element in his final bid for 'glory'. The Oberführer was determined to show General Reinefarth the way to break Warsaw.

Heavy fire came from the right, and the Mark IV came to a juddering halt. It moved forward again a short distance, then turned laboriously on one track, slowly, clumsily, like a crippled elephant. The gun turret swivelled round, looking for its target, a pocket of resistance in some ruins where Weise's men were engaged. Then the gun vomited yellow smoke and fire, its recoil causing the tank to shake, sending the surrounding civilians sprawling to the ground like rotten fruit falling from a tree. The steel coffin immediately rolled forward, crushing an old man's legs, squashing a child. It demolished a wall and opened up with machine-gun fire on the defenders. Two or three times, gallant Poles died trying to place Molotov cocktails, but it was hopeless. Death was doing good business in burning Warsaw . . .

But Grzes saw only that his wife Maria and his son Jan had disappeared from the panzer's turret. Perhaps they had escaped, he hoped wildly; or maybe they too had been crushed; anything would be better, anything . . .

The gun-aimer had not yet noticed that the officer beside him had let his arm drop and cancelled the order to fire. Perhaps because he too had to get used to the idea of firing on his own parents and children; or perhaps because the position of the gun had been changed during the night and he didn't want to reveal its whereabouts prematurely. But under any other circumstances, that Mark IV would have made a sitting target.

The battery officer's face was creased with agony. Only a few metres, a few more seconds, and he would have to give the order. He knew he could rely on his men, and on Grzes in particular. In the last few days the gun-aimer had become famous in this sector for his success-rate. And the rest of them would resist until they dropped, until the end came they would defend tooth and claw, whether those damned Russians came or not.

All the Resistance fighters in the position had seen what was happening; there were muttered curses, shouts of outrage, impotent moans. They all knew what they had to do, and they hated each other because they were human beings, not killing machines. Now the human barrier had been reassembled and forced back in place around the tank, complete with the woman and child on the turret. Slowly the great hulk of the panzer wheeled round and set course for the anti-tank battery.

'Range 220,' one of the anti-tank crew shouted. His voice was unsteady, cracked with emotion. But there was no avoiding their duty. It was a case of kill or be killed: war cast the die quickly, and men had to choose . . .

One second more, two, and the tank had begun to move forward again. In the place where Grzes had to place his shell, he saw his wife, Maria, dark-haired, pretty, full of life, and memories coursed through his agonised mind. It had been love at first sight between them. Four years ago, somewhere in Warsaw, in a place where students used to meet in secret to drink, to talk, and to plan resistance against their German oppressors. They had all had a bit too much to drink that evening, and the place had got noisy – much too noisy. Maria had been the one who had wandered out on to the balcony and seen the Nazi security police approaching. They had scattered and he had fled with Maria . . . They had stayed together ever since, and things had not gone too badly, despite the war and the occupation. There had not been much to eat, their room was tiny, but they were happy with each other and sooner or later things had to change foı the better, they thought . . .

'200 metres!'

Sweat was pouring down the battery commander's face. His eyes were bulging with loathing and fear. He tried to raise his arm and failed. He steeled himself, tried again, and this time he managed it. Ready for the signal, and God help them.

There had been bad times too, of course, Grzes was thinking, unaware of the officer, in a dream-world of his own. Such as when the child came. Even before the confinement, the doctor had looked grave, and in their heart of hearts they had both known that having children should have been postponed to happier times. But they had wanted a baby so much, even though it stood a chance of being born weak and undernourished. Yes, the agony of waiting had been bad, but when Jan had arrived at last, a healthy boy, there had been so much joy. Since then he had spoiled them both, Maria and Jan, had promised her that he would do well when all this was over, earn money and live only for her and the child . . .

'150 metres!'

'Fire!' The commander shouted, then turned his face away as if he were about to throw up.

Grzes did not move, just stared straight ahead, thinking of Maria and Jan, and the last time he had seen them before going off to be a 'hero' in burning Warsaw.

'Fire, for God's sake!'

Someone shoved Grzes from behind, and he stumbled

forward and upright, as if deliberately exposing himself to the battle, wanting some stray bullet to cut him down now before he could experience what was to come. As he rose out of his seat he saw the monster coming closer, saw the turret with its obscene tube spouting fire. He heard the grinding and crashing of its machinery, as if bones were being broken to feed it, human beings pulped to fuel its progress towards destruction. With a sinking feeling, Grzes knew that the monster would claim more human victims unless he destroyed it; that if he hesitated, someone else would have to do it; and that Maria and his boy would die anyway, whether he fired or not. Grzes ran the whole gamut of reasons and they gave him just a little strength, perhaps enough . . .

A few metres closer now. Their commander could see that Grzes had the panzer in his sights and that there were no more orders to give.

'130 metres!'

Grzes let the Mark IV come even closer. Hold on for a few more seconds, he told himself; think of nothing, concentrate on hatred and nothing else. You never saw Maria before . . . you never kissed her . . . Jan, your child, was just a dream, and dreams are frauds, and here you are fighting with the others and you will hold on until the Russians come, until they get us out of this, until we are free again. Only that is important, nothing else exists . . .

There were only a hundred metres between himself and the tank now.

I'm lying to myself, Grzes thought wildly, it's all nonsense, rubbish. Maria's out there, and I love her, and I can't kill her . . . Let the tank crew see us, take aim and shoot. *Our Father* . . . he began in his mind, but he could get no further. *Our Father* . . . he thought, and tried to aim at the turret. *Our Father* . . . he saw his commander nod, and knew he had to fire. *Our Father* . . . he heard himself repeating, and thought: the record has stuck, the needle's not moving. *Our Father* . . .

Now, thought Grzes. His body shook with the tension. Then, all at once, the crazy energy left him.

'I . . . can't do it,' he moaned. His head slumped down in abject, total despair.

There was a flash from the panzer's turret. The first shell passed over the gun-crew's heads; the second was too far to the left, and exploded in a nearby house, showering the Resistance fighters with pieces of rubble.

'Idiot!' screamed the Polish officer. 'Fire! Fire, for the love of God!' He looked at Grzes's agonised features, realised he was in shock and acted mechanically. He slapped the man's face, once, then again, and hissed: 'Fire, you bloody coward!'

Grzes was no longer a functioning human being. He was like a zombie, and what he did was a reflex action, as if someone else were carrying out the action on his behalf. *Our Father* . . . the word still echoed in his head, but it was far away, faint and muffled, when he released the firing-button.

And the shell hit home.

The turret flew up in the air and flew several metres backwards to land in the middle of Dirlewanger's advancing B-soldiers. Flames shot up from the hulk, and for a second it heaved up and down, almost as if it were some old performer taking a bow. Then the tank took off almost vertically into the air – the ammunition must have gone up.

Immediately the Poles unleashed a merciless fire into the exposed mass of B-soldiers, mowing them down where they stood. The women, too, and the children and the old men . . . There was no dignity, no grace or chivalry in Warsaw. On that front, the luckiest were those who were already dead.

But young Grzes wasn't watching all that. He was weeping like a child, his head slumped over the barrel of the anti-tank gun. It was a couple of minutes until, still sobbing, he forced himself to look up and saw the officer who had given him the order down in the street, pumping his machine-pistol into the German ranks. Grzes felt a sudden wave of hatred overwhelm him; suddenly the officer was responsible for all this, for this bottomless pit of suffering . . . The young gun-aimer staggered out of the emplacement and into the midst of the battle; lurching up to the astonished officer, he knocked the man's weapon from his hand and grabbed him by the throat, screaming all the time:

'Murderer! Bloody murderer!'

He squeezed the man's windpipe with all his desperate strength. 'You killed them!' he moaned between sobs. 'Maria . . . my child . . . murderer!'

No one else noticed at first. They had their hands full with Dirlewanger's bandits. For a couple of minutes Grzes and the officer were rolling on the ground, completely out of cover, with bullets whizzing all around them. They staggered to their feet, almost at the same time, and it was then that a grenade exploded in the gutter. The blast threw them backwards into a shell-hole, and knocked the fight out of both of them.

The shock brought Grzes to his senses again. It was only now that the officer discovered that he had ordered a man to kill his wife and child . . .

Grzes sat staring into space after he had finished talking to the officer. Then he took a few paces forward to stand with his comrades, unarmed, feet planted apart, shaking his fist in the direction of the Germans. 'Maria!' he shouted. 'They killed her!'

Brillmann's shame at his final humiliation was very soon replaced by relief that he was now free of the special brigade – and out of Paul Vonwegh's power. He was smiling smugly to himself as he picked his way through the rubble. He wouldn't be wearing Dirlewanger's rags much longer.

He was going in the right direction this time – towards the rear – and he would only have to do this short first stage on foot. Soon he would be installed in the comfort of an officer's compartment on the train to Berlin. He would no longer be a pariah but a public prosecutor, with the rank of S S Sturmbannführer. Yes, soon he would be back where he liked to be: holding the whip hand . . .

The thought made him quicken his step.

Brillmann hurried round the corner of a high ruin and then stopped short. A cloud of thick, stinking smoke was coming from a heap of rubble; it was like a garbage-burning. He sniffed and realised to his horror that what was being burnt were corpses. He thought he saw a charred figure move, just recognisable as a woman . . . but maybe it was his nerves playing tricks.

This sort of thing offended his principles, went contrary to his sense of good taste, because Wulf-Dieter Brillmann was a man with strong feelings about aesthetic standards. He felt yet more satisfaction at the realisation. The trouble with the Nazis was they didn't know where to stop. It was hardly surprising that sensible people were starting to think of their own interests again.

With an inward smile, Brillmann knew that in his mind he had already changed sides. He had already transferred his inner allegiance to the right side, to the victorious side, to the only side a man with any sense owed loyalty to . . .

As he walked on, Brillmann began to consider the matter further. Vonwegh would never understand, he thought, that it was not idealists who made politics but tacticians: it was a question, not of ideals, but of aims. The company commander should have had him, Brillmann, put up against a wall; Vonwegh had had the authority, and the means. What was the point of that stupid 'duel of minds' he had got them both involved in? It was the old, familiar liberal rigmarole – all very well in a cinema drama, could be quite gripping in a novel, but a total waste of time in real life. A question of character? That was schoolboy stuff, the kind of classroom morality that Brillmann had seen through by the time he was fifteen.

He heard footsteps and took cover. The sounds came from three men in German uniforms, he saw with relief. Then he realised that they were military police and was suddenly anxious; in his hurry to leave, he hadn't bothered to get written confirmation of the order to report to headquarters.

The police patrolmen had stopped and were talking about the delight of women in occupied Kiev. All that was ancient history now, of course, and they were nostalgically consoling themselves with photographs, which were being passed around with leering comments and mutual digs in the ribs. Then the MPs saw a young soldier on the other side of the street and swooped on him. Brillmann could not follow their conversation with their victim, but after a minute or so he saw them take the man away. His route was open again.

Brillmann started off purposefully, but after a while his thoughts slowed him down. In his mind he had already settled into his three-room apartment in Berlin and was feeling those valuable, antique rugs under his feet, secure in the knowledge that there was nothing to show they had been looted from a Jewish bank. All this shit was behind him; now he was taking a fortifying bath in his deep, luxuriously large bathtub. Yes, soon he would have it all again: the good Virginia cigarettes, the smart suit cut from top-quality English cloth . . . From now on until the end, he intended to enjoy all the comforts of life; others might have to fight for a few grams of margarine, but for a man who enjoyed the privileges of S S headquarters, things could be good, very good.

Mind you, he reconsidered, perhaps he might not keep things going right up to the end – only until the day before. The trick was never to become conspicuous, never to rise too high nor fall too low. When he changed sides, it would have to be just at the right moment, not a day too late and not a minute too soon . . . perhaps he should take a few files with him, evidence of just how much those above him at State Security Headquarters had to answer for. That wouldn't really be treason, he told himself; those people had really gone too far, never thinking of the burden their fanaticism placed on people like himself, who were only trying to do their jobs as well as they could . . .

What can the victors accuse me of, anyway? Brillmann asked himself. He had been a State Prosecutor in the ordinary legal civil service, and had been transferred to State Security, just as in wartime any dressmaker might be drafted into a munitions factory, whether willingly or not. Who was to know that in his case he had applied for the job?

Warsaw was in flames, but Wulf-Dieter Brillmann, who had always known on which side his bread was buttered, was at peace with himself. Close by to him, children were crying;

their mothers had been shot, and they would die of hunger or thirst unless some compassionate soldier finished them off with the butt of his rifle first. Just behind him, seven brutes who called themselves soldiers had just raped and murdered a thirteen-year-old girl, as they were perfectly entitled to under Warsaw's 'order of the day'. The order had come from Hitler, and had been passed on by Himmler to General Bach-Zelewski. Reinefarth had taken it from him and given it to Dirlewanger. The order was death, rape, torture and extermination to every living being in the city who was not a member of the 'master race'. It meant an Iron Cross for Dirlewanger, oak-leaves on his braid for Reinefarth, promotion for Bach-Zelewski, praise for Himmler, and a boost for the Führer's shattered morale. It was the kind of 'national solidarity' the Nazis dreamed of, something the whole rat-pack could congratulate themselves on.

So much the better if I can stay human, Brillmann thought. Today's atrocities will be my alibi for tomorrow; because I was too soft and too humane for Headquarters, they sent me to a penal unit. He was already shadow-boxing, already pleading his case before the Denazification Commission . . . but then a man like him always thought things out in advance, always kept his ear close to the ground. That was the difference between himself and Vonwegh, he decided with an almost light-headed satisfaction: the company commander was narrow-minded where Brillmann was flexible; he dreamed where Brillmann acted. Brillmann made a quick survey of his past and decided that no one would be able to accuse him of anything – nobody except Vonwegh, and the man probably wouldn't get out of Warsaw alive. Brillmann thought some more, and decided that when he got back to Berlin he would have to make sure of Vonwegh; there should still be enough time and opportunity to get him quietly out of the way, if the Poles didn't do it first . . .

Brillmann had unfortunately liquidated his opponent just one street corner too soon. Lost in thought, he wandered round a pile of rubble and straight into the arms of a military police patrol. The men didn't even demand his papers, simply dragged him along with them towards the front line. The Poles had broken through somewhere, it seemed, and they were rounding up any sort of force that could be scraped together to plug the gap. Before Brillmann had time to realise that he was being forced back in the wrong direction, he was confronted by a hail of fire. He managed to dive away into the rubble and find an empty cellar to wait in. The MPs hadn't even asked for his name, the idiots; when the noise of battle had subsided, he would come out again and find his way through to the rear to report.

Wulf-Dieter Brillmann had added up the bill correctly, but no one had presented him with it yet. Unfortunately it was the Polish Resistance who were there when he came out of his bolt-hole, and they were only too willing to demand the full amount of recompense. The group that caught him was composed of two men and a fourteen-year-old boy, ragged and unshaven, with determined faces and eyes that showed only a fathomless hatred.

Brillmann put up his hands and begged for his life, and oddly enough his action earned him a reprieve. A plea for mercy was something new in the Warsaw of August '44, in a city where no quarter was asked or given. The Poles were so astonished and intrigued that they let the man in the uniform of the Dirlewanger brigade live – for the moment.

They locked him in a cellar and placed a guard outside. An hour went by, two hours, a whole night, an endless night. Here there were no deep carpets to tread, no bathtub to wallow in – just a dripping tap, which carried on for hour after hour, monotonously regularly, with insane precision. In the end, the drops were like hammer-blows in his skull; and he was terrified that they would stop, convinced that when the noise ceased it would be some presagement, a signal . . .

Towards dawn, he heard footsteps. Brillmann made to stand, then cowered down like a threatened animal in one corner of the cellar. 'No!' he was howling, even before they opened the door.

They had a fourth man with them, whom Brillmann had

never seen before. The man wore a battered leather jacket and seemed to be some sort of leader. If Brillmann had been able to understand Polish, he would have heard the man saying that the area had been surrouned by Reinefarth's men and was being taken in vicious house-to-house fighting. What the man in the leather jacket was explaining, quickly and dispassionately, was the need for withdrawal. When he had finished speaking, the other two Poles glanced at their captive and asked their leader some questions in low, hissing whispers. Brillmann began to understand only too well . . .

'Please . . . please . . .' he screamed, hurling himself on to his knees.

The man in the leather jacket looked at him as if he were a loathsome insect, then motioned for him to stand. Brillmann got to his feet quickly, eagerly, gratefully, still the model pupil.

It all happened very fast after that, but to Brillmann it was like a weird slow-motion sequence.

The two Poles began to move towards him, with determined looks on their sallow faces.

'You swine . . .' he gasped, backing away, 'you want to . . . you . . .'

There was no answer. One picked up a box and looked up meaningfully at an evil-looking hook that hung from the ceiling.

'I . . . I've got nothing against the Poles,' Brillmann screamed. 'I . . . I like you, really . . .'

'Get on with it,' the man in the leather jacket said coldly in Polish.

The others took hold of Brillmann – they were surprisingly strong for such undernourished-looking types – and hoisted him up. Wulf-Dieter, the rising star of State Security Headquarters, was on his way up again – only this time he would never come down alive . . .

Dirlewanger got his break-through on the corner of Ciepla and Grzybowska Streets, where the despairing young Grzes had sought and been unable to find death. Afterwards, with the strong-point in their hands, Reinefarth's combat-group had driven in an easterly direction from the suburbs of Wola and Ochota by way of Wolska and Chlodna Streets, through the market district and the Saxon Gardens and into the Plac Zwyciestwa. They had reached the bank of the river Vistula and were now fighting in the old city, the centre of the uprising. Dirlewanger's bandits had left moutains of dead to mark their passage. Wherever the B-soldiers went, not a Pole – man, woman or child – remained alive.

The rebels were rapidly running out of weapons, ammunition, water and food; the seeds of death were coming to a barren bloom. But Reinefarth continued to hurl Dirlewanger's men into the uneven struggle with a ruthless hatred founded in a relentless lust for Polish blood.

In his personal success report to Himmler, he wrote:

'Soldiers, S S-men, police, S D-men, members of the T N and the N S K K have all combined to see to it that the Polish metropolis, which has been such a blot on German pride over the centuries, has finally been eliminated as a source of danger. The ancient enemy has been conquered,' he continued gloatingly, 'with the loss to him of a quarter of a million people . . .'

Paul Vonwegh was spared the greater part of this bloody journey into Warsaw. The day after the break-through with the old Mark IV panzer, he and his men had been ambushed by Polish freedom-fighters and forced into a desperate resistance. His men had already been in close combat with the Poles when he had seen Kortetzky's hand-grenades and had hurled them at their attackers. When he had seen that the grenades hadn't exploded, he had stood up to take a closer look, only to get a bullet through his shoulder. Hours later, when he had woken up in a field-hospital, he had learned that the grenades were harmless; the gorilla had emptied them of explosives and filled them with looted diamonds and jewellery. A counter-attack by another German unit had saved Vonwegh's men from being wiped out, and that was how he had survived long enough to be provided with medical attention.

So it was that Paul Vonwegh ended up in the rear with the

camp followers, being cared for and treated. There was still no news from Karen, no indication whether she had managed to get out of the women's camp. It was a time when Vonwegh raged against the fate that had torn him out of the battle for Warsaw and put him in a clean, quiet hospital bed – for he was given the chance to think, to dream, to long for Karen. Then, a few days later, Sergeant Müller-Würzbach turned up to see him.

'Well,' the man said, with wry admiration spread over his plump, pig-like features. 'It seems you weren't so stupid after all . . .'

'Why not?' Vonwegh asked genuinely puzzled.

'As it happened, you got rid of him rather nicely . . .'

'Who?'

Müller-Würzbach smiled knowingly.

'Brillmann,' he said. 'He was caught by the Resistance and hung. Messy business. They found him yesterday and identified the corpse. Anything to do with you . . . ?'

'Brillmann is dead?' was all Vonwegh could say, unable to contain his excitement, feeling the old wound twinge, the old hatred leap for joy.

'Come on,' Müller-Würzbach grinned. 'Don't play that game. This is strictly between you and me . . .'

Paul Vonwegh found himself breathing heavily, fighting against a barbarous satisfaction. From beyond the grave, Wulf-Dieter Brillmann was trying for one last victory over his enemy's humanity . . .

Warsaw was dying.

The Polish capital was bleeding to death with agonising slowness, with a courage and a resignation that should have put its murderers to shame.

Right up to the last hour, the final bullet, the last sigh of pain, the men, women and children of the city waited for liberation by the Red Army. But on Stalin's orders the Soviet advance guard remained stubbornly in the northern suburb of Praha throughout the rising, its weapons sheathed, watching the final destruction of Poland's noblest and best.

Soon only soot and ashes would be the heritage of this city; Warsaw, whose lot was blood, suffering and tears.

Just as Kaminski and Dirlewanger were preparing to stamp out the last, faint embers of the uprising, they were recalled. In his usual unpredictable way, Hitler had decided to placate world opinion by treating the few surviving insurgents as ordinary prisoners of war under the Geneva Convention, so that the newsreels could show how 'humane' he really was . . .

The propaganda coup Berlin was planning made the special brigades a potential embarrassment. They were withdrawn from Warsaw at short notice and condemned to temporary 'unemployment'.

And meanwhile Dirlewanger had a superior who wrote to the Führer's headquarters:

'S S Oberführer Dirlewanger . . . has shown repeatedly by his actions that he belongs among the bravest of the brave. I propose therefore that he be made a Knight of the Iron Cross . . . (signed) Reinefarth.'

Hitler was only too glad to accede to the proposal of S S Gruppenführer Heinz Reinefarth – the same Reinefarth who in 1958, as representative of the 'All-German Block of Refugees and Persons Deprived of Their Rights', would take his seat in the democratically-elected parliament of the German province of Schleswig-Holstein.

After one last, desperate attempt at a break-out, the collapse of the Warsaw Uprising was signalled in the press throughout the world during the second week of September, 1944. In Germany the headlines glowed blood-red; elsewhere they were black, like the crêpe of mourning.

Even in neutral countries like Sweden, people suffered with the gallant people of Warsaw. During those fateful days, the appalling news from Poland was discussed in every cafe, on every street corner. Karen, however, felt little involvement with the destruction of the Polish capital. She did not know that Paul Vonwegh had been in action there . . .

For the moment, all Karen could feel was a complete incredulity at the fact that she was in Sweden, in a neutral country, an oasis of peace in the midst of war. Everything had gone so smoothly that, right until the last moment, she had feared a trap.

Suddenly, all those bureaucrats, the toadies of the system like her cousin Wulf-Dieter Brillmann, the men who usually took such delight in making people's lives a misery, had been so kind to Karen. Perhaps they were already creating their alibis for tomorrow, but she did not care. The important thing was that the necessary formalities were completed with astonishing speed.

Then Karen was able to experience the most thrilling sensation available in the world of 1944: the stillness of peace and safety.

Karen had to start again from small beginnings. She had to get used to the natural things of everyday life, the simple, banal things that are taken for granted, whose value is never appreciated until they are lost: like the singing of the birds, the laughter of children, the smiles of the couples walking arm in arm through tranquil parks, with no need to watch their words, or hide their happiness, or care what anyone thought of them . . .

Now, though, Karen was beginning to feel the weight of her loneliness. In Ravensbrück, Paul Vonwegh had been her constant support, the reality that had given her purpose and direction. But here in Sweden the man she loved was shrinking to a phantom in her memory. She realised how far away he was, how twisted and tortured was the path which perhaps, in spite of everything, they might walk together some day. That was the hope that kept her from lethargy and despair, however foolish it may have seemed to an outsider.

The official from the Swedish embassy had kept his promise and given her Vonwegh's field post number, though with a warning that Karen should communicate with him indirectly, if at all. She had decided to send the letter to a girl-friend in Berlin, who would pass it on to an acquaintance of Vonwegh's, who would then make sure it got to the right place.

Karen's head was swimming as she sat down to write to

Paul for the first time in what seemed like an eternity of years. But when she put pen to paper, her thoughts became as precise and sure as her nature.

'Paul,' she wrote, 'I have counted every minute we have not been together as lost time in my life, and those minutes have added up to hours, days, and months. Despite it all, I want to tell you that I have never missed you as much as I do at this moment.

'Everything has happened so quickly. Before I realised what was happening, I was in the country where my mother was born, feeling like a deserter, feeling that I should have stayed in Berlin to wait for you.

'I know that what I am writing may seem stupid, and will probably make things even more difficult for you, but perhaps my words will work some kind of magic to protect you. Please come back. I don't want to be alone again. I need you. Tell yourself that every moment. I need you, do you hear?

'Your Karen.'

To be on the safe side, she left out any reference to her time in the concentration camp.

She sealed the envelope, stood up, and went over to the window to gaze out on the street. For a moment she felt confusion and despair, then she pulled herself together and called on that innocent, childlike strength that had always sustained them when they were together. Oh God, she thought, let him come back; let him come back safe and sound. She, and the whole world, needed Paul Vonwegh and all the men like him. There were so few of them . . .

Everything was agreed. The plan was going into operation. In the morning, the remaining men from Vonwegh's company would head for the Russian lines.

The war, the orgy of death, was now showing that it too was mortal. Dirlewanger's ragged gang had been used to plug any and every hole in the German resistance, and had now become 'honourable', like an ageing gangster. These days it hid behind the title 'S S Grenadier Division Dirlewanger'.

After they had pulled out of Warsaw, the structure of the

unit had changed. The regular staff were no longer so brutal as before, and life was no longer quite so cheap. For the last time, the concentration camps of Dachau and Sachsenhausen spewed prisoners out to fill the gaps in the ranks of Dirlewanger's brigade. That was in the autumn of 1944. The majority of these human wrecks were men who had been in prison for many years because of their convictions, as socialists, Catholics, Christian pacifists, communists. Their arrival brought the creation of a new platoon, and also a different emphasis. With the injection of new blood, the rot began to set in. It affected Vonwegh's company first . . .

Since Brillmann's death, Vonwegh had stuck to his goal with iron determination. Dirlewanger had tried to frighten the new recruits by telling them that the Russians would string them up if they captured them. It was the old trick: fear as the spur. Paul Vonwegh had worked secretly against the Oberführer's propaganda, doggedly and with gradual success.

During the fighting in Hungary he had taken an opportunity to disprove Dirlewanger's warnings. In Vonwegh's immediate vicinity, under his covert direction, two whole companies had surrendered intact to the Russians. They had been properly treated as prisoners of war; the enemy now knew that Dirlewanger's unit was more than simply a gang of brutes and cut-throats. Deserters were assessed as soldiers and not as criminals – and those of them who had already gone over to the Russians shouted it over loudspeakers to their comrades whenever an east wind was blowing.

Now the dam had burst; Hitler's most pitiable soldiers scented a chance to survive the cataclysm that was coming. The B-soldiers realised that the situation was no longer hopeless; the enemy were beginning to discriminate between those who had killed for pleasure and those who had had no choice.

Vonwegh's company was now in position on the river Neisse, the last line of defence before the capital of the Reich. The regular staff, including Dirlewanger himself, were quartered in Berlin, and Vonwegh lay under the command of

Müller-Würzbach, who had been promoted to commissioned rank as an S S Hauptsturmführer. They were holding a weak position which the Russians could have overrun whenever they wanted to; it was just a few communications trenches running into each other like a spider's web.

The unrest among the men that day was like a physical force, though few enough of them knew what the plan was, and even they were unaware of who had conceived it. Vonwegh had surrounded himself with a group of reliable men from among his veterans, led by young Kordt.

At last darkness fell. The night was impenetrable and starless. When the signal was given that the Russians were waiting on the other side, Vonwegh sent over an exploratory group composed of reliable 'politicals'. Their job was to discuss exact escape-details with the Ivans, ready for the next day.

When a group of shadows left the opposing trenches and began creeping soundlessly in their direction, Paul Vonwegh motioned to Kirchwein, the epileptic, and said: 'Report to Hauptsturmführer Müller-Würzbach that fifteen B-soldiers have deserted.' His face was cool and impassive. Tomorrow, he thought. Tomorrow would be the day of reckoning, the climax of all his work.

Müller-Würzbach, the ex-sergeant, may have been a drunken yokel, but even he had some idea that bad times were coming.

He had made sure he was surrounded by men he could rely on, who would stand by him because they had to. His company were the cream of the criminals, and the Hauptsturmführer kept them faithful to the swastika by giving them licence to booze, rape and plunder.

He had stopped trusting Vonwegh long ago. Men under his command were always deserting to the Russians, and each time Vonwegh seemed to have some convincing excuse. And why did all the politicals end up in Vonwegh's platoon? In the sector held by Müller-Würzbach, a man only had to stick his head up out of a trench and he would be shot to pieces by a Russian sniper. Vonwegh's men, on the other hand, could sun themselves on top of the trenches on fine days without having to worry about the enemy. Müller-Würzbach refused to believe that such a remarkable series of coincidences could have come about by sheer good luck.

So when Kirchwein reported the desertion of fifteen more B-soldiers to him, the Hauptsturmführer decided it was time to settle Vonwegh's hash.

'He thinks he can take us for suckers,' he said to one of his cronies. 'Get me a line to the old man . . .'

It took hours, but finally he got a connection to Dirlewanger. Had anyone known it, the Oberführer was in the process of arranging his own flight, but when he spoke to Müller-Würzbach it was with his usual contempt.

'Put Vonwegh up against a wall! And get rid of the rest of his bunch, too!'

'Yes, Oberführer,' Müller-Wurzbach said, barely able to make out his drunken chief's slurred words of command.

'And your head will roll if any of those mutineers manage to escape . . . any of them!' Dirlewanger yelled finally. Then he hung up.

Müller had two companies under his direct authority, positioned to the right of Vonwegh's unit. The Hauptsturmführer grinned malevolently. Things were quite clear: if he understood correctly, then the deserters would try to make their break to the left. Secretly, under cover of the darkness, Müller-Würzbach re-grouped his men so that they stood between Vonwegh's company and the Russians . . .

Morning dawned after a long night. Somewhere, a long way away, a German MG 42 fired a lone burst. Otherwise, all was quiet.

Vonwegh carefully looked at his watch. Kordt, standing nearby, picked up the signal and motioned to a group of men.

A second later, thirty or more B-soldiers launched themselves out of the trench and began to run towards the Soviet lines.

The whole business was staged. As someone quietly and unhurriedly reported the mass-desertion, Vonwegh ordered the escapers to be fired upon. The crews manning the machine-guns were, of course, reliable men who made sure that their bullets failed to hit anyone. After a suitable interval, the company commander intended to exploit the confused situation to escape with the rest of his men.

With the plan well into operation, Vonwegh maintained his habitual icy calm. Everything seemed to be going smoothly.

Suddenly he was astonished to see a concentrated, witheringly accurate barrage of fire coming from their left. The men with Kordt in no man's land hurled themselves to the ground, but most were sitting ducks. In seconds, the majority had been picked off singly by the mysterious attackers.

It was then that Vonwegh saw Müller-Würzbach appear with a group of heavily-armed bodyguards. He just had time to signal to Kortetzky, who passed on the message to the other machine-gunners.

'You are under arrest, Vonwegh,' the Hauptsturmführer said with grim satisfaction. 'Hands on your head . . .'

The company leader smiled bitterly and slowly raised his hands. A second later, Kortetzky swung round his machine-gun and cut a vicious swath through Müller-Würzbach and his entire group of henchmen. The Hauptsturmführer had an instant to realise how terribly he had underestimated Paul Vonwegh, and his face was still shaping itself into an expression of shocked surprise when he was hurled backwards, almost cut in half by the deadly stream of bullets.

'Run!' Vonwegh yelled. The others followed him, desperately running, forward towards no man's land.

'This way, Kordt!' he shouted.

The ex-student, still sprawled for cover after the failure of their first dash for safety, understood at once. It was no use their going to the left. They would have to get out of the range of Müller-Würzbach's bushwhackers by taking the route to the right.

They all ran with the superhuman swiftness of men seizing a chance for life, but still the way was too long . . .

As the hundred or so B-soldiers under Vonwegh's command dashed across the stretch between the lines, they found themselves under fire from their own people and, increasingly from the Russian side. The Soviets, unaware of why Vonwegh had had to change his plan and break through on the right, feared betrayal.

'Move!' Vonwegh bawled at his men, dragging one who had lost his nerve to his feet and shoving him forward. He made sure a wounded man was dragged along with them, ducked and ran among the groups of escaping men, always heedless of his own safety, his only concern that the others should make it.

There were still 150 metres of ground between them and the Russian lines. It had been a long way from the hell of Lahuisk to this last, tantalising glimpse of freedom, but the final stretch was going to be the most perilous of all . . .

While Vonwegh's company were making their bloody bid for freedom, the fate of the rest of the special brigade was being decided.

Dirlewanger flew out of encircled Berlin in a Fieseler Storch, after one final, crazy all-night drinking session.

Weise, now an SS Standartenführer, donned civilian clothes and, together with his henchmen, managed to break through to the west, where all traces of him were lost.

The main body of the brigade were to the east of threatened Berlin. Yet again, the B-soldiers were herded into battle – to be slaughtered, hanged by roving courts-martial, or hunted down by the Russians like mad dogs. The killer-brigade was wiped out to the last man . . .

Meanwhile, Oberführer Dirlewanger had disappeared in the chaos of the final collapse. He was briefly detained by French occupation forces in the idyllic South German town of Altshausen, but managed to conceal his identity and was released. Of his subsequent fate nothing certain is known. But there is reason to believe that he still lives today in the Middle East – the El Dorado of prominent ex-Nazis, war criminals and Jew-baiters.

Satan will always find his protectors . . .

Vonwegh's only concern now was to see that his men got

through. As they stumbled on towards the opposing lines, Kirchwein fell and did not get up again. He bent over the epileptic; the man was dead.

Vonwegh shook his head in near-despair and straightened up to gaze across at the Russian positions. The idiots . . . their fire was gathering in strength now.

Vonwegh moved out into the open, cupped his hands in front of his mouth and shouted in Russian: 'Don't shoot! Don't shoot!'

This frantic message echoed across the field of slaughter, but to the men of the Red Army, thoroughly confused by this time, he was simply a German in one of those hated black uniforms, unprotected, a gift in their gunsights.

A hail of fire hurled Vonwegh backwards. He crashed to the ground and lay still, while ahead of him the rest of his company neared the Russian lines.

Kordt was the first to realise that Vonwegh had fallen. He knew he should have kept on running – he was so close to safety – but the ex-student just turned and headed. It was madness, but the others followed him: Kortetzky the gorilla, Gruhnke from Berlin . . . by all the rules, they should have been thinking of their own skins, but in that moment they didn't.

Kordt reached Vonwegh, lifted him up painfully, hauled him on to his shoulders in a fireman's lift, then collapsed after managing a few tottering steps. But then Kortetzky was there, and between them they could carry him.

Paul Vonwegh did not move. Perhaps he was already dead; at any rate, he was unconscious. Then the gorilla's heavy body sprawled on top of him. A burst of machine-gun fire had hit Kortetzky full on. Kordt was bleeding from his forehead, Gruhnke had a shoulder-wound.

They knew that they could probably only manage a few more steps, but it didn't seem important. They had waited years for their release, tiny flickers of hope had kept them alive, but now all they could think of was getting Vonwegh to the other side, dead or alive.

And so they staggered on with their burden, slowly, step for step.

By the time the Russians had realised their mistake and stopped firing, only Kordt was still with Vonwegh. As the silence descended on no man's land, he was able to signal to other B-soldiers. Now they could carry their leader openly and with diginty.

Paul Vonwegh had achieved his goal, reached his destination, but he would never know it. The unconscious man's face had the grey pallor of death in it. As they put him down gently in the Russian trench, he groaned softly. Kordt bent over him, biting his lip, incredulously shaking his head; he ignored the world around him, just stared at the dying man, as if by concentration he could bring him back to life.

But Vonwegh could not see him. He would never experience his own final triumph: the sight of outlawed men, ex-criminals, braving almost certain death to protect him.

And Karen's letter would never reach him now.

Perhaps, as he lay there in the brief dream world that presages death, Paul Vonwegh was with her one last time, as he had been when they found each other one mild spring evening. Perhaps he heard Karen's voice again, murmuring to him: 'It's true, isn't it? . . . We two love each other . . .'

A Russian NCO stumped up to Kordt and clapped him on the shoulder, then pointed to the group of survivors who were lining up for the long march into captivity.

Kordt ignored him. He kept peering into Vonwegh's face, seeing how death was setting in and transforming it. Now, when the ebbing of life should have brought harsh lines and sharp contours, Vonwegh's features seemed to be becoming strangely soft, almost relaxed. The mask was dropping; that almost superhuman self-control was losing its grip. Now, at the final moment, this man who had withstood all the hells the Nazis could create for him, was finding the way back to himself, was becoming a human being again, with a right to life, to happiness, to love . . .

'*Davai!*' the Russian bellowed at Kordt, who still didn't

move. He leaned over to give him a poke in the ribs with his gun. Then the Russian caught sight of Paul Vonwegh. He paused, as if some final fascination streamed forth from the man, swore softly and then, almost gently, began to lead young Kordt away.

Kordt turned round just once more to take a look at Vonwegh. He would remember. Then he tramped on, holding the last image as long as he could until it drowned in his mind's eye.

WARLORDS

BY BOB LANGLEY

BRITAIN'S FUTURE?

Britain is on the verge of total collapse. North Sea oil has suddenly run dry. Rationing and unemployment spread like wildfire. And four elections in two months have plunged the nation into a terrifying chaos.

Across the Atlantic America decides it is time to step in and assist their one-time ally. BY FERMENTING NO LESS THAN A FULL-SCALE BLOODY REVOLUTION GUARANTEED TO BRING THE DYING NATION TO HER KNEES AND TO CHANGE THE COURSE OF WORLD HISTORY WITH ONE DEVASTATING, FINAL COUP DE GRÂCE . . .

Fast and furious, WARLORDS is a terrifying and disturbing vision of Britain at the mercy of the powerlords in the not-so-distant future!

ADVENTURE THRILLER 0 7221 54[illegible]9 7 £1.25

HITLER'S SEED LIVES ON . . .

THE WATCHDOGS OF ABADDON

IB MELCHIOR

1945:

A group of SS officers flees in mortal terror from a remote hut in the heart of Nazi Germany. In their wake, a trail of bloody carnage – and in their keeping a secret prized possession: *the son of Adolf Hitler.*

1978:

A motiveless murder, a single photograph and an instinct for trouble plunge Harry Bendicks, ace investigator, into a nightmare world of political intrigue, frenzied murder and power-crazed manipulation. The trail leads Bendicks back 30 years to war-torn Europe and the deadly horror of a lethal conspiracy which threatens to destroy the very fabric of the Western world.

THE WATCHDOGS HAVE WOKEN – AND THEY HERALD THE FOURTH REICH!

THE WATCHDOGS OF ABADDON blazes a trail from Nazi Germany to the heart of Washington, and to the fabulous wealth of the Middle Eastern oil empires, and explodes in a brilliant, nerve-shattering climax of devastating evil.

ADVENTURE THRILLER 0 7221 6023 2 £1.75

IN COLD BLOOD

TRUMAN CAPOTE

15 NOVEMBER 1959

The rich and respected Clutter family, Herbert, Bonnie, son Kenyon and daughter Nancy, were brutally murdered in the small village of Holcomb, gunned down by Dick Hickock and Perry Smith. Truman Capote was fascinated by the killings; by the meaningless slaughter, the lack of motive, by the intensive police operation mounted to track the killers and by their incredible testimony. For each man sought to condemn the other with a devastating confession – and started a relentless ride on the wheel of justice. Their inevitable convictions for first degree murder earned them the death penalty. Numerous appeals – right up to the Supreme Court – followed. But there could be only one outcome. Smith and Hickock were hanged at 'The Corner' in Kansas State Penitentiary. This scene of extreme judicial cruelty haunts Capote today, years after he created his stunning document, a controversial study.

IN COLD BLOOD

GENERAL FICTION 0 7221 2288 8 £1.95

THEORY AND DECISION LIBRARY

An International Series in the Philosophy and Methodology
of the Social and Behavioral Sciences

Editors:

GERALD EBERLEIN, *University of Saarland*
WERNER LEINFELLNER, *University of Nebraska*

1. GÜNTER MENGES (ed.), *Information, Inference, and Decision.* 1974, viii + 195 pp.

2. ANATOL RAPOPORT (ed.), *Game Theory as a Theory of Conflict Resolution.* 1974, v + 283 pp.

3. MARIO BUNGE (ed.), *The Methodological Unity of Science.* 1973, viii + 264 pp.

4. COLIN CHERRY (ed.), *Pragmatic Aspects of Human Communication.* 1974, ix + 178 pp.